D1030740

The Wild GARDENER
IN
The Wild LANDSCAPE

Morning mist on the lake as seen thru white pine, on the property of the photographer. The foreground has been herbicide-cleaned.

The Wild GARDENER
IN
The Wild LANDSCAPE

The *Art* of
Naturalistic Landscaping

by

WARREN G. KENFIELD

Photography by Happy Kitchel Hamilton, FRPS, ASPA.

HAFNER PUBLISHING COMPANY
NEW YORK AND LONDON
1970

ACKNOWLEDGMENTS

Charts and plans drawn by Harry E. Van Deusen.

Drawing, page X, by Lewis Browne, from the World's Great Scriptures, by Lewis Browne, courtesy of the MacMillan Co., New York, N.Y.

Two 19th century woodblock prints, pages 6 and 7, courtesy of the Metropolitan Museum of Art, New York, N.Y.

Line drawings of individual flowers, from the New Britton and Brown Illustrated Flora of the Northeastern United States and Adjacent Canada, by Henry A. Gleason, 2nd ed., 1963, Hafner Publishing, reproduced with the permission of The New York Botanical Garden.

Biographical sketch of the author by Kathryn Whitford, Department of English, University of Wisconsin — Milwaukee.

Printed and Published
by
Hafner Publishing Company, Inc.
31 East 10th Street
New York, N.Y. 10003

Library of Congress Catalog Card Number: 66-19582

Printed in U.S.A. by
NOBLE OFFSET PRINTERS, INC.
NEW YORK 3, N. Y.

In gratitude to those friends without whose encouragement this present work would never have been completed. In the words of Josef Haydn (1732-1809), in a letter to a musical community written under remotely analogous circumstances,

> *You gave me the pleasant conviction . . . that I . . . [may be] the enviable source from which you and so many . . . [may] derive pleasure and enjoyment . . . What happiness does this cause me! Often, when contending with obstacles of every sort . . . a secret feeling within me whispered "There are but few contented and happy men here below; everywhere, grief and care prevail; perhaps your labors may one day be the source from which the weary and worn, or the man burdened with affairs may derive a few moments of rest and refreshment." What a powerful motive for pressing onward.*

The marble not yet carved can hold the form
Of every thought the greatest artist has
And no conception ever comes to pass
Unless the hand obeys the intellect.

MICHELANGELO—1475-1564.
from Sonnet XV,
translated by Elizabeth Jennings.

PREFACE

DO YOU HAVE ONE OR SEVERAL ACRES in the suburbs? Or are you an exurbanite, with a second home on a tract of forest land? Are you plagued with lawn-mowing and weeding? Are you worried at the way "brush" is filling up your old fields, destroying your views? If so, then this book may be for you.

Watch out, though! Are you the tidy meticulous gardener, who cannot bear to see an autumn leaf on an immaculate lawn? Or a johnny-jump-up in the fresh spring earth of the asparagus bed? Do you walk thru the woods, compelled to clean up the dead branches and logs, never noticing the mosses and lichens upon them? Are you unhappy until you have removed the dead hollow tree, home of young raccoons, one branch with a woodpecker hole, and with its crown silhouetted against the sky, perfect perches for the mating swallows? Then do not waste your money on this book. It is not meant for the "pure" among gardeners, landscapers, and botanists. Go back to your little garden and lawn, chained like blinded Samson to a treadmill. My manicured garden and lawn get smaller each year. Someday soon I shall be entirely a free man. But even if you do not intend to be entirely free—your neighbors and your status will probably demand a bit of lawn; and beds of pansies and roses have true virtues, I know. Cast your sights to the farthest slope, and mold the botanical landscape as your fancy chooses.

It might almost be said that there are no other books on the subject I am here discussing. Yes, there are many books on "wild flower gardens," "growing wild plants" and "wild gardening." But these all bear more in common with treatises on the care of polar bears and jungle peacocks in city zoos. (One does keep the poor things alive, at an extraordinary expenditure of time and energy, in anything but a natural environment.) One notable exception: W. Robinson's British-based THE WILD GARDEN, which reached a fourth edition in 1894, a logical forebear of this book, tho I discovered it only a few years ago.

1945; the end of World War II; discontented at being a success in other eyes but not mine, I retired to an abandoned farm. It is still "abandoned" in the eyes of some. Now, after 21 years of joyful research and labor, involving more laziness than labor, I pass on to you some of the things I have learned. For a bit of labor, may you too enjoy your laziness. Laziness, in the form of appreciative leisure, can be among the noblest of human activities.

TO

the ecologist,

      whose brains I have picked so unmercifully
that he has asked to remain unnamed.

Table of Contents

Illustrations

PROLOGUE
Five Modes of LANDSCAPE APPRECIATION

There are very few people in this world who are willing to spend
their entire existence imbedded in the steel, aluminum, glass,
plastic and concrete of the haunts of man. Most of us feel some
deep-seated and unexplainable urge to "return to nature," there to
revive our spirits in peace and tranquility, in an emotional and
esthetic experience that may transcend any obvious understanding.
"Nature" can mean many things to many people. To some, it will
mean a landscape untouched and unmarred by man. To others, it
will mean a landscape idealized and symbolized. A person may be
deeply and profoundly moved by one, but not by the other. Yet
no man should pass final judgment, should overly praise or deride,
that which another holds most holy. And thus, in this prologue, we
will take a quick view of five different modes of landscape appreciation. It is only the middle one, the third, which forms the subject matter elaborated in this volume. You may or may not find that
this third mode creates a deep and satisfying experience. If not,
I hope you have found your metier in one of the other four. Give
them all a trial. You are poor indeed if the artificiality of man
entirely encompasses your micro-environment.

Mode I

THE WILDERNESS AS A LANDSCAPE

The wilderness was once the enemy of man. As man has beaten back the jungle, as the wild beasts have been vanquished, as the frontier advances, he no longer fears the unknown. For the first time in human history, we gaze upon the wilderness in contemplative security. What little is left we are beginning to cherish. And well we should. Unlike all other types of landscape, man can destroy the wilderness, but he cannot create it.

The wilderness is a landscape essentially free from all the effects of man. This is more or less a theoretical definition. There are relatively few parts of the world that do not know the insidious effects of the hand of man. Even in areas with no agriculture, ancient man selected certain trees for his firewood, and certain roots and fruits for his food, and may have markedly reduced or eliminated these species. Civilizations have come and gone on areas that now seem to be wilderness. One small tribe could start grass and forest fires that could change the landscape for many square miles. Be history as it may, the spirit of the wilderness starts to reenter where the effects of man are not obvious.

The wilderness takes a huge frame. A hundred thousand acres is none too much. An entire mountain range. An unfettered river from source to ocean. The whole of a lake from the deepest bottom to the fullest width of its shores. A view as far as the eye can reach. And solitude.

Solitude? He who loves the wilderness is never less alone than when alone. He is a conscious discerning being, a humble spectator of all the glories of creation, and of their integration into the system which is this Earth: of sky and sea, of climate and soil, of plants and animals. I know of no other mode of landscape appreciation in which it can be said that the greater our knowledge, the more profound our appreciation. A meandering river, an electrical storm, an upturned mountain cuesta, a flock of flamingoes against an azure sea and sky, a rainbow or an orchid—all may be moving experiences to children. Only those acquainted with the natural sciences interpreting these phenomena however, realize that with such knowledge they attain to intensities of appreciation previously beyond the ken even of their imagination.

Mode II

THE RURAL LANDSCAPE

Unless you are one of those hardy souls able to go off on camping trips in wild rugged mountains or far into extensive swamps, the probability is that "nature" to you does not mean wilderness, but lands in which agriculture is, or has recently been, the dominant factor. This, to the city man, is "country."

The placidity of the farmer's landscape with its straight rows of bright green crops and its herds of contented cows has long been idealized by the urban dweller. French royalty once played at being shepherds and shepherdesses, and the poetry and art of that time amply reflects this innocent but unrealistic game. However, even as the wild animals of the forest lead lives in which the species survives, but the life and happiness of the individual are passing incidents, so too the farmer's crops and animals have always been at the mercy of floods and drought, insects and disease—and marauding tribesmen, replaced in later years by absentee landlords.

There are magnificent beauties to the rural landscape. The terraced rice fields of the Orient are unparalleled in the world of art. Even the shifting agriculture of native tribes, tho unquestionably an unwise land use, creates pleasing and intellectually interesting variations in the landscape. In this type of agriculture, the native fells and burns the original forest. Among the stumps and ashes, he pokes his crop plants. Then, as the ash fertility is leached out by tropical downpours, and as uncontrollable weeds take over, he moves on, to fell another stretch of forest. Under more advanced agricultural techniques we are treated to broad open stretches and distant views that would otherwise be closed with forest. We have the tilled cleanliness of crop lands. Pastures can be areas of superb beauty, for while cattle produce a fine sward on the spots they trample and graze, other plants they will not touch. These untouchables are often bright wild flowers, handsome shrubs like laurel and juniper, or magnificent conifers like cedar and pine. A pastured landscape is an unintentional work of art.

Mode III

THE HERBICIDE–SCULPTURED LANDSCAPE*

If you do not have the flying capacities of a condor, and a 100,000 acre wilderness to enjoy, if you do not have cattle and till the land and a horse with which to ride around your farming domain, you may still be lucky enough to own a few acres, maybe even 10 or 100 acres. Now "wilderness" has its place, but when your abandoned farm land becomes entirely and homogeneously covered with impassable and impossible brush, you have a problem. You cannot farm it. You cannot garden it. A bit of brush may be nice, but you do not want to drown in an ocean of it.

Herbicides to the rescue! This magnificent tool—even tho oversold by the hucksters of Madison Avenue, capital of the advertising world, and overused by utility and highway engineers and others—can become superbly powerful. It will allow you to work with nature, not against her. It will allow you to carve out, carefully to excise, what you do not want. The view-hiding thicket, the poisonous ivy, the rank weeds, will vanish. In their places will emerge the landscape that you yourself choose to sculpture, waving grasslands dotted with bright flowers, backed by curving borders of shrubs, surrounded by a varied forest of boldly contoured evergreen and hardwood trees. Perhaps also you can ornament these natural plant-communities with a few bright gems, special plants chosen from far-off lands, or even hybrids that always could have existed but never did until man brought the parents together. Such hardy plants, judiciously used, will "belong" to your natural landscape just as completely as if a wild bird had dropped the seeds and nature had raised the seedling.

The herbicide-sculptured landscape is the subject of this book.

---

* Herbicides need not be the "poisons" that some uninformed people think them. All substances, even the pure chemicals sugar and salt, are poisons in undue quantities. The chlorophenoxy herbicides are non-poisonous to animal life and man as here suggested. Applied discriminately, they only rootkill the plants they touch. Then the chemical is utilized as food by soil bacteria, and vanishes.

Mode IV

THE OCCIDENTAL
LANDSCAPE GARDEN

An appreciation of the wilderness (I) requires observation and comprehension, but not manipulation, of nature. Appreciation of the rural landscape (II) depends on the manipulation, often laborious, of someone else—the farmer. Appreciation of the herbicide-sculptured landscape (III) is related to the "triggering" of changes in natural processes, such as by the elimination of certain plant species. When we move on to the consideration of the Landscape Garden, we enter an entirely different world. "Gardening" can be defined as the art or culture of growing plants, individual plants, under optimum conditions for their finest growth. Gardening involves the growing of potted plants in the home, of plants in the conservatory, of lawns and shrubbery around one's suburban lawn, of the geometrically formal gardens of our city parks, of our large estates, and originally of royalty, as at Versailles. The professional gardener is a very different kind of individual from one who seeks the wilderness. That is evident even from the illustrations of authors themselves as they appear on the dust jackets of their books. They are antipodal in several respects, each to be admired for what he is, not for what he is not. The wilderness man accepts nature. The gardener improves on nature—until it is beautiful but unnatural. Like a striking woman prepared for presentation to the Queen: one wilted flower in her corsage is as intolerable and unforgivable as a fallen flower on a bed of roses.

The Landscape Garden is a garden first, and a landscape second, even tho gardeners may call it "naturalistic landscaping" (not the Naturalistic Landscaping in the title of this book). The highly cultivated plants are arranged in pleasing landscape effects. Hills are utilized. Ponds, streams and rocky outcrops are worked into the scene. The effect is indubitably a landscape, a beautiful landscape, a completely unnatural landscape, and one that requires an enormous amount of time and energy to keep in condition.

Landscape Gardening has progressed along two quite dissimilar lines in the Occident and the Orient. The Occidental Landscape Garden has several historical threads. It is an outgrowth in part of the private hunting preserves of the aristocracy. It received tremendous impetus in the days of Romanticism, when ruins were created de novo to give that wild and ancient look. Ideals of shepherds and shepherdesses played their part, and grazing sheep. Occidental Landscape Gardening is still a living art, as is evident from the spacious lawns and tended shrubbery of our large Western city parks. Possibly the finest and most recent examples are the post-World War II gardens in the Royal Park at Windsor, England. Maximum advantage has been taken here of the natural terrain, with its streams, lakes, rocks and hills. Species of plants have been introduced from all over the world in absolutely bewildering variety. They are tended with extraordinary care. Water is piped to all parts; pruning and fertilizing are done seasonally. All these plants are arranged around lawns and grassy trails in pleasing effects of flower borders, shrubbery masses and background forest. Occidental Landscape Gardening is a profession and an art. Lesser mortals may aspire, but even if one has the knowledge, one may have neither the time nor the money for such elaborate indulgences.

Mode V

THE ORIENTAL
LANDSCAPE GARDEN

Quality and quantity more vast than an ocean separates the landscape garden of the Occident from that of the Orient. The Oriental Landscape Garden, receiving possibly its finest flowering in Japan, is an exquisite work of art, one of the noblest contributions of any race to human culture. One should "listen" to a Japanese garden as one listens to the intimacy of a string quartet from the decades near 1800. It has no relation to the brass combos of the 20th century.

The Japanese Landscape Garden is by no means a large wilderness. It is a small, sometimes exceptionally small, area, completely "artificial," but representing a most extraordinary perceptiveness and sensitivity to the characteristics of a wild landscape. These characteristics are both idealized in the sense of materializing their most important aspects, and symbolized in the sense of relating those aspects to matters of human significance. It is this combination of idealization and symbolization which is unique to this school of gardening.

The Japanese Garden has had a long history. It was already developed 13 centuries ago, when the West still thought that a garden was a matter of growing things in pots, or in straight rows outdoors—if gardeners were that advanced. Since then, minor changes in style have come and gone, but the basic principles of the oriental garden remain much the same.

One will take a diminutive area, what we would call a back yard perhaps, with a rumbling street car nearby, and electric power lines in view. Topography is important. If the area is flat, it may soon cease to be. Valleys are dug, even 20 to 30 feet deep. Hills are made, perhaps symbolic of Mount Fujiyama.

Water is introduced. It plays a most important role in the landscape, as ponds, as streams, as waterfalls. Where else in the world would one so plan a stream that scattering petals from an unseen plum tree are observed from a guest-room window as they go floating past? Where else would the quantity and height of falling water be so gauged as to produce just the right tinkling pitch as heard in the home? Islands are built in the pond, often of such shapes as to symbolize the crane and the tortoise, the most long-lived of animals. Where water is not available, white sand or pebbles can be used, in representation of a water-formed landscape.

And stones. Stones are chosen with infinite care. In shape, size, color and texture, they become as important in a garden as the plants themselves. They are moved from long distances, often from old gardens being dismantled. Individual shapes are symbolic; and their arrangement in small groups carries abstract meanings.

Then the plants are introduced into this idealized landscape of rock and water. Many of the plants come from other gardens, grown for decades into naturalistic yet symbolic forms.

The Japanese garden is a place of retreat for contemplative peace and meditation in a crowded world. It satisfies a yearning for wild nature, even while it re-creates that nature in a form that idealizes it, in symbols representative of our highest spiritual aspirations.

PERSPECTIVES

REVOLUTION IN LAND–USE

The Home "Subdivision"

In these middle years of the twentieth century, many developing nations are witnessing a greater revolution in land-use than at any time in their previous history. Land-use patterns are now being formulated which may well set the stage for succeeding centuries.

Two separate factors are contributing to this change. One is the extraordinary explosion in population. With old people living to be older, and fewer dying in childhood, the human race is increasing like an agricultural weed, like maggots on dead meat. What happens when the meat is gone, does not worry the flies—or the optimists.

The second factor is the removal in many countries of the average family from the crowded conditions of walled city, of slum and tenement, to the expanses of his own home and grounds, with an enormous increase of acreage requirements per family. I am not sure I understand, psychologically, the reasons for some aspects of this second explosion. For example, in America, many an average sociable family is now isolated on some country road. He does not "see" the forest around him. He must commute long distances to work; she must drive long distances to shop and market; sonny must be driven long distances to school; repairs and maintenance of home and grounds add to the chores of life. Perhaps this was a tawdry attempt to emulate the privileged of a previous age, with their country estates. Perhaps our minds are manipulated and persuaded more than we think by the advertising hucksters of industry. After all, homes, and all that is used in on and for them, are what raise our Standard of Living, and our Gross National Product. At the individual and at the social level, these are twin idols in America and places emulating America. As good Americans, it is expected that we of a "higher" civilization should worship such standards.

While the concrete and steel of the city proper expand, the periphery is generally lost to housing developments. Here the lots are measured in terms of tens of feet, and the architecture exhibits such a sameness that I marvel at the homing instinct that leads one to find his own nest late on a Saturday night. As remarkable in its way as the avian intelligence that leads a booby to its nest among the thousands that dot a guano-covered islet. Of these populations, we are not here concerned.

Farther afield from the urban loci, there is—as yet—more elbow room. The homes may be just as be-gadgeted and overly applianced. (For which reason, shares in the securities of modern corporations are among the soundest of financial investments.) The difference lies largely in the "grounds."

On the one hand, we have an extension of the area of lawn, of manicured flower beds, and of clipped hedges. The area in this type of land-use is often correlated indirectly with the ages of the owners: the younger the age, the more such land.

On the other hand—like an ogre in the offing, forever ready to encroach when one's back is turned—lies "waste land," "brush." Here were the lawns, kept mowed when you were younger, the ornamental shrubs planted by your predecessor who could afford several gardeners.

This book is meant for those to whom fate or fortune—or misfortune—has given a tract of land of greater size than their lawn-mowing propensities can control. It is no ogre in the distance, when you get to known it. To the contrary, with a very minor amount of acquaintanceship and taming, you may find it is your truest friend. But do not expect a clipped and beribboned lapdog, neurotically demanding and temperamental. The land is a rough and shaggy animal, as gentle and true as a St. Bernard.

HORTICULTURE
The Gardening Addict

"Gardening" is not a pastime. It is a fine art, a philosophy. I greatly admire the magnificent gardens of our large estates and formal parks. Gardening is also a compulsion, a mania, an emotional disturbance with masochistic behavior patterns. The American wife, fatigued by manipulating the control panels of the household appliances, by committee meetings, by taxiing the children to school, is pulled relentlessly to the garden. Many of my friends drive to their suburban homes after a frazzling day at the office, or have a hundred-mile bumper-to-bumper parade at the end of five such days, only to find their garden fairly screeching for attention. Lustrous foreign beetles rustle in the rose buds. Dandelions smile seductively from the lawn. Birdseed-producing polygonums peep attractively from under the coarse foliage of the zinnias. Oak twiglets lie scattered on the fresh soil of last week's weeded bed, eagerly sought by that song-outpouring wren who must express his exuberant masculinity in building a second nest. Possibly he will build it in the old shoe that the neighbor's brat tossed into the lilac bush. And so, man and wife, in touching togetherness, doff their respectable clothes and don the ritualistic garb. Armed with knives, clippers and pokers of sundry shapes and sizes, sometimes made fiendishly effective with electricity, and with chemical poisons that would have made the Borgias blush with envy, they go their murderous way. They seem to like it! But masochists and sadists do.

The results of this behavior are truly extraordinary, even tho "green thumbs" (symbol of the gardener) have turned to red raw meat, and backs are painfully bent in premature senility. Suddenly "harvest time" is here. Tulips or roses or dahlias or mums come to full glory. Like vain women, they cry out for admiration; like vain parents, you want them to get attention. They want to be looked at; they want to be picked; they want to be "arranged" in the house. But you are far too weary to enjoy them, even to lie in a hammock with a good book and in the shadow of their color and fragrance. Your neighbor? He is equally weary, and with an equal abundance of his own riches.

Then the vegetables suddenly ripen. Peas, beans, cucumbers, corn, tomatoes, pumpkins, pumpkins and more pumpkins. They well up in the garden with cornucopial profusion. The vegetables are particular fiends. They demand to be picked, washed, shelled, stringed; and finally packaged and frozen, or cooked and canned. It has always seemed to me an especially exquisite torture to be so immersed in a vegetable between meals, just at a time when the meals themselves are so overloaded with that same vegetable as to make a dead dietician disintegrate in his grave.

This is gardening. I should know. Many and many a time I have been at the receiving end of large quantities of flowers and vegetables from my worthy neighbors. I know the work that lies behind it all. I try to soothe my conscience by profuse appreciation. It is difficult though, for I value a few flowers in the house just as much as a mammoth mess of them; and the vegetables just then are at bargain prices in the stores. This is gardening.

The Lawn*

THE LAWN is one of the most interesting sociological and psychological phenomena of our times.

It is a sort of living fossil, having evolved several thousand years ago in the history of our West European culture. Not a fossil in the sense of the coelacanth, which fish, until found recently off the African coast, had been considered extinct for 70 million years. It is still very much at home in those waters. Lawns, to the contrary, are kept alive only by an exorbitant amount of nursing and babying, otherwise they would disappear, to be as extinct as the dodo.

The Lawn arose early in our cultural history, certainly before the days of gardeners and landscape architects. When we first domesticated cattle, goats and sheep, we kept them fenced and tethered close to the hearth. This action was to protect them from marauding animals, especially human neighbors. (The custom of fencing still persists, for tho we have made the former animals extinct, the latter still exist.)

Vegetationally, the practice was a logical and esthetic coincidence. The hooves of the animals compacted the soil to walkable firmness. By their excretions, a high fertility-level was maintained. By trampling, only grasses survived. By grazing, a close-cropped sward was maintained. The result: a Lawn, a beautiful expanse of emerald green.

Times have changed. The original top-soil has been exchanged for "fill", called top-soil by the man who sells it to you. The tethered front-yard cow has vanished, replaced by chemical fertilizers and herbicides (quite fine in their limited way) and by mechanical monsters (that keep the repair man busy, even when Junior does not pour water in the gas tank). The Lawn? A living fossil in a modern human zoo.

---

* I really like Lawns. They have the pure clean simplicity of a freshly painted floor, or a bolt of mono-colored cloth. I like them as I like sheathing evening gowns on other men's women, beautiful to look at, but horribly expensive to support. The economic theory of "costs vs. benefits" is apropos. I prefer a bed of moss, the subtle satisfaction of a stretch of periwinkle, or the inviting expanses of an unmowed grassland rippling in the breeze.

Grow that Hardy Flower!

THE HARDY FLOWER is an idea. It involves a concept unique to the gardening profession. It is a rough and rugged garden plant, which can survive our severe winters. It is advertised as "foolproof" (i.e., fit for fools to grow). *If*, to abstract from leading gardening books:

Soil improvement must be considered. Drainage is possibly poor. Dig out to a depth of three or four feet. Put in special kinds of drainage tiles. If there is a hardpan or an impervious clay layer, this must be broken, possibly with dynamite. Then simply replace the ton or so of overlying dirt.

If you wish to slouch on the job, dig down only a foot or so, and spread a layer of ashes or other such material to effect suitable drainage.

Your soil is probably low in organic matter. Grow leguminous cover crops for a year or so, ploughing them under at the proper time. Then start gardening. Or you might use well-rotted manures. If not well-rotted, pile the material near the back, by the kitchen door, or in front by the patio for a few seasons.

Sands are too light; clays are too heavy. You probably have one or the other. Get an adequate amount of what you don't have, and mix thoroly. (A large concrete mixer is suitable. You merely have to shovel stuff into the mixer.)

Fertility levels must be maintained from year to year. Use well-rotted manures or proper (known after laboratory tests) chemical fertilizers. Too much, or too little, would be disastrous. Spade in thoroly. A compost pile is highly desirable (a ritualistic "must," for one cult). If properly located near the kitchen door, things like coffee grounds and orange peels can be applied without leaving the house. (Odors can be called "healthy" and "natural".)

After due attention to seed source, coatings with disease-protective chemicals, and depth of planting, the seeds may germinate. So also will hundreds more of very hardy "weeds." (It is an absorbing incidental scientific study to find out how many different kinds of seeds, and what large numbers of them, exist in the soil—in addition to what you have planted.)

Then starts the jolly game of weeding. You can assume that the hardy weeds are not only more numerous than what you planted, but that they grow far more rapidly. By diligence precision and constant effort, you may eventually turn the tide of battle, without uprooting that which you planted. You think the last weed seeds have germinated? Come back a week later; a totally new kind of weed has suddenly germinated; threatens to produce a forest.

Need I mention the legions of pests? Bugs and beetles. Fungi and virus diseases. Moles, mice, rabbits, woodchucks, even the birds. Cheer up. There are books galore on the subject. (Buy that extra bookcase. You will need it.) There are new chemicals for each and every trouble. (But watch out. Some of them have the selectivity and discretion of a bulldozer, killing what you want and allowing other pests to multiply.)

You probably will not appreciate the way the plant grows. When the plant is six inches high, pinch off the tips. Pinch again at the second six inches, etc. Stake it, tie it, support it, otherwise it will sprawl indecorously.

Then it blooms. You have a few days of grace with which to enjoy it. (If you can spare the time from other plants.)

Those dead blossoms. They must be removed. Then the foliage starts to wither and yellow; unsightly. It is best carefully to transplant entirely to a hidden corner, so that the foliage can continue to nourish the roots.

Autumn arrives. All dried parts must be carefully collected and burned, so that the propagules of disease (which you did not control after all) do not survive the winter (tho you know they will). The frosts come. (You carefully mulch, knowing that frosts will heave the roots if you don't, and mice will congregate if you do.) It is better, the books tell us, to take a few plants indoors (ugly things, now); make cuttings in midwinter (buy that greenhouse), transplant to suitable flats; put them out in early spring. Of course, such care means you cannot take that cruise to a warm climate during the winter, but the satisfaction (they say) is worth the deprivation.

(I think of the huge mass of peonies on the slope below my home, all but thrown into holes over a decade ago. The only labor in ten years has been that of picking some blossoms each spring. That is naturalistic landscaping!)

PLANT ECOLOGY

"If Naturalistic Landscaping is not gardening," you ask, "then assuredly it is plant ecology; and I must read the ecology books." You are right on two counts, wrong on two counts; four counts to be considered.

As for gardening, I have already shown that the answer is not to be found in the gardening books. But gardening knowledge is very very pertinent. The more you know about garden plants, and the scientific reasons why such irrationally laborious efforts are necessary to make the blessed things grow, the more successful you will be in Naturalistic Landscaping. It is the gardening spirit that is completely out of place, the spirit that prefers a clipped yew in a formal garden to a curvaceous coconut on a wild shore, that prefers a Roxy Rockette to the original South Sea lass.

So we turn to plant ecology. I raise my eyes from my typewriter as I write these words, avoid the tendency to look at the deep snow blanketing my natural grassland, unmowed for 21 years, and glance at eight feet of shelf space frowning with the world's leading texts and surveys of that science. Not one mentions this subject! And yet, the more factual information you possess about this science, the more successful you will be in Naturalistic Landscaping. Read those books!

A paradox? Not at all. It is true, however, that gardeners and plant ecologists will rarely help you, if at all. I should know. For several years I tried to interest botanical gardens and university botany and landscape departments in projects on this subject. Everyone was extremely interested, cordial and polite. Said the botanist, "Go to the landscape department. That is their field." Said the landscaper, "Go to the ecologists. That is their field." So I found out for myself. In the last few years, there has been one exception. Dr. William A. Niering, at Connecticut College, is establishing his own herbicide-induced landscape at the Connecticut Arboretum. As such, he can almost be said to be the exception to prove the rule. His professional interest has enormously encouraged me, tho I should add—to protect him—that he by no means shares my flippant, irreverent, and unbotanical enjoyment of the subject.

He would have been far happier had I cut the length of this book most drastically, preserving only its botanical facts.

The Ecology Devotee

Ecology is a strange subject; the ecologist is a strange individual; but the ecology devotee is the strangest of the three.

Ecology as a science has had a strange history in America. It began about the turn of the century, tho its roots stretch far back. Ostensibly it was involved with the description and understanding of natural and seminatural Vegetation (i.e., plant communities). Actually, it became side tracked into a body of esoteric doctrines involving "plant succession" (a very orderly idea, which in most cases nature, not reading books, does not know about) and the "climax," or "virgin vegetation" (strictly an anthropomorphic concept; nature does not believe in virginity). Furthermore, the science has been defined as "all forms of life in all relations to all the environment." Thus, it has slipped over into an all-embracing environmental-causationism, encyclopaedic in scope, and excellent for a scatter brained general-ist who wants to be thought a special-ist. Whether as a biological science investigating environmental relationships, or as a study of Vegetation in all its relationships, ecology has a fine future.

Ecologists have much in common as a professional "type." They are really admirable individuals, and you will find them intelligent and cooperative, tho not always sympathetic with Naturalistic Landscaping. The ecologist to a certain extent represents a contemporary version of an age-old phenomenon: the "return to nature," the avoidance of the "artificial." He studies the wilderness, untouched, "natural" vegetation (or what he thinks is natural). He studies old-fields only insofar as they are undergoing "plant succession" back to the original climax. Such inordinate meddling as invoked by Naturalistic Landscaping is simply not to his taste.

The meddling to which the ecologist is opposed is not only on the sociological, Vegetation, level. It is also on the floristic or species level. Most ecologists have a strong contempt and resentment for the introduced and alien species. For them, horticulture is scarcely to be considered a branch of botany. Vegetation possessing such Ausländer is not natural, not worthy of being studied (unless to study what it was, before the aliens entered). We find an analogue of this situation among some gardeners, especially those who only have "wild flower gardens," and belong to such societies as the Daughters of the Original Barbarians. These are the true natives; it would be better if everything else were eliminated, even still older antecedent "barbarians." Personally, I think this may be an extreme view. Whether a Japanese iris arrived on American shores on a log drifting on an ocean current, or by jet plane, is a difference of degree, not of kind. On the contrary, the alienophilists can become extremists to an obscene degree. Some will shun every native plant as common and vulgar, to be yanked up and destroyed, while their gardens are crowded with "exotics" (say the word as tho you are describing some rare carving of white jade). There should be a happy middle-ground, says the Naturalistic Landscaper, where hardy carefree peonies from the Orient can merge their pink perfection with that of the superb Occidental mountain laurel (Kalmia).

Thirdly and lastly, the ecological devotee results when the science of ecology acts thru the ecologist upon a layman. Beware of becoming one! The devotee uses the word "ecological" with a sense of infallible authority, to allay all doubts in the hearer. He alone has access to the Truth. He knows just enough of the jargon to impress a circle slightly more illiterate than himself. A lilting lingo, tho a language, is not necessarily literacy. Be modest. None of us, certainly not myself, know very much about this subject.

Vegetation Management

If academic ecology is not going to help us, at least directly, can we expect aid from some of the more practical fields—forestry, range and pasture management, and wildlife management? Here too, the answer is "yes;" and "no."

Forestry, as a profession, is highly developed, with an enormous literature. The main purpose of forestry however is to produce and harvest timber. The forester is a man who gauges the beauty of a tree in terms of the board feet of lumber he can get out of it, and the dollars it will bring. Forestry as a profession has largely been concerned with an inventory of our forest resources, and the handling of them so as to harvest the most timber now and in the immediate future.

Range management is involved with the handling of grasslands, primarily for their forage values. Beauty is in terms of the number of cattle that can be nourished on an acre. We can learn much from the literature of range management, but we must pick and choose with considerable discretion.

Wildlife management, historically, is the youngest of these three fields. The wildlifer is primarily a hunter. He wants more game to shoot; he is a sports-man. He is learning that wildlife is a product of the habitat, the Vegetation habitat. The more game to kill, the more beautiful the land. His management of that Vegetation has been heavily empirical: try something, and see if it works. We can learn from what he has done, but we have to adapt his results to our own ends.

———————————

We may look upon Horticulture and Plant Ecology as a kind of Scylla and Charybdis: necessary, important, but dangerous cliffs, past which we must sail our barque, picking up important experience and information on the way, before we emerge into the placid but relatively unknown seas of Naturalistic Landscaping.

Naturalistic Landscaping
a Branch of Vegetation Management

The purpose of the preceding pages has been to show us that Naturalistic Landscaping—a practical art involving the esthetic manipulation of plants and plant-communities to form a pleasing whole—borrows from many sciences, only because it is young. It is fundamentally an independent and distinct branch of the biological sciences.

Naturalistic Landscaping appeals to the kind of person who likes wild nature, modified just a bit. He glimpses a view of a distant hill, marred by a big unnecessary tree. He sees a scraggly spot on the marsh edge, and wants to convert it to a grassland, the better to sit in the sun and watch the beaver. He spots that colony of berry-laden viburnums, and knows they will grow far better along the stream side if he removes the miscellaneous things now competing with them. His eye envisions daffodils under the bursting buds of the white birches. He is willing to tip the scales of nature with one finger, not to spend his life trying to grow plants in anti-ecological unnaturalness.

The rest of this introduction will be in three sections:

1. The major Physiognomic Vegetation Types: grassland, shrubland and forest. The chances are however that you have none of these now, but simply "brushland." To manipulate vegetation types, we must manipulate, not the types, but individual plants. Thus we are next concerned with

2. The Life History of the Individual Plant, with particular reference to its reproduction, its root systems, and the form of its aboveground growth. Then we move on to

3. The "Tools" for managing vegetation. Originally, these were such mechanical tools as shovels and axes. Now we have herbicides (non poisonous to all forms of animal life), without which this book would be impossible.

BOTANY

The Physiognomic Vegetation Types

As our eyes pass over the natural vegetation of the world, in all its manifold complexity, it is convenient for many purposes to classify it. Classification, besides seeming to be a compulsion on the part of many people, is an extremely efficient way of organizing scientific data, of showing similarities and differences, of generalizing, and of showing relationships.

When we attempt to classify vegetation types in terms of gross morphological differences, because of the abundance of certain kinds of trees, shrubs, or herbs, we speak of their "physiognomy." Three of the most widespread physiognomic types are Forest, Shrubland, and Grassland. There is also the low Tundra of polar regions, as well as the Deserts of arid parts of the world, neither of which concerns us here. Elsewhere, trees are scattered in grassland, called Savanna in the tropics, instructive in its phenomena but not of immediate importance for this book.

The Forest

We work with forests often in Naturalistic Landscaping. Most of our readers will be living in parts of the country that either were in a preceding civilization, or are tending to become, forest. We want forest in our landscaping plans, in some places, not in others.

For our purposes it is well to look upon the Forest as an entity in itself, a kind of "whole"—not just a collection of trees. The combined effect of the branches and the foliage produces conditions of shade, atmospheric moisture and other conditions that are unique. The Forest itself is composed of certain kinds of trees. (Many light-needing trees may not be found in it.) Beneath its canopy, only certain shrubs and herbs can grow, and these grow in special ways (not as they would if you put them out in the open). The trees affect the soil; and the soil affects the trees, so that a particular balance, or equilibrium, occurs. Respect the Forest. Work with it, not against it.

The Grassland

Not many people in forest regions know natural grassland. Not many people in the Prairies, Plains and Steppes know natural grassland either! That land is mostly now in corn or wheat, and the forests of the river bottoms have crept up the slopes. The Grassland however is one of the most intriguing and beautiful of natural phenomena. It is true we cannot have it in a thoroly "natural'" condition, for that would require herds of buffalo, antelope and other hoofed animals, with all their trampling and grazing effects. It would also require periodic fires, to burn off the accumulated mulch and the woody plants that may have started, as well as to open up bare spots in which flowering herbs may start.

The Grassland is a thing of beauty. As the season advances from early spring to late fall, one grass after another becomes prominent, in green, yellow, pink and bronze. Each in time waves in the breezes like the proverbial field of wheat—except that a field of wheat is a mighty poor substitute for the real thing.

Furthermore, the Grassland is not just a blanket of green, as monotonous as your lawn. It is a tapestry studded with flowers. From the earliest spring bulbs to the last chrysanthemums they come and go in endless profusion. Sometimes there will be a low-lying carpet of yellow, extending continuously. Then there will be the isolated orange of lilies and the purple spikes of blazing star, or patches of asters and goldenrods. As one vanishes (literally vanishes, without benefit of gardening) another bursts into view. Finally, all turns to magnificent hues of brown in the autumn frosts. It is submerged beneath a sea of snow. It emerges with spring thaws as smooth as if flattened by some conscientious roller.

The Grassland has a life of its own. Many plants thrive in it; others survive; others just won't grow at all. The chances are, you have no natural Grassland. But you can create one. Once created, it is not much effort to maintain. Only certain kinds of invading trees tend to be nuisances. Know your Grassland, and it will know you, reflecting your own temperament and personality.

The Shrubland

There is less "natural" shrubland in the world than either grass-land or forest. Shrubland occurs where there are wet winters and dry summers, as in southern California and the Mediterranean area. There such vegetation is called chaparral, macchie or garigue. How "natural" such brush is, is anybody's guess, for past races and past cultures have had roles in its history, and both forest and grassland are mixed up with it.

Once you have shrubland however, you continue to have it. It "stays put," relatively. There is some on hilltops of the southern Appalachians which has lasted for 200 years. Others, in England, date from Roman times. And Mediterranean macchie may be pre-Roman in part. The Shrubland is another kind of vegetational "entity"—sufficient unto itself. Trees have difficulty in entering it. There is no space for the low-growing grasses and flowering herbs. If destroyed, it tends to reproduce itself in very much the same form. It has its own types of animal life, particularly in regard to song birds.

The Shrubland has especial value in Naturalistic Landscaping, particularly at the margins of grassy areas, where it can form a sort of transition to the high forest.

The Brushland

The chances are that you must start off with neither good forest, nor grassland nor shrubland, but simply "brushland."

The word "brush" is not a good botanical term. It merely in-dicates woody plants, of a kind you do not want. It is probable that the acreage you are eyeing with landscaping intent is only abandoned agricultural land, growing up to a miscellaneous mass of trees, shrubs, grasses and other herbs. Cheer up! This is the best possible land with which to start. You undoubtedly have a tremendous floristic diversity from which to pick and choose. It will be all the easier to convert to grassland, or shrubland, or forest, as you, the creator of the landscape, decide. The marble is an unsculptured block. You, the creator, are free and untrammeled. The choice of what to carve is yours.

Life History of a Plant

Vegetation types, even tho they act in many ways as "wholes" (like a hive of bees) are ultimately composed of individual plants of different species (like individuals of the different species and castes of ants in one colony). Our actual endeavors in Naturalistic Landscaping will naturally be on the species and individual levels of thinking. The more we know at these levels, the more successful those endeavors.

The Kind of Plant

In the first place, know the species or the horticultural variety with which you are working. Our floristic manuals of native plants make it appear that a species is something very distinct in nature. As facetiously stated by some of our more liberal Western plant taxonomists, a species was at one time created by an Act of God. Later, it respectably left the Ark in company with its spouse; and thereafter stayed haughtily aloof from all the de-segregation tendencies in the world about it. No. A "species" is made by a taxoonomist, not by a God. A species is a relatively uniform population of individuals, existing at this moment in the geological evolution of the race. It is a relative continuity between two relative discontinuities, in the opinion of some botanist who has the audacity to break into print on the subject. (I should know—the making of a species was my very first contribution to the scientific literature— a very incidental offshoot of a technical study). A species is a name, attached to that continuity. When, therefore, you are working with a "species," be modest and cautious. It may be quite different, in soil requirements, in time of flowering, in size of flowers, than what goes by the same name in someone else's territory.

Horticultural varieties of plants can be more stable and reliable. These are often propagated vegetatively, that is, without benefit of pollen, ovules, seeds and the associated techniques. They are as alike as different branches off the same tree—which indeed, they may be, as rooted cuttings of an apple. They are as alike as identical twins in a human family. But watch out. Even identical twins can develop very differently when separated and brought up in totally different environments.

23

In the second place, when we become interested in a certain plant, we should endeavor to find out about its normal modes of reproduction. I do not mean its reproduction in floricultural practice, but the way it spreads and disseminates itself in nature. If we know what happens in nature, we can encourage or discourage that phenomenon according to our wishes.

"That is easy," you say, "by seeds, of course." Yes, I once thought so too. But that is only part of the story. The weed seedlings in your garden are overwhelming evidence of the importance of seeds. Young birches, pines and ash in the grassland are further evidence. The heavy production of acorns and beechnuts bears out the tale. But there is also another tale. The more one studies nature, the more one realizes that many of the predominant "plants" in the Vegetation did not begin their present growth as germinated seed. That came several "generations" earlier, from the now-ancient roots. Then why this annual profusion of flowers and fruits on the part of plants? Your guess is as good as mine. Nature is lavish, and irrational. (Only man is rational.) That abundance: to please the bees; to feed the squirrels; to delight man; or—as I am sure they, the plants, would say if they were conscious—to please themselves, for the sheer fun of it. The fact is: they do; and that is all that concerns us at the moment.

Vegetative reproduction is what we should watch for and know about, for it is by vegetative reproduction that many species continue from "generation" to "generation." Vegetative reproduction is that which arises by special development of some vegetative part of the plant, such as leaves, stems or roots. In temperate regions, leaves are of little importance. It is the stems and roots we should know about.

Some plants "get about" largely by specially developed stems. There are above-ground stems that arch down and root at the tip (like some blackberries). Others run over the surface of the ground, rooting at every node (strawberries and myrtle). Others have their stems underground, at various depths and of various sizes, spreading outward, and periodically sending up shoots. Knowing these differences, you can effectively encourage or discourage many kinds of plants.

Vegetative reproduction by true roots may be less common than by stems, at least for herbaceous plants. But in such large root-suckering trees as beech, aspen, locust, ailanthus, sassafras and plum, it may be the dominant factor that changes and controls the vegetational landscape. It is essential to know the root system of the plant with which you are working.

24

Life-form of the Plant

In the third place, the term "life-form" is used in a general way by botanists to refer to the vegetative appearance of a plant at maturity. There are many classifications of life-forms, the majority of which recognize the major groups of: trees, shrubs, and herbs. (The word herb is also used to refer to plants of special medicinal scent or taste value, as in "herb garden.") Herbs (all plants not woody) are conveniently divided into three groups: annual, biennial and perennial, depending on the persistence of the root systems. Ragweed is an annual, starting each year from seed; carrot is a biennial, flowering, fruiting and dying in the second year; irises are perennial, sending up new foliage each year. Another convenient classification of herbs is into: grass-like plants or graminoids (grasses, sedges and rushes), and forbs (all other herbs, including those with conspicuous flowers). We shall be using all these terms in this book.

The Naturalistic Landscaper is especially interested in the forms of the forbs, for these forms can be used to describe or judge the value of the plant in his Grassland. The following categories often need to be recognized:

1. The Narcissus Type. Narcissus, and other spring-flowering bulbs have their own especial role. They spring up as green oases thru the snow-flattened mulch. They burst into astonishing blooms, just at a season when blooms are most appreciated. Then the grasses emerge and overwhelm them. The old foliage is still there, yellowing and eventually browning (as we know from the unsightly garden plants), but in the grassland no one sees it.

2. The Daisy Type (most highly desirable). The foliage is low and inconspicuous. The flowers are raised on high, just above the level of the grasses, where they can be seen best. They form the pattern of our "oriental rug." After flowering they dry and seem to vanish, while some other flower can emerge into new conspicuousness.

3. The Cinquefoil Type (highly desirable). The cinquefoil seems to cover the ground with its semi-prostrate node-rooting stems, thru which the vertical blades of the grass emerge. This blanket is literally sequin-spangled with yellow in its flowering season.

4. The Blazing Star Type (desirable). The Liatrises or blazing stars send up bright striking spikes of flowers high above the general level of the grassland. Many of the lilies belong to this general life-form. These are the "feature plants," not to be used too abundantly, for tho the eye rests on them with pleasure, they break thru the smoothness of the grassland carpet, like a piece of furniture on our oriental rug.

5. The Peony Type. Here are plants that are extremely valuable because of their flowers. Their foliage however is rank and abundant. It persists long after the flowers have disappeared, forming a sort of blot in the fine weave of the grassland. For this reason, such plants must be placed with discretion, as where the summer foliage will merge with background shrubs.

6. The Rugose Goldenrod Type (usually undesirable). Goldenrods are of many types, some highly desirable, but this one (*Solidago rugosa*) forms a heavily foliaged mass, of such aggressiveness that it can eliminate the grasses and the forbs. For most of the season, it is simply a mass of rank foliage; it is colorful for a short time; then the rank foliage again takes over. If used sparingly, andor at a distance, it can have its value.

7. The Summer Goldenrod Type (usually undesirable). Summer goldenrod (*Solidago juncea*) typifies a plant that might otherwise be desirable, but its tall unsightly flowerstalks remain standing thru the winter and all thru the next season, disrupting the continuity of the grassland carpet. One can, of course, cut these down each fall. You may not want an acre of them.

In this discussion of types, you are beginning to form an idea of what is desirable for the Grassland. It is essentially a living carpet, basically of grasses and cinquefoil types. Flowering aspects of plants such as daisy emerge, and vanish, as the season progresses. Here and there are conspicuous feature plants, sometimes with more foliage than we may like, but then so placed as not to detract from the essential continuity of the grassland.

The "Tools" of Management

In Naturalistic Landscaping you are working with plants. You are either putting them in or taking them out. In that respect it is not much different from ordinary common gardening. But there is this difference: in ordinary gardening, you are working in bare soil, on a relatively small patch of ground, and you keep the soil essentially bare, a part of each year. In Naturalistic Landscaping, you are working in plant-covered land, and you shun bare soil, always. Furthermore, in gardening, you are forever clipping, pruning, staking; in Naturalistic Gardening, the plant grows as it wants to. If that way is not what you like, you do not enforce your will on that plant; you change to a different kind of plant. For these reasons, altho the various "tools" may be more or less the same as in gardening, you will use them with differing frequencies. For convenience these tools may be classed as (1) mechanical, and (2) chemical.

Mechanical Tools

I assume you will have all the mechanical tools that are needed in this game. By mechanical I mean those operating thru physical forces, human muscle (increasingly obsolescent), fueled motors, or electrical energy. The ordinary assortment of garden tools is frequently used: shovels, spades, trowels, sickles, scythes, saws, axes, shears, clippers. Do not neglect a small "lady's shovel," with about a 6×7 inch blade. Unless you are in the 200-pound class, there is no sense in jumping on a shovel to cut 12 inches of snarled quackgrass, when six inches would do just as well.

Power tools will not be in great demand, unless possibly at the start when you first enter your jungle of brushland. Chain saws, and knapsack rotary-bladed brush cutters have their places. Lawn mowers are out of place, tho you may want sickle-bar equipment for developing a mowed trail. Tractors for ploughing and harrowing are definitely out of place, unless you want some original construction, such as a small dam; and then it may be best to have the work done by an outside contractor. There is much little dam foolishness in our society, as well as big dam foolishness. You are probably not the kind to have bought a tractor barely able to turn around in your miniature vegetable garden, but even if so, manipulating a stream can be dam foolishness at several different levels.

Chemical Tools

The word chemical is here used in contrast to mechanical. Mechanical energy is a matter of forces and pressures. It is related to wheels, levers, screws, to electricity and magnetism. Chemical energy on the contrary is related to the behavior of atoms and molecules. Chemical substances are those of known composition and organization in regard to the elements, such as carbon, hydrogen, oxygen, nitrogen, phosphorus and potassium. The sugar and salt on our dining room tables are two of the purest chemicals we meet in all our lives, and quite essential to our lives. So also are the anesthetics that have removed the tortures of the dentist's chair and the operating room. Likewise the carbon monoxide of an automobile exhaust that can terminate other tortures; and the arsenicals, that can be as effective as a gory guillotine without the colorful display.

For our purposes, chemical tools have three potential roles in Naturalistic Landscaping: (1) as fertilizers; (2) as controllers of diseases and animal pests; and (3) as weed killers.

1. Fertilizers

Plants, in order to grow and to grow properly, absorb thru their roots both water and a variety of substances in relatively simple chemical form. It has long been known, both in gardens and under natural conditions, that the addition of various substances will improve that growth. These substances may be animal excrements, compost of decayed animal and plant matter, or chemicals. Since natural soils are constantly being leached by rain water, and the nutrients constantly being washed down our rivers (even without floods and soil erosion), and since this loss occurs more rapidly than new nutrients can be produced by weathering of the soil and natural mulching soils are seldom in an "optimum" state for plant growth. They are just in a "natural" state. This natural state can usually be "improved" by fertilizers. Our food, our society, our civilization, are directly dependent upon this artificially increased level of plant growth. Compost is certainly an excellent fertilizer, but unfortunately, there is not, there cannot be, enough compost (even if every mite of it were saved) to maintain the world's agriculture at its present levels. Thus, the importance of chemical fertilizers. In the Rothamsted Experimental Gardens in England, chemical fertilizers have been used for over a century, with no diminution in crop production and with no deterioration in the health of animals eating those crops.

Use fertilizers if you want, in your Naturalistic Landscaping. I do, in a few cases; but I look upon it as "cheating," a return to fussy gardening, even if on one square foot of a one-acre grassland. Ordinarily, if the natural fertility level is not suited for the plant, I let the plant die.

2. Controllers of Diseases and Animal Pests

Diseases and pests are entirely natural phenomena in the life of the plants. The absence of such diseases and pests is a thoroly unnatural condition. In that sense, the completely healthy man is a completely abnormal organism! True, in nature at large. The parasitologist, to study intestinal parasites, takes the first animal he comes upon. The bird-louse scientist finds what he wants on the first bird in the hand. The forest pathologist does not have to look far for the fungus cankers that signify the presence of rots. Diseases and pests are everywhere. They are an integral part of the vegetation around us.

Now our entire medical profession is engaged in the endless, costly, and eventually fruitless effort of keeping us free from diseases and pests. It is still worth while, for the individual. (I am not sure it is of much importance to the race. There is good reason to believe that the practice is dysgenic.) Somewhat similarly, the entire gardening profession is engaged in the endless, costly, and eventually fruitless effort of keeping our garden plants free of diseases and pests. Gardeners think it worth while. I am not sure it is of much importance to the plant races (tho there may be exceptions). Many of our garden plants have to be given perpetual care, equivalent to the best of our nursing homes—parasites in another sense. Eventually fruitless, as judged by the tremendous replacement business—of our commercial nurseries. So maybe it is "worth while."

As for Naturalistic Landscaping, I suggest you throw away all your powders and sprays. (Not too far—you may want them for some especial and critical case). If there are aphids, beetles, cutworms, blights, mildews, molds, rots, rusts, let them come. Let the weaklings die, even if they have the wan beauty of a 19th century neurotic consumptive courtesan. You only want the sturdy hardy individuals. (Or do you still want to be a nurse, a slave, a host organism parasitized by them?)

1. There are many kinds of herbicides, varying from simple and simply pronounced words as salt, gas and gasolene, to such a tongue-twister as polypropyleneglycolbutylether two, four, five-trichlorophenoxyacetate. The ones most useful are chemical derivatives of 2,4-dichlorophenoxyacetic acid and 2,4,5-trichlorophenoxyacetic acid, sometimes called the chlorophenoxy herbicides, sometimes called 2,4-D and 2,4,5-T; hereafter simply referred to as D–T. There are other herbicides on the commercial market; there will be others in the future; the comments below pertain only to D–T.

2. D–T herbicides are non-poisonous to all forms of animal life, including man, as normally used. Those individuals who won't use pesticides, no-how, no-wise, never, they like to refer to "toxicity tests," laboratory experiments in which the organism is fed increasingly large doses of the stuff until he finally gives up the ghost. Could be, just from overeating! Toxicity tests are most important laboratory procedures, for peanuts as well as pesticides, but we should not confuse them with practical everyday uses of such materials. Sometimes government regulation is a bit slow in the coming, but I have no reason to be concerned about the D–T compounds in the present state of knowledge.

3. Grasses are relatively resistant to these herbicides, as well as ferns, and certain deep-rooted rhizomatous perennials such as common milkweed, dogbane, and a loosestrife. Thus, the herbicides are said to be "selective" when they are applied indiscriminately.

4. These herbicides are not soil sterilants, baring the soil and making it unfit for other plants to grow.

5. The herbicides do not persist in the soil for more than one or a few months. They are broken down (used as "food") by certain soil bacteria, and eventually decompose to carbon, hydrogen, oxygen and nitrogen. There are no persistent residues, such as of copper, arsenic, sulfur, lead or zinc.

3. Weed Killers

In Naturalistic Landscaping, fertilizers play a very minor role. Disease and pest controllers play a very minor role. But the weed killers play a tremendously important role. So important is this role that for a long time the title of this book was planned to be "Taming the Landscape with Herbicides."

Words should be used properly. Preferably, herbicide means plant-killer. (The word herb in this case means all plants.) In contrast, zoicides are animal killers, for anything from mosquitoes to moose. When insects alone are considered, the chemicals are called insecticides. Since these chemicals are manufactured, promoted, and sold as killers of organisms-which-we-don't-want, they are collectively called pesticides. Few of them are specific for one pest alone, the so-called target organism. Instead they may kill a vast range of animals, from mouse to man. It is like shooting at one starling in a large flock of swallows, with a high-powered shotgun. You will probably get your starling. Furthermore, what you do not kill (to follow our analogy—like the mole that may be underground) may then increase to epidemic proportions. In addition, we do not know how long some of these other poisons may remain in the environment, in the soil, and carried from one tolerant animal to another that may not be tolerant. Altogether, the virile enthusiasm with which various elements in our society are boosting the use of some (not all) of the pesticides in the mid-20th century is valid cause for concern.

Herbicides are used as weed and brush killers. A "weed" is a plant out of place, that is, a plant we do not want. Most people use the word weed to refer to herbaceous plants only. "Brush" is composed of woody plants. Previously, the word was merely a descriptive term, referring to any mixture of shrubs and young trees. Due to the advertising literature promoting "brush killers," brush has become a derogatory term, comparable to weed. The herbicide kills brush. Therefore all brush must be undesirable. (Else how can the most chemical be sold?)

Do not think you can be a Naturalistic Landscaper without using herbicides. I tried to, back in the 1920's—before these chemicals were even a glint in the eyes of the manufacturing companies. I used a pickaxe and shovel. I did not get very far. It was much too much work. Besides, I left little bare spots of soil, and that is not playing the game properly. Bare soil is an open sesame for starting all sorts of seedlings that you do not want. You produce more trouble than you eliminate. It was only in the mid-1940's, with certain herbicides commercially available, that I could return to this type of work. I've been using them ever since.

How freely and fearlessly should you use herbicides? Yes, there are certain things you should know, and the numbered statements below cover all the important features. Knowing these things, you will be able to use herbicides with the same ease with which you put sugar in your morning dose of caffeine, sprinkle salt on your lunch, gulp down an alcoholic drink before dinner, smoke a stogie after, and go to bed with a barbiturate. All these things are poisonous, or can be, if misused. A "poison" is not in what you use, but in how you use it.

DAUCUS

D. Carota

6. The herbicides can be applied selectively. This is one secret of their enormous value in Naturalistic Landscaping. A young red maple can be removed from the very center of a blueberry bush, with no harm to the blueberry.

7. 2,4-D is effective on forbs, the so-called broad-leaved herbs (but not on some of the rhizomatous herbs that spread by underground stems). It is not sufficiently effective on woody plants.

2,4,5-T is effective on all plants including woody ones. T is more costly than D alone, but a mixture of the two is about as effective as T alone. The commercial "brush killers," which you will use most often, are mixtures of D and T.

8. There can be unwanted damage from both drift and volatility. Drift is due to liquid particles being blown sidewise. Do not spray on a windy day, or hold your spray nozzle up high. Volatility is a gaseous emanation. Early tender spring foliage is especially sensitive. Keep at least 25 feet away from such sensitive plants as roses, grapes, tomatoes, raspberries and blackberries, at all seasons.

9. The effect of the herbicide in the plant is predominantly upward, not downward. This is embarrassing to the chemical manufacturer, exasperating to the Naturalistic Landscaper, and highly advantageous to the plant. Industry has spent large sums of money financing prestigeful university research trying to "prove" that the chemical goes "down" in the plant, i.e., down from the leaves into the roots. The evidence for such downward movement is in terms of a measly few centimeters in isolated strands of the conductive systems. The fact remains that in most practical field applications, distant roots are not chemical-killed. When these roots (as in aspen) can send up shoots, beware! Improper spraying may serve as a reforestation measure!

10. Herbicide treatments of one kind or another are applicable in every month of the year. Do not spray during or after rains (when the bark is wet). To spray before a rain is not advised, tho the oil sprays do not wash off readily. Do not spray in deep snow, since it is important for stump sprouting species like maples and oaks to soak the root collar, the part at the soil line, where shoots can emerge.

Equipment Needed

You will need sprayer, chemical, and a brush hook.

For a sprayer, any knapsack sprayer sold in gardening and agricultural supply places will be suitable. The three-gallon sprayers operate like a bicycle-tire pump and it is difficult to maintain a constant pressure in the tank. With five-gallon sprayers, one pumps with the right hand while spraying with the left. Altho the five-gallon sprayer may be reasonably heavy when full (about 50 pounds), it need not be refilled often. If kept at the proper level on the back, even a light-weight person can carry it with ease.

Keep the sprayer for D–T spraying only. It is difficult and time-consuming to clean it, and even the slightest trace of these chemicals, sprayed onto other plants, will keep them from flowering.

Most commercial sprayers are fitted with nozzles suited for high-volume wide-scattered orchard-tree spraying. You will need another type of nozzle. My choice is a low-volume unit that gives a fine spray in the shape of a flat fan. It is equipped with a check valve, that prevents drip between sprays.

For the chemical, any commercial "Brush Killer" will do. It will contain esters of 2,4-D and 2,4,5-T. Recommendations on the can for mixing are generally satisfactory. Be sure to note the concentration of the chemical you are buying. What is cheapest, may also be weakest. Somewhere, in very fine print, it should state that there are "4 pounds acid equivalent per gallon;" and if you do not understanding what that means, do not worry.

Just see that that is what you buy.

You will be using two kinds of spray: weak water sprays and strong oil sprays.

HIERACIUM

Water sprays are mixtures of one part of chemical to 100 parts of water. Use tablespoons, cups, beer cans or gallon jugs, but keep the ratio straight.

Oil sprays are mixtures of one part of chemical to 8-to-50 parts of oil. Any kind of light oil, such as fuel oil or kerosene. Some contractors recommend one-to-eight (you use more chemical that way). I have for several years been using 1-to-50, with satisfactory results. Effectiveness more often depends, not on the strength of the solution, but in using adequate amounts of it.

I always carry a small brush hook with me, hanging on my belt, or on the pumping handle. Some resistant plants, like white ash, should be cut and stub-sprayed. If one does not spray such a plant at the very moment of cutting, you are likely to miss it (and find three of them next year, four feet high).

(The different spraying techniques, and the special needs of the different species, will be discussed fully in "Part I, The Art of Eliminating Plants." Herbicides will also be used afterwards, in maintaining the landscape you have so created, but in relatively small quantities.)

H. aurantiacum

Part I

INTAGLIO

The Art of Eliminating Plants

Part I

INTAGLIO

The Art of Eliminating Plants

Ordinary gardening is largely involved with putting in plants, and getting them to grow. Naturalistic Landscaping is largely involved with taking out unwanted plants, and simply letting the remaining ones grow. I use the Italian word intaglio for this latter process, since it bears many analogies to the fine art of engraving, to a carving out of unwanted portions of a flat or sloping surface, so that a planned design remains.

This type of intaglio can, conceivably, be the only procedure with which you will be concerned. Intaglio, and intaglio alone, can produce some beautiful Naturalistic Landscapes. Take things out; let nature do the rest. For these reasons, the sections on "Planning" (immediately to follow) are placed in this Part I. Planning, in this game, is overwhelmingly a problem of what-to-take-out. This situation is different from that of the gardener, who starts with "nothing" and is forever concerned with what-to-put-in. I say "forever," for what he puts in is not likely to last very long, even with his care.

In Part II, we will consider the "maintenance" of the landscape. There are some very important points here, but you will find that "maintenance" is generally an absurdly easy task.

In Part III, we will let our meddling propensities get the best of us, and carry on some actual embellishment in the form of planting. We can use only native materials, if that is your preference. Or we can use some hardy plants from other countries, plants which would probably move onto our land naturally, if it were not for the accident of an ocean, a mountain range, or a desert separating their original home from us. Or we can use some horticultural varieties, on the grounds that man has only saved and perpetuated what naturally arose when we brought certain parent plants into congenial propinquity, and which offspring would otherwise have been lost—as have countless other such "experiments" of nature herself.

A. PLANNING THE LANDSCAPE

Whether or not you plan your landscape in advance, down to the last little crocus, will probably depend more on your heart than on your mind. You will find landscaping books, the first chapter of which is entitled "Plan Carefully Before Planting." I am sure there are others who would recommend going step by step, urging you in sage counsel "never to cross a bridge until you come to it." It is fun to plan, especially in the middle of winter. It is fun to change plans. It is even more fun to discover, in a later year, some little swale, a picturesque conifer at the side, a view beyond, which quite simply you never realized had existed.

My advice is to do what you like best. Plan a bit at the desk. Work a bit in the field. Do not bite off more acres than you can chew up and swallow, or you will find that you end up with just as much unwanted brush as you started with—or so it appears.

Get to know your tract of land, in all its messy brushiness, very thoroly. The more imagination, pure and simple imagination, you have, the better. Compare yourself to a sculptor, who "sees" his finished statue inside the block of marble, while his apprentice sees only a hunk of stone.

In general, it may be said that your landscape will be composed of open Grasslands, of irregular shape and contour, surrounded by belts or broken areas of Shrublands, the whole set in a matrix of Forest.

It might be helpful to think of the Grasslands as of six general types: (1) a clear open grassland, with relatively smooth tho curving margins (p. 38a); (2) a grassland spotted with individual single shrubs, such as tall blueberry (p. 38a); (3) a grassland with an extremely irregular "coastline," with numerous "embayments" and "lagoons," each affording its own landscaping surprises (p. 39a); (4) a grassland which is essentially a system of wide grassy trails, either gently curving or tortuously twisted, lying in a "sea" of shrubs, the shrub sea being surrounded by forest (p. 39a); and (5) a system of interconnecting circular or oval grassland "lakes', in its way like the flat, heavily glaciated, poorly drained terrain of Finland and the upper parts of the American states of Michigan, Wisconsin and Minnesota (p. 40a). All the above types are applicable to the "general uplands" of abandoned agricultural lands. If you are fortunate enough to have a flat meadow with a stream, with old drainage channels, you can capitalize magnificently on this gift of nature.

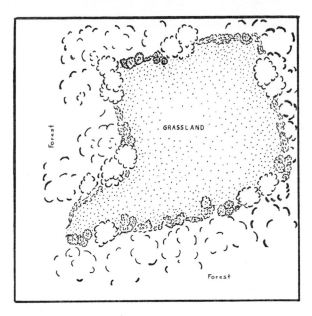

Plan for a clear open Grassland, with relatively smooth tho curving margins. The edges are a highly varied assemblage of tall herbs, more than 25 kinds of shrubs usually grouped in masses of 10 or 20 individuals, and various forest effects including young aspen colonies, dense coniferous stands, the gray boles of a mature maple forest, and white shafts of paper birch. The surface of the land reaches its highest elevation at the upper right, from which an extensive view can be obtained. (From a 7-acre field planned and developed by the author.)

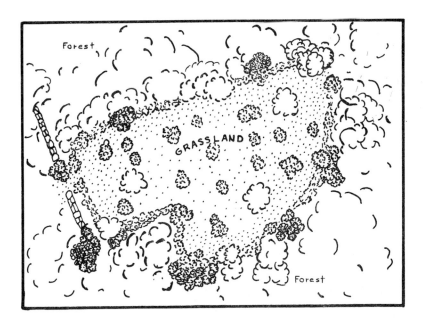

Plan for a Grassland spotted with individual single shrubs. Several apple trees remain from an ancient orchard. Individual native shrubs have been allowed to develop, in full light and without competition from adjacent plants. A few have been planted, but most of them were saved from the original intaglio operations. (From a 2-acre field planned and developed by the author.)

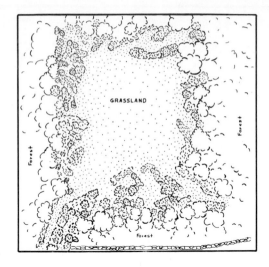

Plan for a Grassland with an extremely irregular "coastline," with numerous "embayments" and "lagoons" each affording its own landscaping surprises. The various embayments were carefully chosen so as to take advantage of large rocks, of berry-bearing shrubs, of certain patches of goldenrods or ferns. The woody vegetation between embayments often rises to heights of 15 or 20 feet, developing a feeling of secrecy and isolation for each such area, as well as a loss of orientation due to the frequent turnings and twistings. (From a 4-acre field planned and developed by the author.)

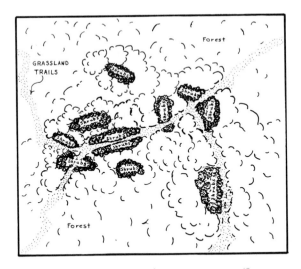

Plan for a Grassland which is essentially a system of wide grassy gently curving trails. Depending upon the degree of curvature, the trail "unfolds" 50 to 150 feet ahead of the walker. Special shrubs or boulders are featured along the sides. By contrast, there are several very narrow and tortuously twisted trails with curves every 5 to 10 feet. All these trails pass thru a series of "shrub seas," themselves surrounded by young forest. These shrub seas are areas up to 300 feet long from which all trees have been removed, and in which shrubs 5 to 8 feet tall cover most of the land. They are not easily traversed on foot, but since one can look over their summits, they are bright and sunny. (From a 12-acre field planned and developed by the author.)

1. Vistas and Trails

Your planning should take into account two elements that can easily be overlooked. One is what you will see, beyond the confines of the immediate grassland, the VISTAS. The other is where you, and others, will walk, the TRAILS.

Vistas are curious things. You may pass by a spot many times, many years. Then, one day you will suddenly "see" it. Rather, you realize what you would see if you removed a few trees and a bit of brush. Wander around your property in winter, when the foliage is gone. Let in more sky. Get a glimpse down that valley. View that distant mountain. There are "Sky Vistas." They are often most effective when at the top of a rise, or a small rocky bluff. If the land drops away in front of you, you may leave attractive shrubs as a ground cover, and get your view right over their tops. Such vistas are utilized constantly along scenic highways. You can probably have your own.

At other times you can remove lower branches and shrubs from the forest, opening up a "Tunnel Vista" to a grassland beyond. Such tunnels are especially effective in summer, when the sunny grassland shines thru like a brightly lit room at the end of a dark hallway. They have the appeal of keyhole-peeping as seen thru the wrong end of a telescope, with the added attraction that you are free to walk right in and inspect at close range.

A trail system demands careful thought. It should be practicable. It should center out from your home. There should be "round trips," of various lengths, so you do not have to come back the same way. If there are flooded sections in spring or the rainy season, or steep rocky slopes that would tax an older visitor or one inexperienced on show-shoes, have alternates available. Do not have needless meanders, or even you will "cut corners." Avoid two sides of a right triangle when the hypotenuse is the logical route. You may have to take such meaningless detours on many college campuses; you never would, on your own property. See that you pass by the more important features, the rare shrub, the gnarled tree, the huge boulders, the views and vistas. Trails thru grassland can be marked with boulders or cairns, or kept mowed once to thrice a year. Thru the forest, they require initial clearing and herbicide treatment, after which one need only remove falling branches. The author maintains a mile of mowed grassland trails (about ten hours of labor a year, much more if the power scythe becomes temperamental), and about 5 miles of forest trails (needing just occasional pick-up, as one walks them).

2. Plans for Spring

Imagine what a spring would be. Wait to live thru a spring. Plan for spring. Spring reveals features in the landscape that are invisible in other seasons. The pale green of the new foliage of a clump of birches or of aspens, the gray of the pussy willows, the white orange and yellow of the daffodils, these are elements in the landscape that should be set against backgrounds of coniferous trees or evergreen shrubs.

Actually, early spring is not a blazing glaring spectacle, as it is in well-kept gardens during tulip, peony and iris times. Yet spring has moved men's souls more than any other season. Those pagan priapean festivals of ancient Greece apparently had a sufficient hold on Western peoples so that the Christian Easter was undoubtedly scheduled as a lucky substitute, not always successfully. After all, what is the Easter Parade on New York's Fifth Avenue but a latter-day emergence of tribal custom, under the relatively moral but certainly a-religious display of beautiful bonnetry, which is worn in the belief that it enhances the beauty below, tho at times it only diverts the eye from the bulges below. There will be no such display in your Landscape, but the spirit and feeling may be just as intense, and far more sincere. Plan with spring in mind.

Wild plums (*Prunus nigra*) in flower on a rural roadside. Ten years before, these plums were all but invisible in a tangle of maple, oak, ash and choke cherry.

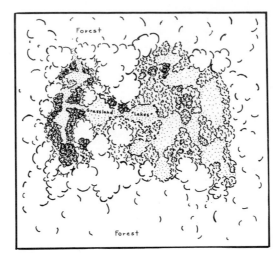

Plan for a Grassland composed of a system of interconnecting circular or oval grassland "lakes," in its way like the flat heavily glaciated poorly drained terrain of Finland, and the upper parts of the American states of Michigan, Wisconsin and Minnesota. The edges of these "lakes" are not smooth, but are a series of swept-out areas, often with radii up to 10 feet (a reasonable limit for knapsack-spraying when standing at one place). Intervening woody vegetation, 10 to 15 feet tall, promotes a feeling of secrecy and isolation for each such "lake." (From a 2.5-acre field planned and developed by the author). These figures can only indicate the larger and grosser features of planning. Many of the attractive elements are on a size scale too small for inclusion. Single unusual shrubs, the clear bole of a tree, a cluster of boulders, a swept-out arc of wildflowers, a distant view under the branches of a coniferous tree, these are elements of the landscape that can only be incorporated by careful on-the-site planning.

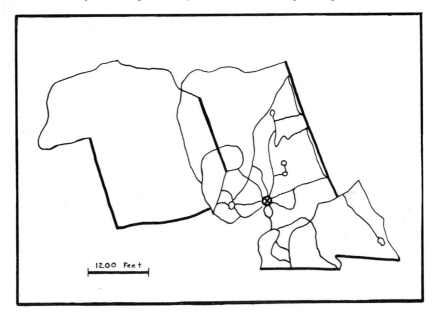

A trail system planned and executed by the author, with eight trails radiating from the main residence. The system reflects not only property lines and stone walls, but streams, pools, cliffs and special aspects of the topography.

3. Plans for Summer

Summer will surely take the least imagination, if only because you will probably be out in summer more than in any other season, and you will be aware of every flicker of her eyelash.

There will be one continuous succession of changing surprises, as flowering aspect succeeds flowering aspect in your Grassland. Never a dull moment.

It is the "feature plants" which demand most thought, in saving, or in planting. Put them in compact groups that appear solid at a distance of one or two hundred feet. A single one is simply lost. Most of the shrubs flower early in the season. They also look better 6, 8 or 10 at a place. (You are no longer restricted to a 100×100–foot city lot.)

Late summer demands more careful thought. Fewer plants give color. This is the time when the horticulturist talks of "bridge plants." He is plainly at a loss to keep your garden brilliant. It is the dowdy down-at-the-heel late-middle-age of garden life, before that final flowering which so gloriously crowns the entire flowering—for a chosen few. Pay particular attention in summer to Japanese iris, the milkweed called butterfly weed, tiger lilies, monardas, and phlox. Here is where nature needs some help if the dry hot days of summer are to be kept brightly hued.

4. Plans for Autumn

When autumn comes, I am sure it is the finest season of the year (but I feel the same way at three other seasons). Buzzing and biting "bugs" are gone, the sun is invigoratingly warm. The grasslands are first gay with the yellows of goldenrods, then with the blues of the asters. Then the rainbow hues of the chrysanthemums take over (if you can convince them to grow by themselves). All this while— if you live in one of the Deciduous Forest regions of the world—the autumn foliage puts on a display unrivaled anywhere else on earth.

It is wise to plan for this foliage display. Each species of tree, and many of the shrubs, have their own shades of reds and yellows. What brighter deeper red than a mass of blueberry or huckleberry bushes. The fine yellows of the birches, the incomparable golden of the aspen, both contrast with the brilliance of the red maple. With these colors on your palette, you can paint in huge gorgeous masses. That which all summer had been a homogeneous green background of shrubs and forest suddenly assumes new significance, each kind of plant no more to be mistaken for another than an iris for a peony.

Keep in mind also that each species has its own time of maximum color, with enough odd-ball individuals to make life interesting. Some consistently reach their peak of color earliest; others hang on and on, like a prima donna taking too many curtain calls for an enthusiastic audience. Keep careful notes on these differences as they occur in your locale, and you will find that you can encourage a clump of aspen in a distant corner, or a glowing red maple at the top of the hill. Such plans pay unbelievably rich dividends in the years to come.

An herbicide-managed grassland, with 20-year old junipers (*Juniperus communis*) selected for the variety of their shapes.

Winter view of a forested rural roadside near a property managed by the author. Note the inconspicuous utility pole in the background. This particular scenic road will be the subject of a special bulletin to be published by the Connecticut Arboretum.

5. Plans for Winter

"Plan for winter?", you say, "Nonsense." Nonsense to you. Winter is a symphony of brown green and white. Green on the forest floor with the lycopods. Green among the shrubs with junipers and laurels. Green among the trees, with pine, hemlock, spruce and fir. Plan to feature the evergreen trees and shrubs in large bold virile masses, slashed by the immaculate whiteness of birches, and you will think yourself an architect, designing a fairy castle, with all its wings, courtyards, and turrets.

Plan for snow and ice also. Every species of conifer, and every deciduous tree and shrub take on new and distinctive forms under the white drapery of heavy snows or the crystalline casings of ice that can serve as twinkling prisms in a bright sun. That same ice weighs down the branches to reveal a whole new world of harmonious arcs and curves, an unimagined transformation previously unimaginable. There is no finer snow sight than the spun delicacy of a cluster of bending birches set beside the mammoth blanketing fans of a group of pines.

Plan for all the seasons. Your landscape is like some extraordinary combination of the Mozart concertos. The full symphony is always there, playing in combination, well worth listening to. But as time progresses, instrument after instrument finds itself in the spotlight and demands attention. Every instrument with a dual role: as a soloist for a short time, as part of the background symphony the rest of the time. One must know his instruments before he can compose a successful multiple concerto.

B. TECHNIQUES FOR ELIMINATING PLANTS

Initial planning, as discussed in preceding section A, will allow you to lay the major areas of grassland, of other types of herbland such as those involving ferns and goldenrods, of shrublands, and of background forest. Your problem is to "take out."

You will take out all trees, and trees only, if you wish a shrubland.

You will take out all woody plants, both trees and shrubs, if you wish to be left with an herbland. If you later wish a grassland, you will also take out the more coarsely growing herbs and those ferns that are not desirable for your purposes.

It is a great saving in time and energy to know in advance where you are going to end up—with shrubland, heavy herbland, or grassland. If you go step by step, you may find that certain shrubs will completely take over the land when you remove the trees. Then, after removing the shrubs, heavy herbs previously rare will form a solid mass of vegetation. By that time, the few grasses may hardly be in a position to cover the land without an intermediate bare-soil stage, which in turn, may allow trees to seed in. Do not let this happen.

KNOW THE COMPLETE FLORISTIC COMPOSITION of your area, once you decide what vegetation types you want to end up with. This may sound like a formidable botanical task, and it may be, to a few people. If you have known nothing but carnations, roses and chrysanthemums from the florist shop, or tulips and peonies near the lawn, you should spend one season living with your land. You do not have to know the Latin names of these plants, but get to know them, as individual species. They are all distinct, and have personalities. Look at these plants as tho you were a deaf man watching a stage play. You can still separate Beauty from the Beast, negro from white, grandpa from baby. You might even be able to see differences between twins. Decide what you want, and what you don't want. Surely there is someone in your neighborhood who can then put names on most of these things for you. It might be the local biology teacher, or any of the government extension agriculturists or foresters.

THE ECLECTIC VS. THE BLANKETEER. Once you have decided what Vegetation Type you wish to develop (young forest, shrubland, heavy herbland, or grassland), once you think you have a knowledge of what kinds of plants are involved on the tract, then you have to make an important decision: will you be an eclectic or a blanketeer? The eclectic is the man of knowledge, who goes in carefully and picks and chooses. The blanketeer is the man with the attitude of driverless bulldozer—enormous power and action, but hardly discrimination. "Foolishness," you say, "there is nothing in all that rubbish and brush to save. Let's clean it all out, every damn bit of it. I can hire a man with a power saw to cut it all down in no time at all. Then we can spray the whole area. Sure. Junk. Clean it all up at once..."

Just possibly you may be right! In about one per cent of the cases I have known, the blanketeer approach might be justified—after a thoro inspection of the area. But if you really feel any deepseated compulsion to tear into the land in bulldozer fashion, I strongly urge you to drop this book, give it to a friend, and go out and get yourself a job on a highway labor crew, or as a highway engineer, or in the commercial herbicide field. They are looking for such people. Quite simply, your God did not design you for Naturalistic Landscaping. You are out of tune in several respects:

Just because you seem to see undesirable kinds of "weeds" does not mean that there is nothing worth while saving. The rare plant of today may become the dominant plant of tomorrow. The rare plant of today may be the feature specimen plant of tomorrow. The rare plant of today may be grown for a time, and then transplanted to a favored spot tomorrow. Some of the finest plants are the rare plants. Sometimes (but not often) their very rarity makes them "fine." Yet such superiority may often be the evaluation of the character who considers rarity and quality synonymous—a type of snobbishness, for the man not the plant.

Furthermore, what you see above ground is not always indicative of what there is below ground. A few measly sparse scattered shoots of huckleberry can indicate a root system that fairly well ramifies all thru the soil. On cleaning out the overstory, huckleberry can blanket the area. A few sterile shoots of colonial goldenrod can be saved, to spread in the subsequently open soil to form a large solid clump. The gawky viburnum which never flowered in the forest can be cut back, and allowed to regrow and flower in the open. The pink azalea may be surrounded by miniature seedlings, kept nibbled down by rabbits and mice for the last 20 years. If you protect them by wire screening from the animals, you will soon have some superb young shrubs for transplanting. Woodland ground covers of various kinds can be moved to new sites. They will be lost anyway, for they do not thrive under a dense shrub cover, and grasses will crowd them out.

In short, there are 99 chances out of a hundred that your brushland should be treated with eclecticism. Take out only those things you know you do not want. Leave untouched what you do not know. It may prove very valuable.

ARE YOU IN A HURRY? The next decision to make is concerning the quickness with which you want results. There are slow ways of doing these things, and faster ways. For example, basal-bark spraying is one of the most effective and cheap ways of killing some trees, but it is also one of the slowest, for it may take a year before the plant is killed. Then you can either chop down the dead tree, or let it stand and slowly crumble under the interesting impact of animals, insects and fungi.

There is good reason for being relatively hasty if you are a retired senior citizen in his 60's, 70's or 80's, and are fearful of cancer in the bargain. Some day I may be so myself. At least I hope to live that long. But if you are 20 or 30, being in a hurry is another problem. The normal American is neurotically hurried. That sometimes-admirable trait has made them leaders or near-leaders in a great variety of human amusements, involving telephones, radios, TV, automobiles, airplanes and flush toilets. A musician can now set someone to banging on a piano, while another pushes the piano screechingly over the floor; the recording of the noise is called music. An artist can stand on the top of a step ladder, yelling to his naked model as—with her foremost parts paint-smeared—she slithers across a huge canvas on the floor. A sculptor, sitting beside a pile of metal junk gathered from the town dump can, blindfolded (so as not to let his sight interfere with blind creation), take the debris piece by piece, sticking the things together into some contraption that does not collapse; it possesses "balance." A gasket-like design can be repeated 24 times in each square of a checkerboard pattern, on each of four sides of a cube-shaped building, and the result is "architecture." Some literary editors discuss, analyze and compliment these contemporary fashions with solemn pseudo-erudition, while the sheep-like public follow, with over-display of their democratic freedom. I am not so sure that Mozart, Da Vinci, Michelangelo or Christopher Wren would approve. Nor do I have the arrogance to say who is "right." But I do say that if you are in this kind of hurry, and have these standards of craftsmanship and esthetics, I urge you most seriously to put aside this book, and turn to your nearest landscape contractor, who is only too anxious to convince you of the merit of his highly costly plan, to start with complete bulldozing. He will even supply a gardener each season in the future, to keep it in order—at only triple the minimum legal hourly wage.

So—if you have decided you are not under a compulsion to transform the entire area into a finished product in one year; if you have decided that you are an eclectic, with discrimination, able to utilize all the potentialities that nature is offering; if you know the plants on your area reasonably well—then you can start operating. We have already discussed the "tools" that you need (pages 27 to 34), both mechanical and chemical. Now we will approach and re-approach our subject from three different aspects:

1. The kinds of techniques, such as peeling, stub-spraying, basal-spraying.
2. The kinds of plants, not by species, but by "types," such as stump-sprouting trees, root-suckering woody plants, rhizomatous herbs, etc.
3. A calendar, indicating the sequence of events around the 12 months of the year.

1. Kinds of Elimination Techniques

a) Mechanical Techniques

In these days of power tools and mechanical monsters, many Americans are almost ashamed to use a simple tool, or even simple muscle. In this game, if you have such ideas, you had best try to lose them. Power equipment has its place, but in some instances there is no practical substitute for mind and muscle, even if you have very little of each.

CHOPPING. A hatchet or an axe is a valuable tool. This technique for felling a tree is as old as primitive man—and he merely learned from the beavers. With few exceptions, the conifers do not resprout from the stump. Consequently, if you want to remove small specimens (up to 3 or 4 inches in diameter), particularly if they are mixed up with shrubs, or are a long rocky walk from your headquarters, you may find that a small axe is much the more sensible way of destroying them, in terms of time and money, than packing in a chemical spray. The tree should be completely severed from its base. Whether you leave it leaning against the shrubs (it will decay, and drop, in a couple of years), or knock off the branches and leave it flat on the ground, is a matter of taste. There is nothing "wrong" about seeing such dead branches among the shrubs. They are always occurring under natural conditions. And you may find that rare warblers will alight on them, giving you a chance to see some you would otherwise miss, if they had nothing but leafy branches upon which to perch.

RINGING AND PEELING. Another long-known way of killing a tree is to ring it, to cut off the bark in a complete circle around the trunk. You will recall that the cambium is the microscopically thin growing part of a tree trunk, lying just between the bark and the wood. It produces both wood (inwards) and bark (outwards). Thus, it itself is pushed outwards by the growth of the wood, and pushes the bark outwards (so it cracks, or thin layers fall off). To remove the bark is to dry and destroy the cambium. Furthermore, the conducting system in the bark (by which food goes from the foliage to the roots) is severed. The roots starve and die. The rest of the tree dies. (Some trees can send up new shoots from different parts of the roots. These we will discuss later.)

Trees may be ringed at any season of the year. A hatchet or an axe is desirable. It is best to remove a vertical band of four inches or more, or new growth may grow over, and reconnect the severed parts. It is also wise not to cut into the wood any more than necessary. Cutting into the wood means that you sever the conducting tissues for moving water and nutrients from the roots up into the foliage. If such conduction is stopped, it appears that new shoots below the ring may be stimulated. Such new shoots may develop into new trees.

The cambium is most active in spring and early summer. At this time, it is a slimy slippery layer, and the bark breaks very easily from the wood. This is the time for SPRING PEELING. In fact, spring peeling is so easy and so much fun that I could never understand why anyone exerts the extra energy and effort to ring trees at any other time! You can use a hatchet. With thin-barked trees like birch and beech, I use a special thick-bladed tool. By pushing it in at one place, one can enter between bark and wood, and work around the tree, somewhat as with an old-fashioned can opener. This is by far the cheapest, easiest, and non-intelligence-demanding way of killing larger trees. With some species like red maple, I find it desirable to keep a glove on my left hand, soaked in a D–T oil mixture, and slide it around the exposed trunk of the tree, thus killing the cambium which, in moist weather, might otherwise reform over the entire surface.

PULLING. It seems rather strange in this day and age—with all our pride in chemical and mechanical controls—that simple Neanderthal-like yanking is still the quickest, cheapest, and most effective way for handling certain unwanted herbaceous plants, at least on small areas. That is, unless you are too proud to stoop to conquer. There are certain herbaceous plants with deep-seated underground rhizomes. The chemical herbicides we have do not travel "down" significantly enough to kill them. If anything, such herbicide treatment stimulates the roots to send up additional numbers of shoots. Mowing is sometimes satisfactory, but that only severs the plant near the soil surface. The full rhizome is left in the soil, to provide nourishment for future shoots. I should know: it was ten years before I had sense enough to give up some relatively futile "modern" techniques, and return to good old-fashioned pulling.

Pulling, if done properly, serves to pull up several inches, sometimes 6–8 inches, of underground stem or root. Considerable nourishment from the remaining parts is then used up in sending a new shoot to the soil surface before that new shoot can form leaves and start replenishing the depleted roots. Thus, pulling—per treatment—can be more effective in reducing root health than any treatment which only kills or removes to the soil surface. Do not think that pulling is suited only for morons. Even a Neanderthal would have to think about it (and he had a larger cranial capacity than yours). A gentle firm tug is needed, so that the stem does not snap in the air, and that it breaks at the deepest possible position. If the stem grows on a slant, you will learn that pulling in the direction of growth, or sometimes in the opposite direction, will be the better. In other cases, a firm pull will lift up 3–10 shoots radiating from the main stem. These shoots would have formed that many plants the next year.

Pulling is highly desired for large rank goldenrods and asters. It is recommended for Canada thistle (if your hand is gloved). Dogbane and bracken, with their flat-topped foliage surmounting a naked stalk, are also good pulling subjects.

SICKLING, ETC. A curved sickle is an extremely handy tool for undesirable herbs with the foliage raised on bare stalks, like the bracken and dogbane mentioned above. One can clip the heads off these plants very very rapidly (and with very little stooping). True you do not "get" as much of the plant each time, but you may prefer the ease of operation.

Mowing, with scythe or power scythe, is not a selective technique in most instances, and is not recommended unless you wish a mowed trail. A heavy bladed brush scythe is useful in cutting some types of brush up to one inch in diameter. "Brush hooks" of various kinds are highly useful for woody weeds up to about 3 inches in diameter. Beyond that you will probably want to use an axe.

POWER SAWS. Rotary saws are available, with knapsack motors. Chain saws, with self-contained motors, are extremely efficient. With such tools, you can quickly cut a swath thru dense brush that will give you a trail-like access thru an area otherwise inaccessible. But do not let your enthusiasm run wild with you. Think twice before you tear thru a whole acre of young forest and tall brush, elated to "see it all come down." You will be left with a mess of stuff that will probably have to be stacked and burned. Then you will go thru and spray the larger stubs you see. You will miss an even greater number of the smaller ones. And in a year or two you will have as much brush growing as you had before. Think before you act. Look before you leap.

b) Chemical Techniques

Chemical herbicide techniques at this time revolve mostly around the use of 2,4-D and 2,4,5-T, called for short D–T*, in oil or in water. The method of application is by a knapsack spray-tank, either 2-gallon or 5-gallon. The nozzle should be suited for the purpose, to give a concentrated cone-shaped or fan-shaped spray, not a diffuse mist such as is used for orchard tree spraying. (Paint brush or garden watering can may be used, if you have only an hour or two of work—but this is not Naturalistic Landscaping.) Do not plan to use these cans or tanks for any other purpose, as it is difficult to wash them clean of the chemical, and the slightest trace of it will affect the growth of other plants. Since practically all your chemical control will be done with two kinds of solutions, a water-borne one, and an oil-borne one, we will divide our discussion accordingly. It is highly desirable to have two such spray tanks, one for each spray. In this way, material can be left in them, and can be ready for use again at a moment's notice.

---

*Completely unrelated to DDT, the insecticide that is critically poisonous to all forms of animal life.

WATER-BORNE SPRAYS. The standard concentration is one part chemical* to 100 parts of solution (i. e. 99 parts of water.) Water-borne sprays are often called "foliage sprays." It was said that the mixture was drawn in by the foliage, moved down to the roots and killed the roots. This was a nice advertising story, apparently based on the study of small germinating bean seedlings, where the chemical moved downward a few millimeters. Actually, most of the chemical stays in the leaves, and dries them, creating the highly undesirable "brown out" seen along many of our roadsides. If supplied in sufficient volume, the solution soaks the buds and the bark of the stems, resulting often in a kill-to-ground (but not necessarily a rootkill). Thus, this spray is now being called "foliage-stem spray." It is still a very poor rootkill, highly undesirable for taxpayers, but highly desirable for commercial interests. It is easy to sell to some government officials and taxpayers, because it is the cheapest per spray, like painting your house with calcimine or whitewash. In Naturalistic Landscaping, water-borne sprays can be used for special purposes, for both woody plants and for herbaceous plants.

The use of water-borne sprays for woody plants I find very limited. I used them extensively in 1946, 1947 and 1948. In 1949, I gave up the use, in preference to oil-borne sprays, and never returned. Since no dye has been found to add to the solution, it is extremely difficult to know what you have sprayed even a few minutes after, much less a few weeks later. Eventually the foliage browns. By next spring, the dead shoots may lead you to think you have had success. Soon the plants are resprouting gaily. Things like ash and basswood may have had nothing more than a leafburn. Root-suckering weeds like aspen, choke cherry, meadowsweet and steeplebush will be sending up more shoots than you had before. The actual volumes of spray required for this work are 10–20 times greater than for oil-borne sprays, and since this is all carried on your back, you have an added reason for avoiding this method. At the present time, when I am using water-borne sprays,

---

*When the commercial material carries four pounds acid equivalent per gallon as may be seen by reading the very very small print in the label.

I usually do not hesitate to wet any small woody sprouts I may come across, up to two feet in height. Anything over that height I do not treat. Not only is an excessive volume needed, but I will be soaking the land underneath, destroying valuable herbs, and the slightest breeze will waft the spray to distances of 20 feet or more, affecting all the flowering herbs in that stretch.

The use of water-borne sprays for herbaceous plants is important. Keep in mind that new soft spring foliage is much more sensitive than the hard foliage of autumn. Species which may be found easy to kill back in early summer may not react at all later in the year, or with only a little distortion in their growth. This is especially true of the coarse goldenrods. Realize also that the very quantity of foliage is important. In spring, plants are but a few inches tall, and you can easily distinguish the different kinds. By mid-summer, you are confronted by a tangle four feet high or more. By that time you will need 20 or 30 times the volume of spray, and the spray will be relatively ineffective. Know the root-systems of your plants. If the roots or rhizomes are deep, the most you can do is to soak the foliage and kill that. As soon as there are new shoots, go back and do the area again. If the growing bud or a short rhizome is at the surface, wet the foliage, but see that you thoroly soak the position of the bud. In this way I have killed several thousand plants of the summer goldenrod (*Solidago juncea*) with less than 1% survivals, and they were "personnel misses," to use an industry term.

Some of the ferns have their rhizomes close to the surface (interrupted fern, sensitive fern, New York fern). The water spray will not affect the foliage, but by soaking the soil you will get the growing ends. This treatment is fairly "rough," and will probably bare the soil. Watch the spot for the next year or two, or you may have an abundance of plants you do not want. In general, I would avoid spraying anything over 2 or 3 feet high. Better to cut it down first. At the higher levels, your spraying is hardly "selective," and both by drip and drift, you will find that you are affecting a very large area.

OIL-BORNE SPRAYS. Oil-borne sprays are "stronger" than water-borne sprays in regard to the quantity of D–T. The standard concentration is one part of chemical to 10–50 parts of oil. I find that 1-to-50 is satisfactory for my work, tho industry likes to use 1-to-10, or stronger. The oil (kerosene or fuel oil) may have some toxic effect in itself, but apparently its chief function is to "wet" the bark. Bark is normally impermeable to water. Its impermeability is essential to the life of the plant, for if not, the plant would shrivel, like a filmy fern in the sun. Thus the ordinary water-borne sprays to a large extent merely run off the bark like rain. Oil, however, wets the bark, and permeates to the cambium. D–T is carried with the oil, and kills the cambium. Once into the woody part of the plant, it moves downward very inefficiently, unfortunately, for we want it to kill the roots. It moves upward however very very quickly. Once in the smaller branches and leaves, the foliage browns and dries. This browning is ideal for color photos, and salesmen and advertisers always have a gullible public to fool. Actually, the quicker the kill of the upper visible parts of the plants, the more likely is it that the underground roots are left in a healthy condition, ready to send up new shoots, requiring new spraying! This re-growth—judging from what industry usually recommends—is a desirable situation—for them.

Oil-borne sprays may be considered in three categories: basal-bark spraying, stub- and stump-spraying, and spraying of herbaceous plants.

Basal-bark Spraying is a quick easy and efficient way of killing many woody plants. The kill is related to the wettability of the bark. For practical purposes, thin smooth bark is easily wettable. Thick corky bark (as on cork-bark oak, or California redwood) I would not attempt. The idea is to soak, not just spray, the lowermost 18 inches. Let the spray roll down and soak the root crown, the part in contact with the soil. The root crown, as on birches, may be a myriad of dormant buds, which will sprout profusely if they are not killed. In general, I would basal-spray only sprouts and young trees up to 15–20 feet in height and 3–4 inches in diameter. Beyond these dimensions, the quantity of spray needed makes the procedure costly. Under exceptional circumstances, you may want to so kill large trees. I have myself killed a 50-foot thick-barked sugar maple, but it took over a gallon of spray. Large beeches have been killed in South Carolina, even tho it took three years for them to die.

In interpreting the results of your basal-bark spraying, be patient. Don't start barking too soon. The chemical ringing may be the most important part of the procedure, and this may not have an effect on the life of the plant until one year later. If you get a quick effect within a few weeks, you can assume the herbicide has moved to the smaller branches. But you do not want the branches to die first! You want the roots to die first. The roots won't die first after chemical ringing unless the top keeps on growing while the roots are being starved, since they can no longer get nourishment thru the bark which has been severed. This little bit of commonsense plant physiology, industry seems to choose to ignore.

Whether to basal-bark spray, or to stub-and-stump spray, depends on both experience and individual preference. Altho plants differ in their resistance—and that you will learn by experience—the decision often depends on whether you mind seeing the standing dead brush, and how much work is involved with clearing away, or at least flattening to the ground, the brush that results from felling a large tree.

Oil-Spraying of Herbaceous Plants, essentially a leaf-burning procedure, is a sort of "chemical mowing." We all know that repeated mowing eventually kills plants. For this reason, young maple seedlings in your lawn eventually die. A browsing cow has a similar effect on many—but not all—the woody plants in a heavily grazed pasture. This is not a poisoning of the plant. It is merely a "clipping." But for a clipping, it is remarkably quick and easy. With some experience, you can give the undesired plants the lightest of sprays—just a flashing "spritz" as you walk past. Being oil, your spraying will be noticed if you return to the spot 5 minutes later. Within a day, the foliage will be withering. Thus, the number of personnel misses will be much reduced, for on walking thru the area a second time, the unsprayed plants will show up as conspicuously as breakfast egg on a man's necktie. True, such spray-burned plants will resprout rather readily. Then the sprouts are sprayed. You will find each resprouting much smaller than the last. Apparently, other competing plants also exert a strong effect. Before you know it, your unwanted plant has vanished. This technique is suited for rhizomatous and resistant species, especially ferns. If the herbicide won't poison the plant, at least we can mow it, and mow it, and mow it, until it finally succumbs from sheer weakness, and from the competitive onslaught of other plants.

Stub- and Stump-Spraying is highly recommended for many purposes. See that the stubs and stumps are fairly close to the ground. Tall stumps require far more spray, and have more opportunity for resprouting. See that the stubs and stumps are thoroly soaked with spray, not the central woody portion (spray hitting such central parts is completely wasted), but the outside bark and cambium. Small shoots up to 2 inches in diameter can easily be cut with a brush hook, even while you have a spray tank on your back. I advise one man handling both procedures, otherwise the second worker is likely to miss many of the small stubs. Large trees can be downed by saw or axe at any season. It is not necessary to spray immediately after cutting. I have had excellent results several months after cutting, and even after small shoots have started to grow. If such new shoots become too large, you can still kill the whole plant, but you waste too much spray simply "burning off" the new foliage.

2. Kinds of Plants to Eliminate

From one viewpoint, the experienced professional Naturalistic Landscaper might say that every species of plant must be dealt with as a separate entity. He might say that each is a problem by itself, and can be eliminated best with its own distinctive combination of chopping, sawing, peeling, water-spraying andor oil-spraying. It is true that when one gets to know a species, one gets to know its weak points, its Achilles' heel. But none of us is born with that knowledge, and there are certain generalizations which may be made which will allow one to be highly competent right from the start. Woody plants and herbaceous plants differ in the treatments they need to eliminate them.

a) Woody Plants

NON-SPROUTING SPECIES offer only a minor problem. In this category are most of the conifers: the pines, spruces, hemlocks. Pitch pine of eastern North America is one of the exceptions. It regularly sprouts from the stump. Shortleaf pine in the southeastern United States will also do so. Most other trees and most shrubs will sprout after being cut or mowed. Under some circumstances, sprouting will be less than normal after cutting, or may not occur at all, but these cases are unpredictable, and have not been fully explained by the scientists.

For the spruces, hemlocks and non-sprouting pines, it is well to remember that the foliage, at least after the flush of their spring growth, is highly resistant to water-borne D–T sprays. This was early discovered in the ill-advised rightofway spraying by many American electric power utilities. Their spraying, rather than killing the entire tree growth, only served to kill the associated hardwoods, and thus release the conifers. Essentially it was a reforestation procedure. At the present time, such blanket spraying, selective in its effect, is being used in Christmas tree plantations, and in silvicultural practices to promote the fast-growing conifers.

For killing larger spruces, hemlocks and non-sprouting pines, chopping or ringing seems to be the most effective. I have used herbicides in many ways, for many years, on such conifers, but the time and energy I have put to such matters has never been practical.

For the smaller conifers, it is sometimes easiest to give them a soaking with oil spray. Such treatment is essentially a foliage burn and a bud killing. If all the buds are so killed, the plant dies, for adventitious buds are rarely formed. How small is "small" is for you to decide. It depends on your judgment between the energy of chopping and possibly removing the plant, and the carrying and the cost of the spray. For the common pasture juniper, I prefer spraying, even tho the plants may be several feet in diameter. This juniper is sharply prickly. Some people are allergic to the scratches. I aim to avoid handling the thing. I prefer soaking the plant with oil spray. After several weeks the foliage browns. One can see what one has missed, and spray again. After a season, the brown needles have dropped. The plant soon vanishes into the grassland. If one is bothered by small pine trees, two feet or less in height, a flick of your oil sprayer will solve the problem. Surrounded by grasses as they are, the browned plant is all but invisible.

For sprouting woody plants, be they shrubs or trees, you must know whether they are "stump sprouters" or "root suckerers." The stump sprouters are those which send up new shoots from the base, like birches, maples, ashes and oaks. The root suckerers are those which can send up shoots from the roots, and thus the new shoots can form a large colony surrounding the original trunk. The root suckerers include beech, sassafras, aspen (which has been recorded as developing a shoot in the grassland over 30 meters from the parent tree!), ailanthus. Some of the shrubby oaks belong in this category, as do plums, fire cherries, choke cherries and many of the blueberries and huckleberries. If in doubt as to whether you have a seedling or a rootsucker, dig up a plant. Do not trust other people, especially engineers, and even some foresters. If the plant you are digging belongs to a colony, and if it is connected to a heavier horizontal root, the chances are that you are dealing with a root-suckering species.

STUMP-SPROUTING WOODY PLANTS are fairly easy to murder. You can kill or remove the upper branches by any one of the several mechanical or chemical methods. The most critical and important aspect is the "root collar," that part of the plant at or just below the soil surface. It is the root collar which will develop adventitious buds and send up new shoots. It is seldom practical to remove this part mechanically, unless indeed you want to go to the trouble of digging out the entire stump.

The most feasible procedure with stump-sprouting species is to see that the root collar is thoroly soaked with oil spray. This is most easily done at the time of stump spraying or basal-bark spraying by putting on ample volume and letting the spray roll down and soak the soil line. If there is loose soil or dead leaves at the base, it is best to kick them aside, for your aim is not to soak the adjacent soil, but the lowermost bark.

It is important to realize with these plants that it is not necessary to poison or to kill the roots themselves. The roots are entirely unable to develop new shoots. Bereft of their "head" they die just as surely as the torso of a beheaded man will die even tho everything below the head is entirely uninjured.

ROOT-SUCKERING WOODY PLANTS must be treated with a very different understanding—or you may end up with an actual forest of what you are trying to get rid of. Many railroads and power companies, ill-advised on the part of the herbicide industry, are now burdened with solid stands of sassafras, ailanthus or aspen, simply because their spraying predictably stimulated the growth of root suckers.

Knowing that the chemical does not effectively move into and poison the roots, one must guard against the possibility of stimulating the roots to produce suckers. One of the best ways to so stimulate the roots is to cut off, or kill, the main tree. And one of the easiest ways of killing the main tree is to cut it and stump spray it, or to basal spray it in such a way that the chemical quickly moves out to the branches and kills them. The chemical industry loudly advertises this as "control." True. It is not kill! The roots are left alive, and quickly develop suckers. There are suckers and suckers in this live-ly game.

Present recommendations indicate that rootsuckering trees should be basal-sprayed in late summer, not at any other season. When so sprayed a chemical girdling occurs. Relatively little of the herbicide moves upward. Possibly some moves downward, linked to the sugars that are moving down into the roots at this season. Furthermore, the girdling soon stops all downward movement of starches; the roots are starved for lack of nourishment; the roots die; then the top dies. This procedure is a bit slow for hasty engineers—but with these plants, haste makes waste—for the home owner (but more business for the contractor, who gets it from the tax-paying home owner).

b) Herbaceous Plants

Annual herbs are no problem, for if one keeps the plant sprayed, no seed is formed, and no seeds will be available the following year to germinate. If bare soil is turned up, buried dormant seeds may germinate. In fact, it is quite remarkable what enormous numbers of seeds will lie dormant in soil, waiting for suitable conditions of light temperature and moisture in order to start growing. Since, however, bare soil is rarely met with in Naturalistic Landscaping, this factor can be all but ignored.

Perennial herbs may be thought of as being (1) clumped, and fibrous rooted, forming single dense plants, or (2) rhizomatous and spreading, forming colonies. Another type (3) spreads by arching branches, or runners, which root at the tip. Such plants, if sprayed before the tip roots, may be treated the same as clumped plants.

1. Clumped herbs can be treated with either water-borne or oil-borne sprays. Water-borne sprays are effective early in the season, when the foliage is young and tender. Later, there may be no effect whatever. Oil-borne sprays may only burn the foliage, with no effect on the growing buds at the soil level. In general, it is wise to treat these herbs early in the season before the mere bulk of foliage becomes a hindrance to effective spraying. What you should be trying to kill is not necessarily the expanse of above-ground foliage, but the growing buds. For this reason, be sure you soak the soil where these buds are. The spray on the soil and on the surface mulch of dead leaves is wasted, in a sense, but there is no other way to get at the growing buds of the plant.

CIRSIUM

C. arvense

2. Rhizomatous herbs are real problems. For some plants, like Canada thistle, dogbane, and the common milkweed and certain goldenrods, the plant spreads by pencil-thick underground rhizomes, sometimes at depths of 12 inches or more. Since the herbicide does not move "backward" to poison these rhizomes, spraying often acts to stimulate the development of new shoots, very much as for sassafras and aspen. Herbs are not constructed, in the anatomy of their stems, like woody plants. The bark, place of major downward movement, is not on the outside. The wood, place of major upward movement of water and nutrients, is not on the inside. To the contrary, the inside of the stem is composed of a lot of little bundles, somewhat like a handful of spaghetti. Thus, one cannot "ring" an herb, and basal spraying only serves to soak thru the stem and kill the above-ground parts. The most that one can do for rhizome-killing of rhizomatous herbs is repeatedly to "mow" them, either by a quick oil-spray leaf-burn, or a slow water-spray effect. Where the rhizomes are close to the surface, as with some ferns, then one can soak the soil. True, one kills most other plants at that particular spot, but in a few months other plants will invade the place. Just see that the wrong kinds of plants do not do the invading and never forget the importance of stooping to yank.

3. A Calendar for Elimination thru the Year in Eight Periods

We have already considered the kinds of chemical and mechanical material (with what?) and techniques (how done?). We next described the general types of plants (to what?) and the different techniques to be applied to each. What remains is the matter of "when?," the problem of laying out an actual program in time, of when we do what and with what and to "whom".

The process of Intaglio in connection with Naturalistic Landscaping is a year-round procedure. There is no month in which you cannot do something, depending upon your ability to bear with, and even to like with exhilaration, extremes of cold or heat. There need be no great hardship here. I assume that if you yourself were the hothouse blossom that needs a totally air-conditioned environment, you would not be reading this book. Cheer up, tho, there is one pleasant "don't:" don't do any spraying while it is raining or snowing, or while there is snow on the ground, or after a rain when the bark is still wet. The spray, to be most effective, must permeate bark and in most cases must be applied close to the soil surface. Thus, this is no job for rain or snow. Mechanical operations yes, but not spraying. The following calendar is suited to regions in either Temperate Zone where there is a cold-dormant season with snow. It is easily altered for the Tropics where there is a dry-dormant season. In the humid Tropics, one easily adjusts to local conditions, when growth is more rapid or more slow.

1. MID-WINTER. DEEP SNOW. This is the most quiescent time of the entire year from the standpoint of Naturalistic Landscaping. It is one of the most beautiful from the viewpoint of skiing and snow-shoeing around the areas you have landscaped, or will landscape. It is an excellent season for clearing some of the higher branches along your woodland trails. Branches which in summer are far out of reach are now within comfortable chopping distance. It is also a good time to knock off the lower limbs of conifers which you intend to ring-peel in spring. These trees may form solid tangles of lower branches, and the preparatory work of getting in to them takes more time than the actual peeling. If you are more or less clear-cutting any extensive area of larger trees, it does not make much difference whether or not snow is on the ground. Just be sure that stumps are not too high. And, of course, be absolutely sure that if you are having someone else do it, he knows what not to cut. Tie a big red rag on every thing you want saved. Even sometimes that is not enough for some operators, who operate more like a butcher than a surgeon.

2. DORMANT SEASON. NO SNOW. In the snowless dormant season, one can often accomplish nine tenths of all woody plant removal—if one knows his woody plants in winter. Recognition of plants at this season is mystifying to the layman, but really very easy. Bereft of their flowers and clothing verdure, of their necklaces and stoles, one merely learns to recognize certain basic features of their morphology and anatomy, the silhouette against the sky, the size and shape of the branches, the nature of bark and buds.

I would recommend the end of winter in general, not the beginning. At the beginning of winter, dead herbaceous material and fallen leaves lie heavily on the ground, and prevent or hinder one from spraying the basal parts of woody plants. At the end of winter, this material is flattened and partially rotted, and one can move around far more easily.

This is one of the finest times of the year for planning, and for preliminary opening of woody trails. One can now sight thru the woods for long distances, for several hundred feet even, whereas in summer the visibility will be limited to a dozen feet or so. One can see interesting rock formations, and general contours of the land, and plan his trail accordingly. The perspective at this season is almost like a bird's-eye view, in comparison to the worm's-eye view later on.

Both mechanical and chemical techniques are applicable at this season for woody plants. Trees can be cut down. Shrubs can be cut. Wherever you would use an axe or a chain saw, this is a fine time for the purpose. With no foliage on the plants, the cut brush is far more easily disposed of.

I would recommend that you do as much as possible of your basal-bark and stub-and-stump spraying at this season. Pick a quiet sunny day. It will be warmer then, and the spray won't blow. Whatever inconvenience you may feel about the lower temperature will be more than offset by the fact that you are not encumbered by low-growing herbaceous material (on which you would waste a lot of spray), or by biting insects (causing waste of time and motion). I would go thru the area basal-spraying thin-barked trees like maples and oaks, being sure to soak the soil-line root-collar. Trees known to be very resistant, like ash, require cutting first. White ash seedlings have the unfortunate habit often of being in a zig-zag-zig shape, the "zag" being a horizontal part of the stem. The zag must be fully soaked also, and this requires nosing into the surface litter with your spray nozzle until you find where the plant turns downward into the soil. For root-suckering plants like aspen and sassa-fras (tho not the best season for treating them), your aim is chemically to girdle the shoot; and thus soaking at the ground level is not so important. Psychologically, it may not be as satisfactory to spray at this season, for you cannot quickly "see results." Worse, spring comes, and the tree leafs out as tho your spray "failed." Have patience, the plant may not die until midsummer. Sometimes one must even wait until the second year. The top does not die until the roots first die, and thus this technique is by far the most efficient in the long-term picture. If you get too impatient in spring, cut out a little piece of the bark, where you sprayed, and see whether the cambium between it and the wood is black and dead, or white slippery and alive. If it is alive, you did not spray with sufficient volume and over a tall enough vertical section.

For certain evergreen shrubs like juniper, this is a good time to soak the foliage. In the summer you will see what you missed, and can complete the job. For smaller non-root-suckering deciduous shrubs, in addition to basal spraying, you may like to give them a light overall spray. In this way, you will kill most of the buds, and your results will be quickly seen in spring, including the branches you missed. I would not try this with the rhizomatous and root-suckering shrubs like huckleberries and trailing blueberries, unless you intend to follow up with additional sprays every time the underground parts send up new shoots. When the new shoots are short, 18 inches or less, there is not much else you can do. Be persistent in the follow-ups tho, or otherwise your effort will be lost.

3. BURSTING BUDS. There is a period of two or three weeks when buds are so swollen and differently colored that they stand out clearly from among dead stems. Then comes the time when green shows. And finally, the new small leaves have popped open, miniature but perfect in shape. If you yourself also feel bursting with springtime energy, by all means utilize it. The grass has not yet grown up to hide the bases of the trees, and it is still time for basal spraying and stump spraying. Furthermore, the new green leaves will show up all that you missed on the winter overall spraying. The smallness of the foliage will be no hindrance to such oil spraying as you may still wish to do on smaller woody plants, or on branches of larger shrubs. Such spraying of shrubs, even ones 6 to 8 feet tall, will not now damage the grassland underneath, for the spray will fall on the dead mulch, thru which the grasses and forbs will later penetrate unharmed.

4. FLUSH SPRING GROWTH. You who grow "flowers" in gardens may think that plants "grow" all season long. You are right, in a way. Actually, however, the greater part of the growth occurs in the first six weeks or so of spring. It is as this time that the cambium of woody plants is most active, and forms the greater part of the year's increase in diameter growth. The twigs now grow rapidly in length, 6, 12, 18 inches or more. Then they stop growing, and the bud is formed, not to break until the end of the next winter. The foliage grows and reaches its full size. Herbs shoot up, and do most of their growing in this period. The result of all this extraordinary above-ground activity is that the roots of plants are in a state of relative exhaustion and depletion. The wise landscaper, knowing this, will often time his activities accordingly. The roots are more easily killed when they are depleted. Each species is slightly different, and knowing your species you can often time your spraying so as to give a knock-out punch. (After all this flush spring growth, the plants settle down to serious summer "growth" of another kind. The green foliage then manufactures carbohydrates, which in turn are moved to the roots and stored, ready to be utilized in the next season's flush and excitement.)

If your herbaceous **g**round vegetation is not so dense as to cover up the bases of the trees, basal-bark spraying and stub-spraying can be continued. For small tree seedlings, the new-expanded foliage stands out on your "misses" like a minute thorn in your finger. They can thus be "lapped up" as you are casually walking around the fields.

This season is one of the best for water-spraying undesirable herbs. They are now large enough to be seen, but not so large as to require exorbitant amounts of spray. Furthermore, the foliage is tender, and far more reactive to the chemical. The worst problem is that there is no "color marker" in the chemical, and a few minutes later—unless you have an inhuman memory—you will respray, or miss, plants. Under some circumstances, I would suggest keeping yourself aligned with markers temporarily stuck in the ground. Be sure you soak the foliage to the drip-off point. And for clumped non-rhizomatous herbs, or in situations where the rhizomes are close to the surface, snuggle your spray nozzle into the base of the plant while you take a second or two in a look-around pause-that-refreshes. In a few days, the growing tips of the plants will curl twist or bend, and you can recognize what you have missed. It may take the rest of the summer however for the plant to weaken and die.

Now is the ideal time for ringing and peeling trees. The bark literally cracks off and slides off. Don't forget to use a D–T sprayed glove to slide around the exposed wood surface, to prevent regrowth. You can keep up peeling as the weeks advance, until the bark becomes "tight." You can keep on for the entire year if you want, but it is too much work for me at these other times.

5. MIDSUMMER is a time of dog-days and general relaxation. You can keep busy, but there is no longer a sense of urgency. Except for resprouting and regrowths! There you must go back and respray, or your first spraying will be totally wasted. I used to wait, thru the season, thru another year, thru still another year, hoping the things would die. They don't. If anything, they grow all the better!

Personally, I find water-borne sprays not of much use at this season. True, the commercial people recommend such spraying, but that is only because you get a color effect in the foliage within a short time, which they can point to as "results." The fact that you usually do not successfully kill the roots is all to their advantage. If you have some "woody brush" around, water-borne sprays will kill them to the ground, and they will show "dead" the next spring. Frankly, I gave up this type of spraying in 1949, and never resumed it. I was not killing the roots as successfully as I was with other techniques. Furthermore—and this is only a very tentative hypothesis—I strongly suspect that such light water-borne sprays may induce a dormancy on the part of some plants. They will be "dead" thru an entire growing season, or even thru two seasons. Then suddenly I will find I get a new "invasion" of the plants. On digging them up, one finds they come from old root systems. An ideal situation, for certain people in the business, no?

In situations where you want a fern bed, at present mixed up with asters, goldenrods and other forbs, this is an ideal time for using water sprays. The fern foliage is now hard enough to be totally resistant to such sprays. The forbs however will be badly set back, even if they are not browned. The end result is a tipping of the competition scales in the direction of the ferns. Your aim is accomplished.

If your ground vegetation is thin, you can keep on with oil-borne sprays, for basal-bark and stubs. I very much recommend going over your land at this time to get not only the "misses" of earlier spraying, but the resprouts from root-suckering plants. Unless these are burned off, they will be replenishing the roots with food, and you will have greater growth the next year. At the same time you can oil-burn the foliage of deep-rhizomed herbs, providing you do not choose to cut them or pull them.

Midsummer is the time for pulling the large rank rhizomatous herbs, such as large goldenrods, asters, common milkweed, dogbane, bracken. I am perfectly willing to recommend some mechanical or chemical technique, when I find such a technique that is more efficient in terms of time, energy, and human cost. With the present state of technology however, and recognizing that this is a small-scale landscaping problem, and not one involving a hundred acres of flat open land, an old-fashioned yank serves in a most satisfying manner to pull up a large amount of healthy root that is not otherwise to be had—unless you use a pick and shovel. There is also one indirect advantage: you will be convinced, as nothing else can convince, that your problem does not lie with new invading seedlings, but with old root-systems (despite all the ecologic theory of "plant succession"). In other words, if you can clean up those old root systems, you have not "controlled" the plant, you have probably "eradicated" it.

6. LATE SUMMER. Late summer deserves special recognition mainly for one type of spraying, basal-bark spraying of such root-suckering woody-stem plants as sumach, aspen, sassafras and ailanthus. Most herbaceous plants are now too hard-foliaged and too large for effective water-spraying. Resprouts of woody plants should be burned off with oil spray as they may be found. But if you are attacking for the first time a colony of root-suckering trees, I recommend that it be done sometime between mid-summer and when the foliage begins to turn in autumn. Research data from several parts of the country indicate that there are fewer resprouts when the spraying is so timed. If you ask why, it may be said that in late summer the manufactured carbohydrates are moving down to the roots, and carry along some of the herbicide with them. Regardless of the "explanation" in dignified scientific lingo, you get better results that way.

This is the time when commercial people spray roadsides with water-borne sprays. If they put on enough gallonage, they may get the equivalent of basal-bark spraying on root-suckering woody plants. Their main reason for doing it at this season however is so that the resulting brown-out merges with fall coloration, so that the public is fooled. For many scientific reasons however, unrelated to brown-out, this spraying is economically (for the taxpayer), and conservation-wise unsound, and legislation should make it illegal.

7. AUTUMN FOLIAGE. Of the eight seasons into which we have divided the year, Indian Summer provides no "must" or "best" for the Intaglio activities of the Naturalistic Landscaper. The cool nights have all but eliminated the nuisance insects and give an invigorating start to the day. The warm quiet sun seems to gain additional fire by reflections from the brilliant foliage. Leaves are no longer sending carbohydrates back to the roots so there is no use burn-spraying them, even while they get in the way of bark-spraying. Take it easy. If your herbaceous ground covers are fairly thin, you might still basal-spray or stub-and-stump spray woody plants that are stump-sprouters. In fact, this is as good a time as any for doing this work. Otherwise, sit back and enjoy what you have done in preceding months, while planning for coming months.

8. EARLY WINTER. DORMANT SEASON. The leaves fall. The trees and shrubs are bare. The grass dries. By tradition, the hunting season is on. The larger mammals dangerous to man have long since been eliminated from our woodlands. But not so with the human hunter. Along with what he calls "game" he continues to take an annual toll of common ordinary laymen like you and me, of other hunters, and sometimes the breed even becomes suicidal. The last two situations, however, are statistically insignificant in reducing their population. Thus I would recommend that, for some parts of the country, you develop the habit of singing or whistling in an unmistakably human manner. (Brightly colored clothing is not enough, nor huge labelling like MAN. Some hunters do not read, judging from newspaper accounts.) Such noises as whistling even tho non-musical, may serve to make both hunters and other such animals flee the area. I know one individual who attached a whistle to the nozzle of his sprayer, but it only drew the hunters, who thought it was some new game bird. In general, the accumulation of dead plant life on the ground will hinder efficient bark and stump spraying. On the other hand, your local vegetation conditions may still permit such spraying. The foliage of unwanted evergreen shrubs can be sprayed at this season, and even of the evergreen lycopods that may be along a foot trail. Do what you can—it may be quite a bit, it may even be the major amount of your woody plant spraying—but do not waste spray on dead leaves and grass that may be covering up the bases of the stump-sprouting trees. The cycle is complete. The snows will soon come. Don't go south. The white snows usher in one of the finest of the seasons.

C. THREE SPECIAL SITUATIONS

The elimination procedures we have already discussed (Section B above) can be an extremely disruptive operation to the botanical landscape. It may leave "holes" in the vegetation tapestry, much like moths operating on a carpet. This carpet can repair itself however, and it promptly starts to do so. Furthermore, there were some weak spots in the vegetation tapestry to start with probably, and these spots can be improved in chosen ways. From the viewpoint of logically developing our entire Landscaping program, it is wise to consider the immediate reactions to our elimination procedures. Later (Part II, p. 77) we will consider the long-term natural changes in the vegetation types we have produced. Finally (Part III, p. 100) we will discuss the art of embellishing with new plants.

In this section, we have three related but none-the-less distinct problems. The first concerns the avoidance of making unnecessary "holes" in the vegetation cover. The second deals with the natural filling of those holes if you have accidentally or intentionally made them. The third puts emphasis on the encouraging and manipulation of remaining plants so as to most quickly fill the holes. These three procedures are very closely related, and you will find that in actual practice you are involved with all three procedures at once. For purposes of discussion and for your understanding, however, it is best to keep them separate.

1. Avoidance of "Holes"

To make a hole, or not to make a hole, that is the question. Many and many a time you will be confronted with a situation which poses this serious question. There will be patches of undesirable vegetation 10, 25 or 50 feet across that seemingly have nothing worth while in them. The temptation will be strong—even if you have been an eclectic in most other instances—to give free rein to the bulldozer element in your personality. (And who does not have it, to some extent?) My advice is not to give in, not to decide on the flip of a coin, but to stop, to look, and even to listen to that feeble inner voice. Put your knapsack sprayer down, and take the time to walk over the whole spot, carefully looking for desirable plants. There may be a thin sparse spot of grass, a few shoots of a desirable forb, the mouse-bitten stubs of a handsome shrub. If so, get back into the eclectic spirit again, and plan to spray discriminately, even if it will require your coming back several times during the season. These things that nature planted are probably a lot hardier than anything you might introduce. They have already survived a lot of competition.

And even if you find nothing worth saving, it might still be wise not to act like a bulldozer, and tear over the entire patch. This is where the "divide and conquer" technique of military strategy can be utilized. Hem in the little spot by spraying all around the edge, thus "containing" it. You will find the plants stay contained very easily. Plants are not nearly as aggressive, not as likely to jump your barrier, as are animals and man. Then in your leisure and in the future, you can draw your net tighter and tighter, eventually pinching the enemy out of existence. More often than not, you will find that a remaining small clearly demarcated little spot has an actual landscape value, and you will keep it!

2. Filling of "Holes"

Where you have chosen to spray out a patch of a colonial fern, where there has been a dense clump of some low colonial shrub, where you have removed a group of trees that had previously cast a very dense shade, it is quite possible that you may be left with a spot of relatively bare ground. Don't itch, and get worried. Don't rush to "plant it up" with some ground cover that an agriculturist recommends. Let Nature take her course. If the course is not exactly what you want, you can gently nudge her into another course. Only once did I ever consider that She was not cooperating with me as fully as I wished. I once blanket-sprayed several hundred square feet of rich sloping surface that was 99% covered with unwanted plants. I used 2,4–D alone, not a mixture of D and T. Brambles are resistant to D alone, and I was rewarded for my endeavors with a bed of 8-foot tall brambles, 99.9% pure. I saw no virtue in such a prickly situation. Furthermore it was absolutely sterile; not a fruit in the lot. Then I used 2,4,5-T. Root-killing was so rapid that I began to get soil erosion. The blackberries and the blanket-spray had killed out whatever plants might have been around, and which would have spread and held the soil. So I slowed down my anti-blackberry campaign. Unwanted rank goldenrods, asters, and ferns continued to pour in, while I continued to peck them out. Finally, 8 years later, I succeeded in obtaining the smooth grassland that I wished.

If there is anything for you to learn from my mistake: Don't get overenthusiastic and "spray everything," unless you are sure that something desirable will survive your murderous activities. If your spraying does leave small holes, just keep watching them. The chances are that rhizomatous grasses will creep in from the sides. Watch for unwanted tree or shrub seedlings. Let nature take her course, yes, but ever be ready to give a push and shove if She gets off course—in your opinion. And this idea leads us to the next section.

3. Encouraging of Remaining Plants

As you keep wandering around your natural-landscaped fields and forests, your eyesight will become sharper and sharper. You will see things you never saw before. You will wonder how you ever missed them. Or if you had seen them, you will wonder how much more they mean to you now. You will gradually get to see plants that are barely surviving in the competitive struggle with other plants. If it is a desirable plant, you will wonder what you might do to tip the scale of competition in its favor. There are many things you can do. Keep in mind that a plant in nature is not the ideal, perfect, hothouse-bred individual that you yourself are, among human beings. A daisy plant in the garden is a huge bushy affair, with a hundred blossoms. In the grassland, it may bear only 2 or 3 blossoms. A tree in the open is a rounded symmetrical specimen with many lower limbs. In the forest, with bitter competition from neighboring trees, it is tall and slender, and probably survived by a narrow margin over countless other slender trees that died in the process. They all are beautiful depending on your viewpoint, tho I doubt that I would consider an overpopulated starving part of the world, surviving as a human community only by a birth rate higher than a high death rate, as beautiful in respect to its individuals. But then, I am prejudiced.

You will find both herbaceous plants and woody plants that will repay a bit of encouragement. The herbaceous plants, possibly some unusual aster or goldenrod, may become 50 times larger and handsomer if you give it a helping hand against its adversaries. As for woody plants, if you see some little azaleas or mountain ashes in the grassland, they will probably be old as well as little. Actually, you will learn in the next section that seedling invasion by shrubs is very rare. What you do find may come from very old root-systems, barely surviving as each year's growth is clipped off. Give them a chance, and they will grow up.

These small plants have remained inconspicuous and small for many many reasons. In general, however, it may be said that they have failed in competition (a) with other plants, and (b) with animals. Other plants may have the advantage in taking water and nutrients from the soil. The above-ground foliage may grow over and shade out the weaker plant. Among animals, insects may continually eat off the foliage. Larger animals, like mice, rabbits, woodchuck and deer may browse it off.

Competition from those other plants can be controlled by killing out the adjacent plants. One of the simplest ways is by applying a blanketing mulch. A few flat stones will often do the trick. There are many ways of mulching, and the subject will be discussed in detail in Section III. If you find caterpillars are eating your plant, use some powder. Very often these insects will only attack weaker plants, and protection for a year or so may be all that is necessary. Rodent damage can be really critical, and these little animals may be directly responsible for the continuance of a grassland that would otherwise become shrubland. For mice, caging with wire mesh is effective. At greater heights, deer browse is a factor. In this case, dead brush stuck into your shrub will be a deterrent. Large dead twigs mixed with small live ones do not please a deer's palate.

Live in all these procedures, keep in mind that your function is to give "one-finger aid" to nature. You are not trying to establish a one-plant garden out in the wild. If the plant becomes neurotically demanding for care and attention, my advice is to let it die. There are plenty of fine hardy plants to work with, without your becoming a slave to an invalid. At this point, the analogy to a human society breaks down. Do not be sentimental about the plants, even if you are incorrigibly, sentimental otherwise.

Part II

MAINTENANCE

The Art of Perpetuating the Landscape

Part II

MAINTENANCE
The Art of Perpetuating the Landscape

The day will come when your Intaglio procedures are essentially completed, when you feel you can sit back and enjoy the landscape that you have sculptured out of the formless brush acres. True, very true—but only quantitatively. It is not as tho you have sculptured the sphinx, to stand unchanged for millenia. Even the sphinx had enemies shoot away its nose, while the desert sands poured upon its paws. Nor should we forget that the sphinx will someday vanish, but an episode in geological time.

The Naturalistic Landscape you have erected is a living growing phenomenon. The plants composing it are growing, are tending to reproduce themselves. The shrubs that now look so fine against the 20-foot conifers will one day be overshadowed and killed out by the 60-foot trees. The clump of pure white paper birch at the forest edge may grow old and ungainly, scarred by ice storms. An undesirable herbaceous weed may overspread your grasslands before you realize what an enemy it is. And you yourself will not climb the ledges with the same agility, nor take the same pleasure from summer heat waves or the below-zero blasts of winter.

You have created a "semi-natural" landscape, a healthy thriving "organism." It is not a gentle fragile hothouse flower that needs constant attention. You will find that it needs watching, and a bit of corrective medication once in a while. But it will be a relatively easy task. And a most interesting task. In my opinion, far more interesting that the previous strenuous sculpturing. Now we have to "understand" the organism we have created. We must realize the way it changes and grows naturally. My own personal interest and enthusiasm always has been in this phase of the work. Here we have an intellectual challenge far superior to the heavy-handed removal procedures that went before. I never would have become so deeply involved with Intaglio activities had not my agricultural predecessors filled up the fields, even if unintentionally, with a lot of brush that I did not want.

One word of caution tho: If you have been interested in outdoor natural history, you have probably somewhere picked up the idea of "plant succession" and of "succession to climax." These are hypotheses that have been inordinately popular with academic plant ecologists, especially in North America where the ideas originated. They are not only easy to understand, but emotionally very satisfying. And these things do happen in Nature, once in a while. But Nature is proving far more complicated than the minds of those ecologists. Do not expect your landscape to have read the ecology books on proper behavior for old fields. And if you yourself are in doubt, read Nature, not books. I find Nature a lot more interesting.

A. VEGETATION DEVELOPMENT

The sequence from community to community

The chances are 99 to 100 that your Naturalistic Landscaping will be on lands that have at one time or another been used for agriculture. That is, they are thick-soiled, and capable of growing crops or of being pastured. We will orient our discussion around this type of land. If you ever start operating on such boulder-strewn slopes or on such ledges and cliffs as to be fit only for goats, you will probably not be dealing with "communities" of plants, but with individual plants in crevices. And if you come to a pocket of soil, even a few feet across, it will be a Lilliputian field. Then borrow from your knowledge of larger fields.

1. Physiognomic Development

As a starting point for our discussion, let us assume that many years ago your field was growing a crop, corn for example, perhaps a century ago. Then the family was massacred, or for some reason we do not entirely understand, the family abandoned all the work that had gone into the homestead and the farm, piled its possessions into a covered wagon, and drove off to New Frontiers and a literal wilderness. Most historians follow the family. We shall follow the field. Corn is an annual crop, and does not survive a winter. Change comes quickly.

a) Annual Weeds. If you were around to see this field, you would have noticed that for the first several years the prominent plants were annual weeds, large rangy things that start from seed each year. Most countries have them, and they go by such disparaging names as pigweed, gooseweed, ragweed, beggarweed.

79

b) Grass Stage. Come back a few years later, and the chances are that the vegetation looks quite different. The weeds have all but vanished, and in their place are grasses. Now whether this abundance of grasses is due to cattle (for grasses can stand being trampled and being grazed off) I am not sure. It is very rare to find an old cropland that is not used for grazing before it is completely abandoned.

c) Large Forb Stage. The next time you will have returned to the site of the old homestead, there will probably be less grass, and heavy non-grassy herbs will predominate. They may be goldenrods, asters, eupatoriums or any of many others. These forbs are larger, and more aggressive than the grasses, and tend to kill them out by competition. I am assuming of course that there is no pasturing and no fire and no mowing. We are considering the natural developments when these other factors are not operating.

d) Shrubland. The years go on and you scarcely know the place when again you return. This time the land is covered with shrubs. There will be a dozen different kinds that are abundant, and many lesser ones. If they are over six feet you will easily lose yourself in the tangle of brush, and find it difficult to force thru an escape route.

e) Forest. The next and last time you come back, an even greater change strikes the eye. A forest has come into existence. You walk thru the deep shade. You see the remains of the shrubs that are dying. You see young trees starting in the shade, perhaps of different kinds than those which are now overhead.

We have seen the changes in physiognomy (p. 80a). That is not enough!

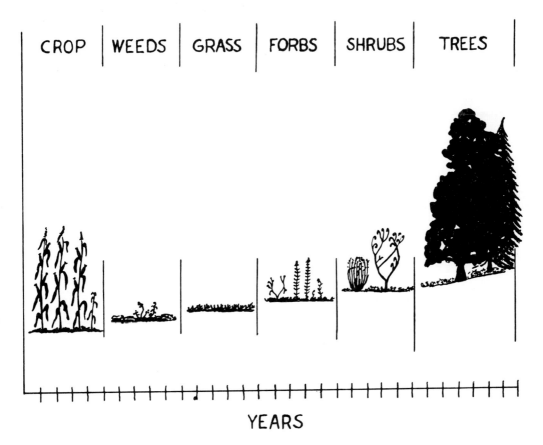

CROP | WEEDS | GRASS | FORBS | SHRUBS | TREES

YEARS

Changes in physiognomy in the development of vegetation. The vegetation on old fields, corn land for example, undergoes superficial changes in appearance as the years progress. Consecutively, these stages are often dominated by (a) annual weeds, (b) grasses, (c) large forbs, (d) shrubs, and finally (e) the forest.

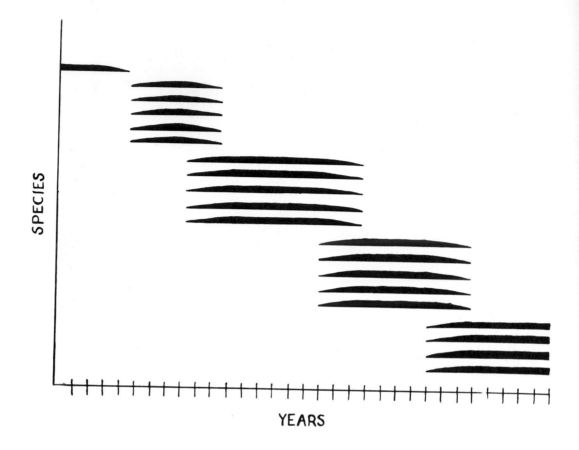

The concept of "Floristic Relays." By this concept, physiognomic change is interpreted in terms of Invading Relays of plants. Each relay inavdes and kills off the preceding relay. In turn, it modifies the local site, making it suitable for the invasion of still another relay, and is in turn killed off by it.

2. Development by "Floristic Relays"

It is one thing to see that change, from corn to weeds, to grass, to shrubs, to trees. Most laymen, even scientists, even ecologists, do not see that much. They look at a dozen old fields that have been abandoned for different numbers of years, and then assume that any one field has gone, or will go, thru such stages. It is sometimes best to leave the state, before the years prove to you how wrong you were. If you cannot leave, you learn to look the other way. This physiognomic change we have described however, from corn to forest, very often does occur. But *how* it occurs is another question.

One way it can occur is by "waves" of invading plants, each coming in, ousting the previous plants, and taking over the land. In time, they are ousted by another invading group of plants. This particular method—it does sometimes occur in nature—is especially easy to understand, and has fired the imagination of the scientists. They say that wave after wave comes in. Each wave becomes dominant over the preceding stage; the plants in turn change the soil and the microclimate near the ground; in time they make the site unfit for themselves and fit for other plants; a new stage of succession comes in. The idea is likened to waves of human populations. First we have the hardy native tribes in an area. Then the explorers and the frontiersmen. The early settlers arrive. They move on when the place gets too civilized for them. Farms develop; first the exurbanites, then the bedroom towns of the suburbs, and finally the city itself. (They do not talk about slum development.) Like most analogies, they serve until facts make them untenable.

This notion can be portrayed graphically (p. 81a). Insofar as your plants do behave in this manner (and this is where you must observe more, and read less) you know some of the secrets of maintaining the landscape as you wish. If trees invade only under a shrubland, you can anticipate that they will give you a problem amongst your shrubs. You will notice however that in the diagram no trees invade a grassland. It will only be the shrubs that give you a problem there. Furthermore, you can have forest and grassland side by side, and neither will invade the other. The "missing link," the shrubland, the "nurse crop" as the foresters call it, is absent. In other words, where you have grassland, you will tend to get shrubland. Where you have shrubland, you will tend to get forest. As often as you destroy one group of plants, you will tend to get back the plants of the stage that immediately precedes. *Unfortunately for this particular theory, it does not often work this way, at least in the humid forest temperate areas of the world.*

81

3. Development by "Initial Floristic Composition"

You do not have to be a scientist to realize that more than "floristic relays" are involved in the ordinary course of vegetation development. Just go out and look for yourself, carefully. Sometimes plant ecologists have not done that much. You see a large forb, a shrub, or a tree. How old is it? If it is a woody plant, cut it off, and count the rings? Wrong, that only gives you the age of the above-ground shoot. Having watched a peony for one year, would you say it is one year old? Actually it can be quite difficult to tell the age of the root system. Microscopic studies may be necessary, and even that may not be enough, for part of a root system may be dead and decaying while another part is growing. Do you know a seedling when you see one? Dig it up. You can generally tell from the shape and appearance of the roots. A shoot of goldenrod or aster or milkweed that is attached to a fat horizontal rhizome is not a seedling. A two-year-old above-ground oak shoot that comes up attached to a root as large as your wrist is no baby. It may date back a century or two. A tree shoot that comes off a deep underground stool-like structure probably was old when your country was young. A few-inch-tall shrub that shows a dozen or so little dead stubs is probably kept that size by the mice and the rabbits, and will be so controlled for the rest of your life, if you leave it. A bit of huckleberry or plum pulled up and found to be attached to a horizontal root coming from a colony of the plant is no youngster. On the

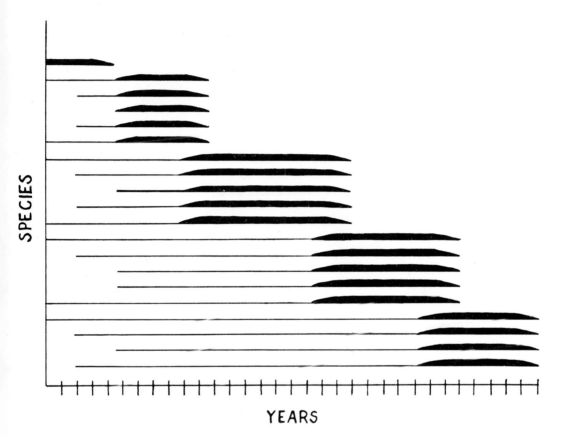

The concept of "Initial Floristic Composition." By this concept, physiognomic change is interpreted in terms of a floristic composition determined when the land was abandoned or last used for agricultural purposes. Physiognomic change is then not related to newly invading plants, but to plants there from the start, and developing into prominence only at a later time. These then die, or are overtopped, by still other plants which also had been there from the start.

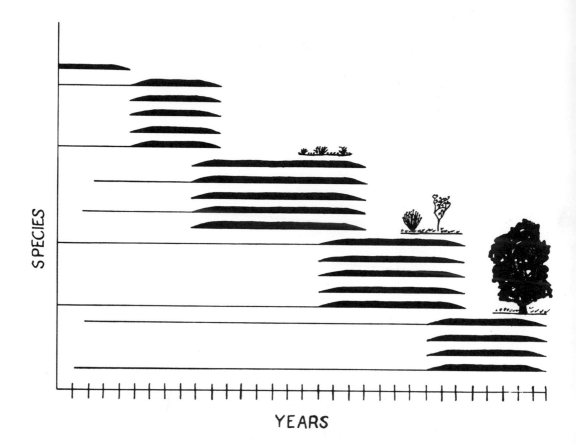

YEARS

SPECIES

A theoretical type of vegetation development in which half the pre-dominant plants of each stage are part of the Initial Floristic Composition, and half are part of an Invading Relay. In this situation, if four kinds of trees are removed from a Shrubland, two kinds may return. Since for example the returning two kinds may be evergreen conifers, while the non-returning two were common deciduous hardwoods, the physiognomy of the returning forest can be quite different than that of the preceding forest.

other hand, a small oak with the acorn still attached, a small ash with the fragments of the cotyledons still hanging on, a small pine showing a few annual rings when cut at the soil line, these will be seedlings in the true sense of the term. Only such seedlings are "invading," *and even for these there is no assurance they will "grow up."*

If you will take the time to observe the plants of the so-called later "stages" of vegetation development, you may be surprised to find that a great many of them are not young by any means. They have been there for a long long time. It is only recently that they have grown up, and dominated the physiognomy of the vegetation. Graphically, we can portray this new idealized situation (p. 83a). In this theoretical case, the plants all started back at the time the field was abandoned. The changing physiognomy occurs when different kinds of plants grow up and dominate the landscape.

From the standpoint of maintenance of your landscape, it is very important to know what plants are behaving according to this principle. For example, if you do not wish trees, and rootkill them, you need not fear re-invading trees unless you repeat the conditions under which they started, the bare soil of the ploughed field. If you eliminate the shrubs, they neither will return, unless you have bare soil. Furthermore, whether your grassland develops naturally into shrubland or into forest will not depend on what currently reinvades as seedlings, but what did reinvade back years ago. Knowing this situation you will consider the unwanted already-removed trees and shrubs as a problem in original "construction" of your landscape. They will be no problem at all in current "maintenance."

4. Development by Combination of #2 and #3

The two preceding theoretical and idealized situations rarely if ever occur alone in nature. Rather, they are to be considered as "factors" which combine in various ways to form the vegetation development that we actually observe.

Page 84a expresses a combined but still theoretical situation in which half the plants of each stage occur as invading relays. The other half are there because of initial floristic composition of the old agricultural field.

Here we have a new problem in the original Intaglio, and in the subsequent Maintenance of our landscape. We may want no trees, so we remove the four kinds that are present. Two of them however are capable of returning, and do return, amongst the shrubs. These two can cause us a considerable amount of trouble. Furthermore, any one or more of these four trees may be conifers, in contrast to deciduous hardwood trees. Thus we may radically change the physiognomy of the landscape by altering the proportions of deciduous and evergreen trees.

The situation becomes more complex when we want to remove the shrub stage also, and obtain a grassland. Some of the shrubs are part of the original cropland flora; a few may invade the grassland. In this case, we find that those shrubs and trees which are part of the Initial Floristic Composition and were removed in the Intaglio process cannot reinvade grassland, and thus will not give us any Maintenance problem. It is the shrub relay which we will have to watch for. Actually, this relay may involve species that previously were very rare. Now this invader is finding extensive grasslands to enter that it never had before. A population explosion is in the making. The idea is to catch the plant before it so explodes. Sounds easy, but the human race is certainly not controlling its own explosion. As for the shrub-invading relay of trees, we need not worry about them at all—as long as we keep the shrubs from becoming abundant. As in the tree situation described above, whatever does come in as an invading relay may very much change the physiognomy of the landscape. It may be a needle-leaved coniferous shrub, or a broad-leaved evergreen shrub, or a deciduous shrub. In other words, developments subsequent to our original Intaglio efforts may be quite "natural," but they may still be vastly different in appearance from the "normal" vegetation development one sees on old fields. What comes, or does not come, I cannot always predict. That is your problem. I am sure you will be fascinated by what does happen—for better or worse.

To this point (Sections 2, 3, and 4), we have dealt with idealized abstract theoretical situations. This approach has probably bothered the realistic ecologist who can only think in terms of concrete facts, or what he thinks are concrete facts. I consider this approach however absolutely essential if you—and he—are to grasp the complex nature of Vegetation Development, and also that you may control it in a practical manner.

SPIRAEA

S. tomentosa

BEFORE INTAGLIO

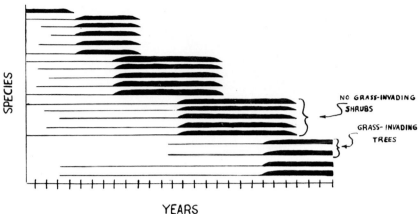

NO GRASS-INVADING
SHRUBS

GRASS-INVADING
TREES

SPECIES

YEARS

BEFORE INTAGLIO. Probable and actual type of vegetation develop-ment occurring on old fields in deciduous forest regions of the world, and in other regions. Note that the bulk of the plants entered the vegetation as part of the Initial Floristic Composition. Note also that all of the shrubs entered at the time of agricultural abandonment. Consequently shrubs should be eliminated with caution, for once gone they may not reinvade the grass-land. Note also that most of the trees were part of the Initial Floristic Com-position, that none of them are an Invading Relay of the shrub stage, and that a few can invade grassland. For this reason, it is economically desirable to root-kill (not merely top-kill) these trees, since once gone, they will not return into shrubland. It is also apparent that shrublands can be extremely stable vegetation types, resisting invasion by trees. The grassland-invading trees, such as pine and ash, can be real pests in Wild gardening.

AFTER INTAGLIO

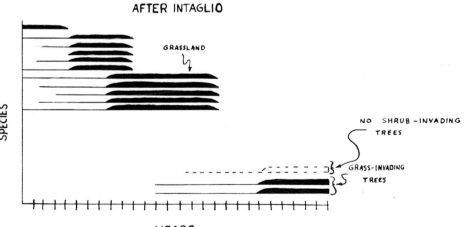

GRASSLAND

NO SHRUB-INVADING
TREES

GRASS-INVADING
TREES

SPECIES

YEARS

AFTER INTAGLIO. Maintenance problems of herbicide-induced grass-land are usually not serious, providing original root systems of unwanted woody plants are actually killed. Grassland-invading shrubs are not likely to cause any trouble. A few species of trees may become troublesome as invading seedlings. A single parent tree may be responsible, and if so this itself may be killed, as for example, a seed-producing ash tree.

Older stands of white pine (*Pinus strobus*) may become cluttered with undesirable tree seedlings, shrubs, and herbaceous plants. These before-and-after views were taken one year apart. Other stands managed selectively with herbicides have required very little maintenance thru the years.

5. Probable Developmental Trends in Your Fields

On the basis of our existing scientific knowledge for humid temperate forested parts of the Earth, there is a strong probability that the situation which you yourself possess can be represented by the diagram on p. 85a. Note that in this diagram the vast majority of the plants get into the vegetation by the Initial Floristic Composition of the old field. All of the intermediate-stage grasses and forbs so arise. This is an important point, for it means that the kind of grass you have now you will probably continue to have. And if you do not have certain asters and goldenrods to begin with, you probably will not get them invading in the future. If you do want some other grasses and forbs you will probably purposely have to introduce them, but that is a story for Part III of this book.

The status of the shrubs is highly important. You will notice in the figure that all of them are part of the Initial Floristic Composition. For this reason, if you remove them in order to obtain a grassland, you will not be troubled with their reinvasion. For the same reason, if you are not sure but that you may want some of them, go slow on destroying them. They will not return. This has been the colossal stupidity in blanket-spraying rightofways and roadsides. They have not only more or less lost the unwanted trees, but they have also lost the highly desirable shrubs, and this is a costly loss of "capital." The fact that shrubs in general do not invade closed grassland as seedlings (tho they may, by underground roots) runs counter to established comfortable armchair ecologic theory. This theory has always supported the "succession" indicated on p. 81a. I am well acquainted with the existence of certain grass-invading shrubs, especially in the tropics. The shrub lantana, for example, has covered thousands of acres in certain Pacific islands. But for the northeastern United States, I know yet of no shrub which in the absence of fire, mowing and grazing, can massively invade by seedlings a closed grassland! I ask the co-operation of my readers in finding an example for me.

The situation with the trees is extremely interesting. You will probably find that most of the trees, those which dominate the last stages of the natural development, probably arose far back, at the time of agricultural abandonment. You will rootkill them. Forget them; they will not return. It is worth spending more time and energy to remove them, for you are "eradicating" them, you are not "controlling" them. On the other hand, note that one line on p. 85a. indicates grass-invading trees. There are some trees that can invade your closed grassland, and they may cause you a considerable amount of trouble. They may be species quite different from those in the "normal succession." Many of the pines can invade grassland. This is a big joker in some commercial rightof-way practices, for the chemical industry has taught the utility industry to spray for grassland, which in turn is a come-on for pines, especially in the southeastern United States. And to get rid of the new crop of pines requires even more costly spraying procedures— all to the good of the chemical industry. Once in a while gray birch and paper birch can invade, but not nearly as often as the ecologists have been inclined to believe. Sometimes oaks may invade the edges of grassland, but only within the distances that squirrels choose to carry the acorns before burying them. Maples may invade, but apparently only within the distances where autumn leaf-fall tends to blanket out the grasses. White ash is one of the chief offenders. It is remarkably successful in invading unmown grasslands, often at distances of a hundred feet from the parent plant. It will survive for several years, showing only two or four leaves (not leaflets). Each season, the falling grass mats it flat. The next spring, the tip grows up. Eventually, it shoots up and puts on 2 or 3 feet a year. Mice disdain it, and I have not found a way to spray it with a cheese-flavored herbicide. (Industry! Get busy!) Furthermore, it is remarkably resistant to 2,4-D and 2,4,5-T, and I find I have to cut and stub-spray each separate seedling unless I get them as 1 or 2 year old seedlings. Their abundance is extraordinary. In forestry terms, it is "full stocking" that soon needs "thinning." I never could understand why some foresters always claim that hardwood reforestation is impractical, and they must plant conifers. I have great difficulty controlling such reforestation—when near a parent tree. And therein lies the weak link in this chain. White ash—alone among ashes—is polygamo-dioecious. That is a fancy way of saying that this thing could not make up its mind whether to be all male, or all female, or some sort of combination, and ended up by being several things. The polygamo means that both hermaphroditic and unisexual flowers occur. The dioecious means that these male and female flowers tend to be on different plants. In simple terms, white ash trees are mostly male, or mostly female; and it is the female ash—as you might expect—which causes all the trouble. Fortunately, they are not fertile every year. They go to fruit heavily only at irregular intervals, maybe every 3 to 7 years. At the present time, I try to control my ash trouble at its source. Every female ash within a hundred feet of my grasslands is under close surveillance. At the first sign of fertility in the spring, she gets ringed. Fertile ash has become a rare event in my managed landscape.

B. BEHAVIOR OF COMMUNITIES

We have been talking about the sequence from one community to another. It is now time that we focus our attention on a single community. Much fine scientific work has been done in the study of these individual communities, a study generally known as phytosociology. If you go into this literature, you will find that some botanists draw a distinction between Phytosociology with emphasis on these separate communities, and Vegetation Science with emphasis on the mosaic or tapestry of communities that occurs in the landscape, such as we have been doing until this time.

1. Position of a Community in the Sequence

Since your interest as a Naturalistic Landscaper is in the manipulation of these different communities to form a new mosaic in the landscape, you are very definitely concerned with the status of your desired community in the sequential development.

It is rather reassuring to know that, under subsequent natural conditions, the community you wish has one, and only one place in the total sequence. It can invade, or come after, only certain communities. Knowing this, you need not be worried by grasslands invading your shrubland, or shrubland succeeding upon your forest. I do not wish to infer that there are not alternative possibilities. For example, there may be several different types of shrubland which might follow a grassland. These could be called "phytosociologic equivalents." In addition, either shrubland or forest, or any one of several different kinds of forest, might invade a grassland, if there are appropriate invading relays of such species. Furthermore some other "natural" phenomenon, like a fungous disease, may as completely destroy the trees of the forest as you have done with herbicides, so that a forest can be succeeded by a grassland. But in the otherwise normal sequential development of plant communities, you can rely completely on the fact that "before" and "after" are relatively fixed phenomena.

One common mistake that has often been made has been the assumption that each stage is "higher" than the preceding one. Tall forbs succeed the lower grasses. Taller shrubs succeed the forbs. Trees follow shrubs. And the tallest trees come last. This was a nice idea, that nature is not interested in following. White pine stands, for example, are followed by less high beech birch maple and hemlock, and this obvious fact seriously disturbed the ecologists some years ago. Furthermore, there are some forests with dense shrubby understories. When their natural development is hastened, that is, when the death of the overstory trees is hastened by cutting them for timber, the shrubs take over, and no trees may return. A shrubland is a "later" stage! This is one of the facts of life not tolerated by decent ecologic theory. Keep your mind open. Read nature first, books second, and you will be more successful.

2. Stability of One Stage

In terms of our discussion, once we have obtained a certain semi-natural plant community, a grassland, a fernland, or a shrub-land, we are concerned with its stability. The more stable it is, the less effort to maintain it. The less stable it is, the more costly to keep it from changing. Following the Intaglio procedures (which you now understand as being to a great extent the removing of those un-desirable plants that were part of the Initial Floristic Composition), your problem is related to invading Relays. The more species that can invade, and the more abundant they are, the less stable will be your desired community. Consequently, one of your chief problems will be to make acquaintance, just as soon as possible, with those species which occur "after" in the total Vegetation Development, and come in as an invading relay. Unfortunately, this information is not readily available in books. In fact, it is largely non-existent. In the first place, before the days of herbicides there was little or no experimentation with Vegetation Development: there was only interpretation, in terms of fields of different ages, all studies maybe in the few years, of a graduate-student thesis. In the second place, these herbicide-induced communities may never have existed be-fore in history. At the most, they are only a decade and a half old. It is quite possible that some of the very worst "weeds" have never been near enough to such landscaped areas to show what they can do in invading. On the other hand, in the light of general back-ground and experience, I am reasonably sure that you will not find any pernicious weed which cannot be reasonably controlled in your Maintenance procedures. Your unsprayed unmown grasslands are really a very "closed" community, more closed than scientists had originally thought, and as closed as some of their minds still are.

3. Fluctuations within a Community

When you see one of your communities beginning to alter, do not get excited and think that it is unstable, and beginning to change into something radically different. It may be only a "fluctuation." Plant-communities are live biological phenomena. You yourself are constantly changing, yet remain the same. You take in some chemical compounds and give off others. Your bones of last year are totally different from those you have today, as molecule after molecule is replaced. So also with plant-communities, as individual plants die, and others replace them.

Annuals and biennials are responsible for some of the most prominent fluctuations. They may be extremely abundant for one or two years, and then become quite rare. A great many factors are responsible for their fluctuations, conditions at the time of seed formation, winter severity, and germination and growing conditions the next season. Let them fluctuate. It is one of the interesting natural phenomena.

There are other species which may be called "wanderers." As they die in one spot, they move on usually by underground stolons, to another place. They may form a solid patch one year; open up into a fairy circle several years later, and reform into other patches somewhere else. At least some of these movements are related to self-inhibitory root excretions, but scientists have much to learn on the matter. The necessity of moving garden plants every few years may be a related phenomenon. My advice is to let the wanderers wander where they will. That is one of the fascinating aspects of your semi-natural landscape.

C. BEHAVIOR OF SPECIES

In the last analysis, for the botanist and not the biochemist or biophysicist, the behavior of vegetation and the behavior of plant-communities can be traced down to the behavior of individual species. This does not mean that communities do not "exist." They exist just as much as human cities exist and operate as a unit, even tho the eventual operations are reduceable to the individual level. Some people cannot see the forest for the trees. Some cannot see the trees for the forest. And the chances are that nature often operates at some intermediate position, as with the colonial coelenterates and with bee colonies. Since we are not hydras or bees, there will always be scientific "controversies" on the issue, for scientists like other average people frequently see only black and white, but not shades of gray.

1. Species from "Outside" the Community

A type of situation in which the Naturalistic Landscaper becomes very cognizant of the need for an individual-species approach to vegetation, rather than a plant-community approach, is in the behavior of Invading Species. In terms of our earlier discussion, this is the invading relay. Each species has its own way, or combination of ways, of entering your vegetation. Some of them will be highly desirable species, like a lily. Others may be pernicious pests, like a trailing thorny blackberry, or like St. Johnswort. St. Johnswort in my own local experience is the most dangerous of all herbaceous pests for the grassland. It gives evidence of being able to replace the grassland, killing out other plants, and forming a solid mass of rank foliage about 3 feet high. The more you can understand about the behavior of these individual species, the more you can either encourage or discourage the process, depending on what you want.

Species from outside can in most cases be classed as "peripheral invaders" or "overall invaders." The peripheral invaders come in from adjacent vegetation types somewhat like an advancing wave. They are to be found in marginal belts anywhere from a few to 40–50 feet from the edge. Such invasion can be either vegetative, by rhizomes or runners, or within a "seed shadow" in which the seeds come from an overhanging tree. The overall invaders start in as tho the plants were scattered from an airplane. In a grassland, new plants would start all over the field, without apparent relation to some seed source. Overall invaders are difficult to control if you do not want them. Marginal invaders can be beaten back, and kept out of your grassland. Like the barbarians in Roman times however, they are always at the boundaries of the empire, ready to pour in whenever the defenses become weak. Fortunately for us the natural defenses, the "stability," of such as your grassland can be replied upon. In almost all cases, it greatly resists such barbarians.

Another way of understanding the behavior of these Ausländer is in terms of their way of increasing or spreading. This spread can be sexual or vegetative. Sexual invasion is in terms of seedlings. Note that I say seedlings, and not seeds or fruits. Most people get very worried when they see some undesirable plant loaded with flowers or fruits. They immediately want to destroy the plant, or at least the fruits. To this I say "calm down." The abundance of flowers no more means young plants than a bitch in heat means puppies. And the birth of puppies no more means mature dogs than does the birthrate in a primitive tribe indicate the number that will survive to maturity. Nature is profligate and wasteful, nowhere more so than in sexual processes. Think of the pollen cast upon the breezes, of the milt discharged by fish in the currents—and of the sexual activities of man. It took me a long while to learn too. There was one time, I am ashamed to relate, when I went around the edges of my grasslands cutting all the pods off the pussy willows for (according to textbooks) willow was a proper successional stage following grassland. Since then I have learned more about improper pussies. My advice is not to worry about fruits, or even to plan upon them, until you have ample evidence of their capacity for desirable or undesirable behavior.

Concerning vegetative increase and spreading, the different techniques must be recognized. Knowing them, you greatly increase your ability to encourage or discourage the species. Vegetative spread is either underground, at the surface, or in the air close to the surface. Underground spread is by rhizomes (underground stems) or by adventitious buds from roots. If in doubt, dig some up. Rhizomes can be 18–24 inches deep or more. Or they may be close to the surface. They may be thick and fleshy, or thin and wiry. The knowledge is worth the trouble. There is not much you can do about such spread. But knowing whether it is rapid or slow, you can use more or less effort to control "the front," as by repeated spraying. It is well to remember that invasion into bare soil can be very very rapid, but that it may be slowed almost to a still-stand if another community already exists on the site. This relationship is true of all biologic invasions. The attempted invasion of one European country into another has always been more difficult than was their invasion into the relatively "empty" New World.

Spread at the surface is generally by so-called runners, horizontal stems that root at every node, and establish that many new plants. The best known local plants spreading by runners are the strawberries and cinquefoils. Indeed, I should hate to have to keep these plants out of my grasslands. I know of no northeastern herbaceous species with runners that is undesirable, and the above-mentioned strawberries and cinquefoils are in my opinion very attractive components. Both have myriads of flowers, while the berries of Fragaria are a tantalizing tidbit, tho I should hate to have to pick them in quantity.

In a very different category are the blanketing vines. Japanese honeysuckle in the southeastern United States, and the kudzu vine in the same area, are phenomenal for their ability in rolling over the vegetation, blotting out all other plants, even shrubs and small trees. Gleichenia ferns have the same role in some tropical areas.

Aerial spread differs from that by runners in that the shoot grows up, arches over, and roots at the tip. This is a remarkably effective way for a plant to get about. It can reach up, and over; drop down onto a new spot; and then, with a large amount of nourishment from the original root-system, establish a new and healthy plant. Unfortunately, there is one serious grassland pest that does just this. It is a thorny semi-prostrate blackberry that sends out canes up to six feet in length, which drop down and root at the tip. A jump of six feet at a time can, in a few years, really make headway thru a grassland. Furthermore, an interlocking network of these canes is somewhat like a field of croquet hoops, but worse. First you stumble on them; then you lacerate yourself with the thorns. In this case, it is obviously very important first to get the new canes before they root, secondly to rootkill the plant that is sending out the canes.

2. Species "inside" the Community

After a few years, you will get to know the plants in your grassland. Each species will develop an individuality. You will know
them the way you know your friends. You will know their weak-
nesses and their strengths. You will find that some need an encouraging hand, while others have to be reined in occasionally. You
will find that some are destined to be "leaders" in the community,
whereas others are content to feed on the crumbs that are left. Some
demand the spotlight like a high-C prima donna; others sit quietly
in the cheapest balcony. Much of this knowledge cannot be found
in books. For one thing, it is too variable, from field to field, and
from country to country. Furthermore, the local soil, the climate,
the past history, all play their roles. Your own fields will be different
from any other, and only you will know them. That is part of the
pleasure of Naturalistic Landscaping.

This knowledge of individual species that belong to the community is difficult to generalize about. For our present purposes,
two thoughts can be presented: the "life duration" of an individual,
and its "state of health," using health in the very human sense of
optimum individual welfare.

Life duration varies tremendously. At the short end of the scale, we have annual plants, surviving only a single growing season, and giving rise to new individuals the next year thru overwintering seeds. These plants may be very rare in your grassland, for it is generally difficult for any seedlings to get started. Be prepared for their numbers to fluctuate from year to year, as countless factors in their environment alter. Biennials, surviving for two years, also fluctuate. When it comes to perennial herbs, we should distinguish between short-lived perennials and long-lived perennials. Altho gardeners know about this situation, Naturalistic Landscaping is too new an art for us to have acquired much knowledge. Some herbs will prove short-lived. There will be nothing you can do to keep a plant alive, any more than you can hope your cat will reach the age of 50, or you the age of 150. Unless such plants have a way of re-establishing themselves, you might as well admit they will eventually vanish. Among the long-lived herbs, there are some that just seem to go on and on and on, at least in terms of a human life. When they start spreading vegetatively, and then dying in the original portions (as already discussed under wandering plants) we have a sort of perpetual youth principle. Just see that you do not tend to foster an overpopulation of such youths.

The state-of-health idea may require a readjustment on the part of some people, especially those kind-hearted souls, nurtured on the Garden of Eden, and seeing only goodness and harmony in nature. It is closer to the truth to consider that a plant in a plant-community is an individual which at all stages of its life has been subjected to the severest of vicissitudes without actually being killed. These vicissitudes arise from both its physical and biological environments. It is under the severest of competition with its competitors for water, nutrients, light and space. Rather than smiling sweetly and saying that it is "in harmony with nature" it would be better to say that it has survived despite nature. Its existence is more to be likened to that of a starving disease-ridden aborigene than to your own plushly pampered and health-exuding life. I am not saying which is the better. "Good health" has been a continuing feature of human tribes for only a millenium or so, and for the first time for any biologic species in the history of the earth. It still has to prove itself as a eugenic rather than a dysgenic force. Be it as it may, your plants are having a rough time of it. Knowing this, you can often assume the role of an Olympian deity, and with a grandiose flick of your little finger, you can remove an overbearing branch or blot out an undesirable murine murderer, and thus bestow continued life on a favored mortal flower.

D. MAINTENANCE PROCEDURES

With this background on the nature of plant-communities, and on the vegetational relations between communities, you will not find it too difficult to judge the "what" and the "how" in regard to maintaining the landscape that you have created by Intaglio. Furthermore, your Intaglio procedures will taper off, but still continue, in regard to the hard-to-kill plants. And thus Maintenance procedures can be combined with the remaining Intaglio procedures.

Mechanical and Chemical Tools. For the forest, I find little if any Maintenance necessary. Once your woodland trails are made, and the undesirable woody plants root-killed, you will have little trouble. Dead branches may fall across the trail, and young trees may have ingrowing branches, but that is all. Depending on your interest in herbs of the forest floor, there will be little else to do.

Shrublands are exceedingly stable, even tho highway engineers and utility engineers disregard this common observation. It may take you a period of several years to root-kill some of the unwanted trees. Once however your shrub cover has been established, the shrubs themselves are one of the most powerful influences that will keep out new tree seedlings, and even rootsuckers from adjacent thriving trees.

Certain fernlands (as of hay-scented fern) and forblands (as of dense goldenrods) are also exceedingly stable. Once established, they may stay unchanged for two decades or more.

Grasslands—tho far more stable than some scientists had anticipated—will give you some problems, but none that you cannot handle with about 0.1% of the effort that you would spend on the same amount of garden.

Once the unwanted grassland perennials are eliminated (and this you will not do in a hurry) I doubt if you will be troubled with any seedlings of these species. Keep in mind, however, that such species will start on bare soil. Animal dens, gopher and mole mounds, even the location of an underground yellowjacket nest torn open by a skunk, may supply just such a spot-environment. On such little mounds of soil, the rhizomatous perennial herbs, shrubs and trees may germinate, so keep your eyes always open.

I doubt if seedling shrubs will be any source of trouble. But root-invading sumach, plum, ericads, viburnums, and Comptonia (sweet-fern), may invade peripherally from the margin of the grassland. Since such shoots are drawing nourishment from parent plants off the grassland, you will repeatedly have to discourage such shoots.

As for trees, you should watch carefully for seedlings. A spray in time saves nine. It is extremely easy to give small seedlings a squirt or two with an herbicide spray when they are small. Let them get larger, and your problem is greater in all dimensions.

I would recommend both water-borne and oil-borne sprays for this work. If you must choose one, I would choose the oil spray. The woody plants require an oil spray, and it is easy at the same time to leaf-burn the herbaceous plants you do not want.

Both mulching and animal protection may become desirable Maintenance procedures. Both these activities are more closely related to, and will be discussed in, the following section on "Embellishment."

It has been the general thesis of this book that your landscape operations will be carried on only with means or equipment readily available to the ordinary owner of a few acres, with an axe, a shovel, and a spray can. It has been the assumption that you do not want, or cannot get, the effects of fire, cows, or mowing machines. There are times however when you may be able to utilize these environmental controls both cheaply and effectively.

Fire. All of us dread fire, that is, the fire of the arsonist, and wild-fire that crowns to the tops of the tallest pines. But none of us dread a fire in the stove. The history of fire in natural and semi-natural vegetation is a subject which scientifically is still unfolding. The early explorers of North America recognized that the Indians regularly burned much of the landscape. Altho that view was maintained all thru this past century by a minority of field botanists, it was lost sight of by those academic ecologists who sought to establish all "causes" in terms of the local climate and soil that they and their graduate students could measure. The foresters instituted a complete all-out anti-fire program, wisely perhaps, for escaped fires at the peak of the dry season were doing inestimable damage to forests in which the artificial elimination of fires had built up a tremendous fire hazard—like smoking in a cluttered attic. Then foresters began to experiment with controlled fires. That work started in the early 1920's, and was all but flooded out by a torrent of bigoted and prejudiced verbosity that is little credit to the profession. Today, we accept controlled fires as a valuable silvicultural tool in many parts of the U.S.A. With that preamble, you can see that fire need not be completely shunned or avoided. And if fire does escape, do not think you should sell and move away. Fire is unquestionably a cheap "management tool" to use. In its control of woody shoots, it results in a reasonably attractive landscape. It is however, one of the trickiest of all tools to use. Unless you have expert advice, as to season and the time of day or night, and with sufficient human help around, I advice you not to use fire—or you will be in the law courts for arson, and in damage suits for burning down your neighbor's home.

Grazing. There was a time when pasture lands were some of the commonest sights. Now, within a hundred miles of the exurbanite and lunatic fringes of any city, they can be rare. A cow is a luxury. But if you have an opportunity to put cattle on some of your land, give it a thought. There will be much that you cannot grow, but you will get pleasing lawn-like effects totally impossible by any other means. In some cases, cattle are directly responsible for the abundance of what might be thought as very rare plants. I recall one swampy pasture loaded with large pink orchids. Without the cattle, it soon would have grown over with forest trees.

Mowing. Mowing may have several advantages. If you are a sociological offshoot of suburban lawns, and not from stretches of vast wild prairie, it may take you a time to realize the subtle values of unmown grassland. You will prefer the sterile stubble of a mown meadow, even tho you will have to work the more to remove the hay you have cut. But do not be entirely opposed to mowing. By cutting the high-rising grasses and allowing them to shrivel and dry, mowing actually encourages certain plants that have flat prostrate foliage near the ground and that would otherwise be shaded out. I myself keep a mile-long mowed trail thru my grasslands. Such mowing definitely increases the abundances of such plants as certain violets, bluets, and even the orange hawkweed. Mowing has its place. It lends variety. It makes for easier walking if in a long narrow strip. But for me, it is too much work to do much of it.

Part III

EMBELLISHMENT

The Art of Adding and Aiding Plants

Part III

EMBELLISHMENT

The Art of Adding and Aiding Plants

The third and final step in the logical development of your own attitudes toward Naturalistic Landscaping now surges forward. First you were engrossed with the Intaglio procedures of getting rid of what you did not want. It probably seemed like an overwhelming task. In a short time you realized that not only were you master of the situation, but that there really was not any situation left of which to be master! Then your attention became focussed on the more subtle and interesting changes that began to appear in this newly created landscape. These were changes that would take shape only with the passage of several years. And then, I suspect, another itching attribute of human nature became manifest. You felt the urge to meddle with things, to "improve" the situation. There was probably a conflict of itches. On the one hand would be the desire to be "natural," to leave everything to what the Gods had decreed, and nature had carried out. This, despite the fact that your antecedent agricultural operations were anything but natural, especially in the removal of stones and in the leveling and terracing of the land by many years of ploughing and harrowing, and despite the totally unnatural present operation of your acting as a disease-substitute and killing off many plants with herbicides. On the other hand would be the desire to improve on nature, to ornament, to embellish, to design, to create, to idealize. After all, these compulsions are the very essence of our artistic instincts, and you would be quite pitiful if you did not feel them. Only the most contemplative and introspective of souls are able to obey, fully, any higher injunction to just "stop, look, and listen," even tho many of us die for not doing so.

If you are one who likes nature for nature's sake, and thus feel a hesitancy to move that wild azalea to a place where it will show off to perfection against the white and green of paper birch and pine, may I suggest you take a cold look at your own supposed logic. Is there some fundamental scientific or divine reason why that azalea had grown up in the "wrong" place? Or might it just as easily have been in the "right" place except for some trivial little coincidence? Now actually you can get logical and scientific support for both sides! The scientific environmentalists, the ecologists in the narrow sense (and most of them for the first half century have been narrow) are firmly convinced that vegetation is what it is because of the environment. The environment is mostly (to them) the existing climate and soil. They seldom analyze beyond those factors. The philosophy is a strict determinism. If you like it, fine; leave the azalea where it is, to blush unseen. On the other hand, if you recognize that chance and coincidence play important roles, you give yourself much more freedom. Water molecules in the cooking pot are in constant motion. Just which ones will escape by evaporation? Chance decides. Three hundred people will die this weekend in highway accidents. You are driving. Will it be you? Chance decides. The entire insurance industry runs on the surety of such mass phenomena. Foresters have long realized that you will not get natural reforestation despite climate and soil, unless you also happen to have some parent trees nearby (a brilliant biologic observation!), and happen to have a good seed year, and do not happen to have other plants fill up the land first. In short, in this game, it is your right and privilege concerning the what and where of individual plants, that you yourself serve as—not God—just a mere happenstance.

A. THE ART OF ADDING PLANTS

When you have once decided that you are going to add some plants to your Naturalistic Landscape, you are immediately confronted with several other problems:

1. Will you use native plants, or exotics?
2. Will you plant seeds, bulbs, or larger plants?
3. If larger plants, just how large?
4. Should one transplant from the wild, or raise his own material in a sort of garden?

1. Natives vs. Exotics

The decision to use native plants or exotic plants will probably come from your heart, and not from your head. I advise you to follow your heart. It will make you happier. We have already brought up this problem on page 16 , under the discussion of the ecology devotee. It exists also among those people who rise from the gardening ranks. Those who write wild flower gardening books, for example, are invariably for the natives. They would no more introduce a foreign plant than Mozart would have introduced a shocking dissonance (tho he did in Ein Musikalischer Spaß, and it is a reflection on our times that it no longer sounds like a Spass, or joke).

It is my opinion that the soundest criterion in this problem is not whether the plant is an alien or a native, but whether it is in good landscaping taste. To introduce aliens only because they are alien, and to treat the local aristocracy as podunks, is only the sort of snobbery that leads an ordinary bibber to buy an imported vintage wine, when on a blindfold test he could not distinguish it from a superior local product or a neighbor's vin ordinaire, très ordinaire. To keep to the natives could be the equivalent of preferring a neo-primitive Grandma Moses on your walls, rather than a Da Vinci—if you had the choice. Chacun à son goût. Everyone to his taste, as said Count Orlofsky in Johann Strauss' Die Fledermaus.

If Naturalistic Landscaping appeals to you, I would guess that you are of that temperament that likes nature—but touched here and there with a bit of "management." Thus, I suspect it may be a problem to you as to whether you feel you can introduce some choice aliens without betraying your faith in nature. To this impasse, I suggest you bear in mind the history and development of our own "native" floras. They are what they are only by the coincidental distribution of oceans and of barrier mountain ranges and deserts. Had there been suitable land passages, plants would have poured across them, and started to naturalize themselves in the new world just as human beings have done. You make an exception for yourself. Why not make an exception for choice plants, in which you yourself act as a substitute land bridge? It is true that I am very glad that all the continents are not connected with land-bridges, just as I deplore the so-called democratic mixing of races into a melting pot of pallid uniformity. Differences and variation make life interesting and worthwhile. Furthermore, they are the very stuff and substance of progressive evolution. And when it comes to horticultural varieties, the same philosophy is pertinent. The horticulturist is either preserving chance mutants that occurred naturally, or he purposely pimped to produce a punk that proved perfection, a hybrid which is certainly not "unnatural" but of extremely high improbability in the world outside of man. In your choice of plants, allow yourself to serve as a natural accident!

2. Seeds, Bulbs, and Larger Plants

Once you decide that you are going to plant, and you decide what species to plant, you reach the nagging problem of what to put in, seeds, bulbs, or whole plants.

Seeds come to mind first. Providing you are not dealing with some hybrid or horticultural clone that either does not produce seed or would not come true to seed, it seems perfectly reasonable to broadcast seed. After all, that is what "nature" does. That is the way natural "plant succession" occurs according to the principle of Relay Floristics (page 81). Yes, that is what I thought also, once upon a time. Staunch and firm in pompous convictions of my academic training, I paid much good money for packets and packets of the best seed, and I scattered it upon the land. I now refer to that time of life as my Era of Onanism. Onan knew better than I. To my knowledge, there was only one apparent slip-up, and that strangely is a lone single plant of a species of Coreopsis which to my knowledge was never planted, a contaminant, evidence of the hand of an unknown man. I do not recommend the scattering of seed. Regardless of whether you feed the birds or mice thereby, or whether the seed remains dormant until a new plough turns the soil, your grassland community has apparently shut its gates to most such invading influences.

When it comes to bulbs and rhizomes, your chance of success is infinitely superior. Bulbs, such as those of narcissus or lilies, are essentially entire plants. They already have enough stored food to allow for a full season's growth, and to shoot the foliage thru competing plants so that they can expand their leaves and produce food for the next year. Bulbs are essentially an organ of vegetative propagation. For this reason, all the unusual and delicate environmental balances that are necessary for sexual reproduction are obviated. Sometimes even in the native homes of these plants, seeds and fruits will be produced only at very rare intervals. The plant carries along by bulbs for many many years. The situation is analogous in a way to men living for long times in harsh environments where successful childbirth and child-rearing are impossible. The environment is lethal only for those stages, not for the adult organism. When you plant bulbs, consider that you are planting a mature individual. If it then does not succeed in the community in which you place it, at least it is not because you should have picked an "older" or a "larger" plant.

The transplanting of germinated seedlings and of larger individuals will occupy much of your time. On the one hand, you can put out seedlings a few weeks old. Or you can spend a considerable sum and put out a 50-foot-tall tree. The chances are that you will use the conventional sizes, such as you see in nurseries for balled and burlapped shrubs, and for asphalt-paper potted herbs. Some of the commercial perennial herbs I have received thru the mails have been almost minute in size. Considering that the larger the plant, the larger the hole you have to dig, you will probably tend to keep on with small sizes. You might rationalize this thought by reasoning that the critical stage of invasion is the germination of the seed and the growth of the young seedling. From there on, your plant is able to take care of itself. After you have lost a hundred or so plants, you will realize that the problem is complicated. It will be a challenge—not in hours of "gardening"—but to your powers of observation and comprehension. An Idea is involved, sufficiently important to discuss separately in the next section.

3. The Concept of "Competition Level"

When you put a plant into your grassland, it is a vastly different matter than putting it in the bare soil of your garden. In the garden, you rigidly exclude competition from other garden plants and from weeds. The plant has all the water, light, nutrients and space it needs. It might be said to be growing in a phytosociological vacuum.

When you put a plant in a grassland, however, you are placing it in the heavy competition of a closed community. There is as much difference as between a person moving into a town where food and rent are cheap and jobs begging, or into a place where everyone is jobless and on the dole, and queues for food are the scene of brawls and fights. Whether or not your introduced plant succeeds depends upon the relationship between that particular individual's "competitive rank," and the "competition level" of the community in which you place it. A frail esthete would not have much chance in a brawling street mob; a pugilist would. A sickly child would not have much chance among scrapping playmates; a healthy child could hold his own—but not with the pugilist.

So can we list the different kinds of plants in terms of their Competitive Levels? The answer is unfortunately "no." In parts of New England for example, altho white ash seedlings at any age will grow and thrive in grass, only older azaleas will succeed but not younger ones. In other words, in addition to the kind of plant, the size and health of the plant are critical factors. That is to say, you can think of your grassland community as possessing a certain "competition level" (actually a complex composed of a good many different, and variable, factors). The plant you put in must have a competitive "edge," and this will vary for the kind of plant, and for its size and health. It is impossible to state this situation precisely for your different transplants. One learns by experience, by his failures. In gardening, we call this a "green thumb." Soon you will develop a sixth sense, an intuition. And since you are dealing with living organisms—rather than gambling on a chain with a weak link—you can step into the fray at any time and turn the tide of battle, like Wotan, as Siegfried fought Hunding. Like Wotan, your interference may lead to more than the downfall of both contestants, so be sure your judgment is soundly your own and that you are more of a man than was this god.

4. Use of a Propagating Garden

If you have grown up from the gardening rank and file, you may wonder whether it might not be economical to raise your own material for transplanting. Most assuredly. In fact, it might be an excellent way to work off some of that parental urge to fuss over and to molly coddle helpless little plants. Go to it, and enjoy it.

Actually, there are many reasons why you should not dig up from the wild the larger shrubs, or old clumps of narcissus bulbs. If you must dig woody plants from the wild, I would suggest root-pruning them a year before, so as to adjust the plant to the loss of long straggling roots you will sever, and to encourage feeder roots in the ball of earth you will move. And with such things as bulbs, they will be so hopelessly entangled with fibrous grassy roots that it may hardly be worth the effort to separate them out.

With plants in a small propagating garden, they will enlarge rapidly, and allow for frequent division. I replant my narcissi, for example, every three years. I find I average a 3 to 1 return, which means that for every dozen I keep in the garden, I have two dozen to put out, every third year.

One of the most interesting aspects of bare-soil gardening with plants for naturalization is the knowledge you acquire in their manner of growth. Furthermore, if you are not too fussy in your weeding you will be thoroly astonished at the kinds of volunteer seedlings you get. For the first time you will realize how important that factor of Initial Floristic Composition can be. I am sure my small garden, if it is abandoned, and rediscovered by some latter-day ecologist, would be a never-ending source of novel theories— as to the nature of primitive man.

B. THE ART OF AIDING PLANTS

This parental instinct is one of the strongest in human nature. Whether it expresses itself early, with dolls and doll houses for girls, or late, with our great grand-children, whether it expresses itself wisely as we force independence upon our offspring, or oppositely so, in that great American pastime of momism, whether it expresses itself directly upon our offspring, or indirectly upon the spousine canine and feline members of the family, or upon such non-biological phenomena as literary "creations" (it is not for me to vouch for the role of this book), we gain a deep satisfaction in caring for things, in playing a role in their birth, in raising them, in nursing them and doctoring them. You will have wide amplitude for expressing all those feelings in Naturalistic Landscaping. Tho essentially you are accepting Nature in the raw, she will often be a bit over-raw. Both with the plants already on your land, and the plants you have added, you will be amply repayed by acting as a Good Samaritan.

You may think of your role as Samaritan in terms of (1) what the plant needs, and (2) what tends to damage the plant. This is a useful, but not watertight separation, for what is worthy in moderation can be damaging in excess—like wine, and women, and song. The classification however serves our purpose.

1. What the Plant Needs

The plant's needs are fairly easily grouped. We can think in terms of:

water,	light,
nutrients,	space.

As for water, I cannot recommend regular irrigation. If you make plans for irrigation, you are most certainly creating a very unnatural landscape, even tho it may be well worth the effort from other viewpoints. But the real test of your urge to meddle will come during that summer drouth that is the worst in half a century. Use your own judgment. It is exactly drouths of such severity that are potent factors in shaping the natural landscape. On the other hand, if this is a once-in-a-lifetime crisis, and you can pull thru some special plant by carrying 500 pounds of water up a rocky mountain, by all means I want you to feel free to do so.

Nutrients, under natural conditions, are often in short supply. This inadequacy is true not only for the commonly recognized deficiencies of nitrogen, phosphorus and potassium, but sometimes for other elements like iron, or for the so-called micro-elements copper and cobalt. If you live in some unusual edaphic environment, like shale barrens which are characterized not only by deficiencies but also by some toxic elements, it would certainly be the course of least resistance to accept your environment—or move out of the county. If you are in a very acid region, you will be tempted to apply ground limestone, to make the soil basic according to the actual or supposed needs of some plants. Or if you are in limestone country, you may go to great lengths to make a spot acid. The effort expended is your decision. Remember however that emphasis on soil acidity was definitely a scientific fad for a few decades. Many plants do not give a darn, and "nature" is not always an indication of needs but only of tolerances. Plants may do as well, or even better, under other soil conditions than where you find them wild.

Whether or not you wish to apply fertilizer, that is, "artificial" nutrients, is another subjective decision. You may be reasonably assured that the plants you so treat will grow larger and finer, (and so will the less desirable plants immediately adjacent). Personally, I prefer not to so fertilize. For what time I can expend on this project, I prefer to have a thin spreading of a couple dozen small plants, rather than one huge garish individual that stands out like a billboard on a highway with an enormous photo of an eye-winking cinema actress.

Some of the mulches, to be discussed later, will serve in this capacity. Those who keep compost piles will be amply supplied with material for the purpose. In this connection, I feel I should pass on the recommendation of one of my correspondents who is an avid supporter of composting and other such organic activities. He lives in an extremely isolated area, and at the lowest and most despised standard of American living: he has no indoor plumbing. He does have an outhouse—for visitors he says. For himself, he writes that he makes little individual packets of night-soil, neatly folded in sheets of newspaper. His comments on this worthy use of the news are unprintable. These packets he places around the grass-land plants he wants to aid, and covers them with grass torn from the vicinity. The procedure sounds intriguing, altho I am sure that several American industries would not encourage any spread of this idea, so dangerous to several facets of the national economy. Furthermore, I am surprised that I have never seen this practical thought mentioned in the organic-oriented books at which I have glanced dealing with composting, books which have a strong crusading spirit otherwise, and certainly not hesitant or delicate in other ways.

In regard to light, plants differ. Some plants are widely tolerant of both light and shade. Others actually need bright light for their photosynthetic activities, while some of the woodland plants would be burned with full sunlight. It is not likely that you can do much in regard to light. If your plant is overshadowed by other foliage and branches, simply pull up or break off the offending material.

Space needs are to be handled in the same way. Simple as it appears, many people, even some scientists, overlook the significance of the fact that two plants cannot occupy the same space at the same time. In other words, simply yank up, or chop down, whatever seems to be growing in the space that your desired plant should grow into.

The combined needs for all these things, for water, nutrients, light and space, can be considered together as a sort of "competition" between your desired plant, and the entire plant-community. In this sense, your plant should be protected from excessive competition. We will see later that mulching is one of the best ways of controlling that competition.

2. What Damages the Plant

To refer to "damage" to the plant is to use a term that is far too broad and indefinite. Damage can be thought of as almost any unfavorable effect including oversupply and undersupply of the "needs" discussed on the preceding pages. For our present purposes, we will limit the term to physical damage, to that caused by disease, by insects, and by larger animals.

The subject of plant diseases, of phytopathology, is a separate profession, and there are books galore on the subject, both for the professional agriculturist, forester and gardener, and for the layman. There are virus diseases and bacterial diseases. There are diseases due to small worms called nematodes, and there is a host of troubles due to a long list of pathogenic (i.e., disease-causing) fungi. There is an important philosophical concept involved in the treatment of disease: Do not always focus your attention on the disease (unless you are by personality and temperament a pathologist—a man who *likes* his diseases). Focus your attention on the disease-resistance of the plant. If you want to avoid spending your life being a full-time nurse to pretty posies, don't start curing them of their diseases. Don't even go in for disease-prevention. (That may be suited for human beings, for obvious reasons.) Pick out healthy plants, and your disease problem ceases to exist. Except for certain unusual cases, it is my recommendation that you, the Wild Gardener, should let the diseased plants die off, and make more room for the healthy plants. Yet I know that my advice will not be taken by those people who are neurotically inclined to the unhealthy, not professionally to cure them, but to suffer with them. I do not know how else to account for the lavish attention that goes to certain garden plants.

Insect damage is a field which, in its human relationships, has much in common with the plant diseases discussed above. But to give the devil his due, there are times that young shrubs, for example, will be heavily loaded with caterpillars, while large shrubs growing adjacent remain untouched. I have not had this situation suitably explained by an entomologist. Whether the caterpillars dislike dizzy heights, or cannot see or smell the foliage from the soil level, it is true that if we can pull such small plants thru a few critical years, they will thereafter be independent. Here also, it will be your judgment. It is your objective to bring that individual plant along until its Competitive Level is equal to that of the surrounding community.

Larger animals, which vary greatly from country to country, will give you no end of trouble. But they are delightful beasts nevertheless, pitting their intelligence against yours in fair competition for food and shelter and survival. Your respect for their intelligence increases in direct relationship to the decrease in respect for your own. I cannot say as much for those scaleless, featherless and furless bipeds who steal my blueberries in summer, my grouse and deer in autumn, my young conifers in winter before the equinox, and anything else at any season which has value to them. Fortunately, this aberrant strain places very little value anyway on the other elements of a wild landscape; and these tendencies are so loathed by other members of its race, that there are reasonably effective checks and controls to such predatory behavior. Nonetheless, I recognize the existence of such deviant behavior within the species, and try to keep items of interest to those deviates away from their known routes of travel, which are generally barren and hard-surfaced strips.

Populations of mice, tho usually unseen, can be truly phenomenal. Furthermore, since man has often embarked on utterly foolish campaigns to eradicate such varmints (in his opinion) as hawks, owls, foxes and snakes, he has created a heaven for the mice. And female mice, as you probably know, are the nymphomaniacs of the animal world. They are either lactating, or pregnant, or seeing that they are getting so. They may like it, but the effect is a sort of "pressure" on the plant community. They have their preferred "ice cream plants," and when you find that mice like what you like, you might as well give up growing it. In winter is when they do considerable damage. Life is not harsh for them under the snow drifts. They will keep shrubs nipped to the ground for an entire human life time. They will keep young mountain laurels defoliated, apparently eating the petioles, and leaving the leaves for you to see. They continue to breed all winter. They can climb up to branches previously out of reach, and chew off all the bark. When the snows melt, you are shocked by the damage. Mouse populations rise and fall with the years. After you have gone thru a 50-year peak, you will not be too unhappy with all the other years.

Rabbits can be another active adversary to your interests. A bunny may make a fine playmate for your child and his having a live one may, but not necessarily, destroy the myth that he (yes, he) builds a nest and lays eggs at Easter time, chicken-egg size, and jelly-bean size. But wild rabbits and you often have interests in the same plants. You will notice their effects all thru the year. They enjoy spring violets for example, to the extent that you may not see any. In winter, they can walk over the top of the snow and girdle so many young trees that you yourself may have no spraying job when the snows melt. But they may not have been the kinds of trees you wanted to get rid of. The rabbits are highly selective in their tastes, and I have a strong idea that the common brush on the old fields of New England would be vastly different if the rabbits had not selectively killed back the species they like. Rabbit populations rise and fall also thru the years. Do not be overly content, or overly worried, at what happens in the first 2 or 3 years of your observations. I am sure the situation will change.

Woodchucks are extremely interesting animals. They are nothing but large terrestrial squirrels that dig burrows and chew up some of your finest plants. They have interconnecting underground passages which I suspect of being over 100 feet long. There was a time I tried to clear them out of one of my largest fields, but it was like dipping water out of the ocean. I finally gave up the endeavor, called the place Woodchuck Hill, and we have lived happily together ever after. I was unnecessarily fearful that they would increase like the rabbits on an oceanic isle, eventually consuming every stem of vegetation. Quite to the contrary, they have the same ideas on private property and overpopulation as I do. The field carries just so many woodchucks, and no more. Others get driven off. There is heavy usage close to the home opening. Decreasing usage is in concentric circles around that opening, with various peninsula-like excursions out along definite trails. Knowing this, I do not cast my pearls directly in the path of their swinish (to me) interests. One is still troubled seasonally, at the time of break-up of the young families and when in search for a place in which to settle for the winter. These roaming young bucks and cruising virgins are often found parking in unexpected places, and one has to take his chances with such excusable delinquency.

Porcupines can be a problem, certainly close to their dens. And they can be very interesting denizens of the woods. Our ancestors have killed off most of their predators, so that locally there can now be overpopulations of them. Ordinarily a porcupine acts as a reasonably sophisticated conservationist. He will go daily to some huge hemlock, wearing a trail thru the snow in the process, feasting on the twiglets high up in that one tree until it is dead. Then he moves to another tree. He appears to be wasteful of beech, reaching up only to a height of two feet or so, girdling it, killing it, and moving on to others. But if the beech has too hard and smooth a bark to climb, that is the beech's fault, not the porcupine's. I like them in their way. Tho they sometimes seem inordinately slow and stupid to me, I suppose I might give the same impression, or could become so, if I wore comparable armor and had an unlimited food supply near by. It is only when an unreasonable bloke takes a perverted interest in the foundation beams of your house, and cannot be discouraged in this strange taste, that drastic procedures are needed.

Turkeys. Parts of the country are now witnessing a resurgence of this magnificent bird, long the rarest and the wildest of game. Perhaps you will be fortunate enough to have a family flock decide that they own one of your Grasslands. Such a family flock will be composed of one gobbler, two or three hens (the male is in charge— no anti-bigamy laws here), and a host of young. They will daily stalk the fields methodically, searching for insects, berries and dry fruits. Wildness, however, can be lost as easily as gained. There are kindly souls that feed them in winter. Come summer, there is no human fear. You might not find it very interesting if one chooses your driveway for a dusting spot, or your raspberry bushes for a lunching station.

Deer, fifty years ago, had been all but exterminated from many parts of the U.S.A. Now, quite to the contrary, many of us are seeing the effects of overpopulation: a browse-line thru the woods, and undersized animals starving in the winter. But there is nothing more attractive than a fearless gamboling fawn. You watch it with mingled emotions, trying to tell yourself that you should give it the most serious fright of its young life, or that autumn it will walk right up to the first hunter it meets. Be it as it may, deer can be a real pest in your grassland. They seem to have an appreciation for the unusual the same as you have. With barely a lowering of their heads, they will toss off some of the finest, tallest, choicest herbs you have planted. Learn to put such things close to the house. That is only a measure of protection. I have had deer walk past my front door, and snort at me.

3. Aids in Aiding

On the whole, I am in favor of living with nature, rather than trying to maintain a very energy-consuming and precarious imbalance. There was a time, as I have already implied, when I used to plant young spruces and firs near the roadside, and each Christmas season I would lose a few to human predators. Now I plant hemlocks in those places. There was a time that my specially preserved blueberry bushes would yield their fruit to other human predators. Now I let them pick for several hours, and then expropriate the berries. There was a time I lost many deer by poaching. Now certain representatives of the law have legal right to take a legal personal catch. They have an interest in and ability in maintaining what is their "territory" against human predators; I get what venison I want; I lose fewer deer in the entire process. There was a time I used to shovel snow, and be rewarded with aching muscles and the sight of muddy paths and offensively dirty piles of melting snow. Now I walk on top of the snow, and enjoy its white beauty until it is replaced by the first green blades of spring. True, an automobile is a useless Goliath behind a long driveway covered with snowdrifts. That circumstance not only gives me a valid excuse to be absent from board meetings and executive committees, it keeps all but the urgent and the hardy from my door. (I dread the day when individual helicopters will be standard equipment for all except the underprivileged.)

When it comes to aiding plants, I am not entirely lazy. I just shirk work. I do feel that whatever is done should be extensive rather than intensive, and that the benefits should rate high, in terms of the costs in time and energy. In the light of these severe restrictions, I have recommendations to make only along two lines: mechanical deterrents like wire mesh and brush stakes, and mulching.

DETERRENTS. You will find that it is absolutely impossible for you to nurture along certain small shrubs, or certain succulent herbs, without protection from marauding small mammals. It is extremely easy to use collars or cages of "wire mesh," small enough to keep out a mouse, and merely poked into the ground. Under exceptionally bad mouse conditions, you may have to bury the mesh several inches in the soil. Such wire mesh, crumpled and poked around the base of young laurel bushes, will keep the mice from defoliating them in winter. The mesh is relatively invisible in the tall grass, and will not be offensive to the eye.

For the succulent and the taller herbaceous plants, I find that "pea brush" such as a gardener uses for growing peas, usually young gray birch, is all that is necessary to keep away woodchucks and deer. Apparently the animals poke their tender noses, and with other food readily available, move on. You may know the brush is there, but it easily blends with the landscape.

I have no such recommendations when it comes to protection from hippopotamuses, elephants, and giraffes. If you live in their land—and there is so little of it left, we should not take it from them—a few concessions may be required of you. An elephant is a force to reckon with. One small tree casually uprooted and tossed aside, one mighty footprint in soft soil, would do more than wreck a detail of Naturalistic Landscaping. It would also uproot and stamp out the entire methodology of one phytosociological cult that worships at the shrine of precise little plots (called quadrats, relevés, or Aufnahmen) sometimes no larger than the afore-mentioned foot.

MULCHES. By mulches I mean any materials which tend to mat out and kill what they cover. Usually but not always they may disintegrate and serve as compost. Note the dual function of a mulch: it kills out plants adjacent to the desired plant, and usually serves as a fertilizer. The elimination of adjacent plants is, for us, its most important feature. Harking back to our concept of Competitive Level, the effect of a mulch is to blot out the immediately adjacent competition. It reduces the competition at that point to zero, and thus gives your aided plant an enormous advantage. The aided plant grows luxuriantly, and attains a Competitive Level which allows it to hold its own against the surrounding vegetation. The mulch either disintegrates, or you can remove it. An enormous number of different substances can be used for mulches, and I would advise you to experiment with a variety. Each has its own special purpose and value. Among the more commonly available materials are the following:

Flat stones appeal to many people. Remember however that stones tend to sink into the soil as frosts and mice raise the earth between them. The plants between the stones are also helped by the "mulch." Soon plants have overgrown the stones. You forget the stones are there. They actually hinder the further enlargement of your preferred plant.

Hay or cut herbaceous material is very valuable in its way, but it is surprisingly temporary. Other plants usually work up between the narrow stalks, and in a single season you will find that those are the things that are being encouraged. Pine needles act similarly in sunny situations. In shade, they make an attractive and more permanent mulch.

Leaves of the so-called broad-leaved deciduous trees are a highly valuable mulching material. They will last for two or three years, and their flatness effectively prevents new seedlings from growing thru them. The seedling expends its energy in growing horizontally, and dies before it finds a topside escape hatch. Once the leaves are partially decayed however, grass shoots can pierce them. I profer leaves to all other mulches.

Buckwheat hulls are widely recommended by some people. I would urge caution in some instances. Tho they are more resistant to decay then leaves, if there are mice around, the hulls may work down into the soil, and actually hinder the normal growth of the roots, for the mixture completely dries out in summer. With all divided organic mulches, you should realize that in addition to aiding the plant you are providing excellent winter quarters for mice. Take your chances.

Wood shingles, such as may be obtained easily from some roof re-shingling job (dating from wood shingle days!) adapt themselves admirably for mulching purposes. One may either lay down large pieces in some neat arrangement, or throw down a basketful of small pieces. Being flat, they effectively discourage invasion of grasses or other plants, and continue in that capacity for four or five years.

Rags and cloths. A good use for old rags in the house is to lay them around your plant, densely enough so as to kill out the underlying plants. If the color of the rag offends you, sprinkle it with some leaves and hay. If you are dealing with a ground cover like phlox, it will grow out over the rags, and strike roots thru it. Indeed, this is the best way of enlarging a patch of such a ground cover. Otherwise, you are forever pulling out weeds and in the process destroying the new adventitious roots of your plant. With rag mulching, your ground cover rolls out as a carpet would be unrolled, completely blanketing the defects and scars and weeds that lie below it.

117

Wire mesh is a handy adjunct if you are using freshly raked autumn leaves that would otherwise stand high, and be blown about. Pile on your leaves as you wish, and then lay down sections of wire mesh more or less a foot square. Their weight will eventually press down, and a neat surface will appear. When and as grass may grow up thru this mulch, it is quickly apparent, and one may add more leaves very easily.

Asphalt shingles, even tho they do not decay to form compost in any reasonable period, are one of the very finest materials for our purpose. They can be bought for a greatly reduced price in odd colors or broken lots. Cut into foot-square sections, one can carry a couple of dozen with relative ease. They weigh only a fraction of what stones for the same coverage would weigh. Placed on the soil with their edges overlapping, they mold and fit themselves to the contour of the land. (Boards, and stiff metal pieces stand up from the soil, and encourage plants to grow in the shade below them.) Moreover, the not-inconsiderable heat engendered under these black surfaces is itself a lethal factor for plants. I have only known the tenacious shoots of live-forever to survive in that bake-oven, and grow out from under the edge. One must not overlook the fact that rain is drained one way or the other over these shingles. In most climates, it would be best to drain the rain inwards, upon your protected plant. If you tilt all the shingles outward, you might leave your plant to succumb from drouth on what is a dry mound. After the first year, dead grasses will tend to hide the shingle and make it inconspicuous. After ten years, the shingle will crack up and disintegrate. It is, after all, nothing but paper and organic asphalt. By that time your plant should have obtained a suitable Competitive Level.

Asphalt shingles have the additional advantage of being useful for expanding ground covers. When you are concerned with a solid patch of ground phlox, or of myrtle, or even such enlarging rhizomatous clumps as a daylily or a Monarda mint, these shingles can be laid in a strip around the plant. Freed from the competition of the immediate adjacent plants, your phlox or myrtle grows out over the asphalt. Sometimes you push back the too-straggling runners. Then, when there is a nice compact mass of plant on top of the asphalt, you slily pull out the asphalt shingle from underneath, to a new position. The heavy phlox settles down on the ground. It is dense enough to keep out new grass seedlings, and it soon strikes many adventitious roots and becomes firmly established.

Naturalization Notes

NATURALIZATION NOTES

Systematic List of Herbaceous Plants,
suitable for northeastern North America
and similar regions

Previous sections of this book have dealt with the principles and theory of Naturalistic Landscaping, in terms of the removal of undesirable plants and species, of stabilization of the resulting plant-communities, and of subsequent ornamentation with native and exotic introductions. The ideas are applicable to most parts of the world that do not suffer from either aridity or arctic cold.

In this appendix, we will necessarily place major attention on northeastern North America, and make a survey of the entire plant kingdom, for herbaceous plants that can be considered in any local program of Naturalistic Landscaping. The plants will be discussed in their botanical sequence of plant families, following the arrangement in Bailey's and Gleason's manuals. (See page 222 below for the full references.) The family numbers are those of Bailey. Page references are given for both manuals to facilitate quick finding for those who wish botanical descriptions and details. Trees and shrubs are not included in this list. Woody plants are relatively easily established. Tho they are not necessarily thereby "naturalized," they are generally more long-lived than you. Do not worry whether they will reproduce "naturally." If they do, you will find out soon enough. In the tropics, you will find that many woody plants become pests. In temperate regions only a handful may show the tendency. Take trips to local arboreta and botanical gardens, and you will find a stupendous wealth of choice woody plants, far greater than the common old standbys with which you are probably familiar.

For each herbaceous plant, or plant group, information will be given such as its role in the native vegetation, problems of introducing it, and its behavior after introduction. This information is not a compilation from existing books or scientific papers, for the simple reason that almost no literature on this subject exists. It is based almost entirely on the wide personal observations and research of the author, and on his specific studies in western New England. The particular area in which he has worked is in a beech-birch-maple-hemlock type of forest, with acid podzolic soils.

These same plants may react differently in other regions, and other plants may play analogous roles. The author is interested in naturalization studies in other parts of this country and of the world, and would like to be kept informed of such studies being carried out by Wild Gardeners wherever they may live.

THE FERNS

PTERIDOPHYTA

The ferns are a very ancient geological group, having their origins far back in Paleozoic times. In late Paleozoic periods, woody and arborescent forms dominated the landscape. These have all but vanished, with only a few tree ferns in the tropics to remind us of past glories. Today there are about 9,000 species, mostly small, mostly herbaceous, and mostly in the warmer climates. They are a highly varied group, and unquestionably polyphyletic in origin (that is, from numerous unrelated ancestors).

Ferns fascinate fanciers. The group attracts its own enthusiasts. We have fern societies, and fern journals, and an extensive fern literature, both in the science of pteridology and in natural history. If you like them, develop that interest. It will be most rewarding.

Ferns can be both boon and bane. There can be no more beautiful sight than a bed of pure hay-scented fern at the edge of a grassland, its feathery fronds curving, and oriented with geometric precision toward the prevailing light. Cinnamon fern and royal fern in the forest are handsome additions in the shade. On the other hand, sensitive fern, looking fine until early summer, starts yellowing and drying long before autumn is thought about. Lady fern, quite attractive thru much of summer, is bold and unsightly all thru the autumn. Such ferns must be used in small patches, where the eye will not tend to notice them in the "off season."

For the Naturalistic Landscaper, one must find out whether a fern is "colonial," or grows as separate isolated plants. The colonial ferns are those which grow in solid pure patches, tending to eliminate other plants, and growing outward by spreading rhizomes. Each is probably a clone, starting from a single sporeling. They may extend rapidly in bare soil, but in the occupied soil of grassland and forest, expansion may be slow. Hay-scented fern, thought by many to be "aggressive," has extended outwards into grass only 12 inches in as many years, on test plots. The noncolonial ferns occur in small isolated clumps. Each plant must be treated as a separate individual, and it generally is not feasible to try to develop a solid cover of them. All ferns move constantly, by an extending rhizome. When such growth is slow, and relatively unbranched, a non-colonial fern develops. When such growth is repeatedly branching, colonial growth develops. Actually, the distinction is quantitative, and intermediate types sometimes occur.

Ferns are highly resistant to herbicide treatment. They are almost totally resistant to water sprays. Use only oil spray. To rootkill them requires such heavy spraying as effectively to bare the soil. Such spots should be carefully watched, until they grass over. One way of killing the fern in a grass-fern mixture is to spray the fronds frequently but very lightly, on the principle of chemical-mowing. Perseverence is absolutely essential: five or six times in a season is needed, until the roots are exhausted. Keep spraying every time new fronds appear. Check the following year, and continue such spraying if necessary. Pull by hand when only a few fronds remain. Competition from grasses completes the kill.

We will discuss separately three groups of ferns: the osmundas, the so-called common ferns, and the clubmosses (which are not mosses).

THE OSMUNDAS

2. OSMUNDACEAE. B: 73. Gl I: 25

There are only six osmundas in the world. Three are in north-eastern North America, and all of them have their place in Naturalistic Landscaping. They are large striking plants which, tho they may be frequent at any one locality in nature, occur as single plants, not as a solid ground cover. They transplant easily. Even tho normally a moist soil, swamp-edge plant, they survive well in grassy uplands, but are smaller. Permanent mulching, to separate them from grassland competition, is recommended.

ROYAL FERN. *Osmunda regalis*. This is a widespread species, found also in Eurasia and South America. The native New World form is var. *spectabilis*. It is highly valued for its foliage, and looks well if planted in clumps of six or more, about a foot apart, and if the site is kept free of other plants.

CINNAMON FERN. *Osmunda cinnamomea*. The sterile fronds of this, and the following species look very much alike, and only a practiced eye can differentiate them. They differ strikingly in the fertile fronds. That of cinnamon fern is a tight wand of bright brown, which is highly attractive. This and the following have sterile fronds that arch gracefully, like ostrich feathers. Encourage them in front of shrubs, or at the back of grassy stretches.

INTERRUPTED FERN. *Osmunda claytoniana*. Interrupted fern is fine—if you do not have cinnamon fern. The fertile fronds are fertile only in the middle pinnae, and are merely a dull brown in color, looking very much as tho they were accidentally diseased. If you can pause a moment, break off these fertile fronds. The sterile fronds will look much handsomer.

COMMON FERNS

6. POLYPODIACEAE. B: 77. Gl I: 27

POLYPODY. *Polypodium vulgare.* B: 78. Gl I: 34. The small evergreen polypody fern is generally found in nature on the organic duff overlying boulders and large rocks, where it is not subject to competition from other plants, or to blanketing by autumn leaves.

Emulate that habitat if you transplant the fern. It is apparently not suited for the Grassland.

MAIDENHAIR FERN. *Adiantum pedatum.* B: 81. Gl I: 28. This much-loved plant may be easy to grow in the garden, but it is a different problem to naturalize it. The relatively small fronds on the top of slender stems form a very thin ground cover by itself. You will find it in woods, where the forest shade keeps out competing grasses and forbs. Too much shade, no fern. Too much light, too many competitors. It does not hold its own in grassland.

BRACKEN. *Pteridium aquilinum.* B: 83. Gl I: 28. This is a world-wide species, easily split into numerous forms by the delighted "splitters" among the taxonomists. In the Pacific Northwest of North America, one can bend slightly and walk thru a veritable forest of the stuff. Elsewhere, it can be knee high.

Bracken is rough, tough and aggressive. It is a pest to the range man (cattle won't eat it), a pest to the wildlifer (little food and no cover value), a pest to the forester (it hinders tree reproduction). Unless you grow no asparagus, and have an enormous liking for the slimy fuzzy cooked young fronds (they are good—in moderation), you will be trying to kill out this fern. Men in many countries have tried to develop chemical and mechanical means of destroying it, without much success. My advice is to "mow" it repeatedly, by simple pulling, or by oil-spray leaf-burning, just as often as fronds appear. Six times or so the first season. With a second season of chemical-burning of the remaining small fronds, competition from other plants gives it the coup de grace. I have never seen a new colony of bracken starting in land well covered with other plants! You are probably tackling a colony that started before you were born. Eradication is worth while; "control" is preferred by the chemical industry.

LADY FERN. *Athyrium filix-femina*. B: 86. Gl I: 43. This can be a very common fern. Thru spring and early summer, you will be delighted with it. Then it will darken, become brown, and form a tall bulky eye-sore. For this reason, even if it tends to appear in the middle of your grassland, you will probably want to eliminate it from the open grassy stretches, and permit it to grow only in the marginal areas. To rootkill it, use a sickle for the first two or three times. Then hand pull, or give it a light D–T oil spray as often as small fronds appear.

CHRISTMAS FERN. *Polystichum acrostichoides*. B: 87. Gl I: 56. This evergreen fern does not have as many advantages as one would first think. It develops as individual plants, not in colonies. Where there is enough light for grasses to develop, this plant is too low to be seen properly. Furthermore, the over-wintering fronds are semi-prostrate. Its best location is in the high shade, at the edge of the forest, where local concentrations of it can be attractive.

NEW YORK FERN. *Dryopteris (Thelypteris) noveboracensis*. B: 91. Gl I: 48. This, and the closely related following species, can be used to advantage. They are colonial species which, tho appearing to grow best in low wet areas, can also become established on uplands. When on uplands, they tend to form patches intermingled with slightly taller grasses. If one takes the trouble to pluck out the competing grasses, a pure solid fern area will result. Try a few square feet at a time. Do a small amount well, if you want to see results. The fronds are gracefully erect; in fall they dry to an inconspicuous brown, not unpleasantly noticeable in the Grassland.

MARSH FERN. *Dryopteris thelypteris (Thelypteris palustris)*. B: 91. Gl I: 50. Despite its name, and its frequent habitat, this close relative of the New York fern will also do well on uplands. Treat it the same way, carefully pulling out competing grasses in order to encourage a solid cover. When seen at the same time as the New York fern, there are subtle and fascinating differences in the shade of green, the angle of arching, the height, and the degree of laciness.

HAY-SCENTED FERN. *Dennstaedtia punctilobula*. B:92. Gl I:28. This is the queen of all the ferns for Naturalistic Landscaping purposes, even tho at times it can be a pest to the farmer in his pastures. Roll some in your fingers as you pass—the fragrance is superb.

It will frequently occur mixed with other plants, especially rank forbs such as asters and goldenrods, and with various woody plants. My advice is to have some pure masses of the fern, especially at the edges of the forest, or in small woodland clearings. The woody plants can be cut out and stub-sprayed in the dormant season, so that one need not trample on the fern. Let the branches lie; the fern will grow up thru them and they will not be seen. Heavy asters and goldenrods can be pulled at first, so as to get large sections of the horizontal rhizomes. Thereafter, and once the fronds have attained a hardness by mid-season, spray over the whole colony with a D–T water solution; the fern will be unaffected. If there are intermingled ferns of other species, these should be kept hand-cut, or soak the spots with a D–T oil spray by holding the nozzle of the spray at the point where the fronds emerge. Once the colony becomes established in a pure condition, it requires almost no maintenance. It is remarkably stable, and resists invasion by grasses, forbs, shrubs and trees. In turn, it extends outward very slowly, only a few inches a year. This extension, if you wish, can be controlled by leaf-burning with an oil spray.

You should develop colonies of hay-scented fern with a forest background, and where the morning or evening light strikes them and puts into unexcelled relief a pattern of arching curves and of intricate lacy detail that is not surpassed in the vegetation world.

SENSITIVE FERN. *Onoclea sensibilis*. B:93. Gl I:37. More often pest than otherwise, the colonial sensitive fern looks fine until mid-summer, while the dried fertile fronds have a value in winter bouquets (but one needs only few for this purpose). It is one of the first plants to yellow and dry, before one wants to think of autumn, thus becoming a blot on the landscape. The roots of this fern thoroly fill the soil, and to spray-kill it, one kills other plants as well. Furthermore, in cleaning out various brushy areas, this will often take over, requiring further spraying. I would suggest, in reducing the amount of this plant, you try the military tactic of encircling the foe, and gradually closing in, over a period of years. During one year, leaf-burn a strip around the colony, as often as the fronds appear. By this policy, you will not miss the increasingly smaller fronds that will appear. Such plants if not completely rootkilled may come back to dominance. Besides, you eventually get the colony down to a small clean patch that may itself have a landscaping value.

THE CLUBMOSSES

LYCOPODIACEAE (not in Bailey)

The lycopods belong to that group of plants known as "fern allies," a varied assortment, possibly not monophyletic, which includes also the selaginellas, the isoëtes, the horsetails or scouring rushes, and the grape-ferns. The lycopods are evergreen trailing plants, 600 in the world, abundant in tropical mountains, of very high value in Naturalistic Landscaping. The Lycopodiums are known to most people as woodland plants. In winter, when other plants have dried and disappeared, these ground covers stand out in shining green, and enhance tremendously what would otherwise be bleak and bare. Since they are relatively unpalatable to cattle, they appear to be especially prominent in young forests that had been pastures.

One usually finds these plants very abundant in local spots, then absent for long distances. The evidence is strongly indicative that each colony is a single clone, established long ago, perhaps centuries, as a single individual, spreading slowly outward, and only rarely dying.

The lycopods, tho found most often in the shade, are not adverse to moving out into the grassland. Here they mingle with the grasses, and are relatively inconspicuous components of the community. The high-growing grasses tend to shade them out in summer, and to mat them out in autumn when they fall. You might wish to clean out small spots. The lycopod will take over in a pure stand. The runners, which grow out several feet in a year, can be pulled around and laid onto the cleared spot, as an aid in converting to pure Lycopodium.

GROUND-CEDAR. *Lycopodium complanatum*. Gl 6: 1. This flattened-branchlet species may be the commonest in your region. It has the smoothest glossiest color of all the woodland lycopods, and is a cherished sight before the snow falls.

GROUND-PINE. *Lycopodium obscurum*. Gl I: 4. This plant is so-called because of the resemblance of the erect terminal branchlets, with their miniature cones, to small small pine trees. Pull one up, however, and you will find that it is part of a long trailing branch. I have only rarely found this, or the following two, out in sunny Grasslands, but they grow well in the high shade at forest edges, where competition with grasses is unimportant. It adds a welcome tone of green when all else may be brown.

Lycopodium lucidulum Gl I: 2, and *Lycopodium annotinum* Gl I: 4, are two closely related species with erect terminal branchlets and compactly covered with leaves that look like hemlock needles. The former has sporangia in normal, tho slightly smaller, leaves; the latter has sporangia in a terminal cone. Both these lycopods appear to be essentially woodland species, less abundant than the other two and forming interesting variations in the tone and texture of these ground covers.

THE SEED PLANTS

SPERMATOPHYTA
MONOCOTYLEDONEAE

THE GRASSES

25. GRAMINEAE. B: 133. Gl I: 96

Gardeners think of grass as "lawn;" farmers think of grass as "hay;" cattle men of the open range think of grass as "forage;" the taxonomic botanist thinks of grass as a natural plant family of extraordinary wealth and diversity, 6,000 species in all parts of the world; the economic botanist thinks of grass as one of the most valuable of plants to mankind, for it includes our cereals, corn, and bamboo. To the Naturalistic Landscaper, grass is the very substance of his open areas, not only the warp and weft upon which the tapestry is woven, but also its background color and texture. Furthermore, grasses frequently provide sharp features of striking interest, to be used sparingly and wisely.

Like many of the finer things in life, an appreciation of grasses does not come full-blown. These are not plants that shriek for attention with cheap and tawdry gaud. Not by any means are they nature's analogy to mid-century claims for fame in the realms of music, painting, sculpture and architecture. Their colors are restricted to greens and browns, each species with its own subtle shade that changes thru the season, like the tone of a certain musical instrument, recognizable all thru the playing of a full symphony orchestra. And in its fruiting condition, the individuality of each grass species is not less remarkable. To know them is equivalent to knowing the different art motifs employed in Renaissance and Gothic stone sculpture. It is a world of its own, in pattern line and delicate tracery, each responding in its own flowing manner to breezes and winds. A few hardy souls will take these grasses back to their library. With hand lens and wrinkled forehead, they will unfold new delights, as each species is found to be a logical and understandable product of biologic evolution, variant of a basic type that existed far back in geologic time.

Any manipulation of the grasses in your Grassland must be undertaken with due respect for their own "success" in the natural plant-community, and for their resistance to present herbicides. Insofar as possible, adjust to what you already have. These common grasses are probably rhizome-spreading, and it will be all but impossible to eradicate them. In fact, seedling reproduction is probably unimportant: do not worry if seeds of "weed" species are blowing around. Know the roots of your plants, and on this knowledge encourage or discourage the grasses you have.

It would be well to consider your grasses as belonging to one of two types: the rhizome-spreading turf-forming grasses, and the non-rhizomatous tussock grasses. The distinction is usually, but not always, appropriate. Some species are intermediate in nature, and some act differently in different types of soil. Furthermore, tussock species may occur so abundantly that they give the appearance of a turf.

A. odoratum

The Big Blue-Stem (*Andropogon gerardi*) in an herbicide-induced grassland. This species is a dominant of the Tall-Grass Prairies, and serves admirably as a "fountain" species.

A mowed trail thru a field of redtop grass (*Agrostis alba*) dotted with daisies, at the season when the grass is a flush of pink. Before herbicide treatment this field was mixed brush, dominantly meadowsweet (*Spiraea latifolia*).

The Turf Grasses

Turf grasses are "desirable" insofar as they do not form a dense jungle over three high and difficult to walk thru. They should not form such a tight growth as to keep out many of the brightly flowering plants. Furthermore, they should mat down with winter snows. If they remain erect, they are not only unsightly in spring, but become a serious fire hazard.

RED FESCUE. *Festuca rubra.* B: 151. Gl I: 110. This, the commonest of the fescues, may be tufted at the soil surface, but its occurrence in extensive patches would indicate that at least at one time it may have spread rhizomatously. The turf is fairly thick and solid, and tends to keep out some of the flowering plants.

KENTUCKY BLUE GRASS. *Poa pratensis.* B: 152. Gl I: 118. This common lawn grass is found frequently in abandoned fields, especially in limestone areas. It is desirable in all respects.

QUACK GRASS. *Agropyron repens.* B: not in. Gl I: 139. This bane of the farmer should not cause you any great concern, even tho you find it occasionally. It is a pest on the farm only because the farmer insists on overfertilizing his land. It will die out when these excess fertilizers are leached away with spring rains. If you do have a patch of fairly fertile soil, learn to live with quack grass, for tho dense in summer, it does mat flat during the winter.

It is rhizome-spreading, not seed-spreading, in nature. The writer has successfully kept it from his garden for 15 years by the simple expedient of an Iron Curtain. By laying 2-foot-wide second-hand galvanized iron roofing strips on the land (which strips are now hidden by stones dug from the garden), invasion is completely stalled (except where there are nail holes!). Furthermore, one year under such iron completely kills the incredibly tough snarl of wiry rhizomes. The next spring, the Iron Curtain can be shoved outwards, and the soil under it easily spaded, its fertility enriched by the dead rhizomes.

RED-TOP. *Agrostis stolonifera.* B: 150. Gl I: 166. Here is one of the more attractive background grasses. Flower stalks begin to arise in early summer, and as they open they lend a distinctive pink aspect to the grassland. Furthermore, the colonies on the author's land occur irregularly, in patches 20 to 50 feet in diameter, with similar distances between the colonies, giving a billowy effect, like broken clouds in a sky. In height of foliage, density of growth, and other factors, this species lends itself admirably to admixture with various forbs.

The Tussock Grasses

Tussock grasses may form continuous uniform grasslands, each tussock having started separately as a seedling. Or they may occur as lone isolated plants. These latter when tall serve ideally as a spot of interest, almost like a fountain, rising out of a placid lake formed by a lower mat of grasses. Tussock grasses lend themselves to management far more easily than the turf grasses. They can be blotted out if one does not want them; they can be planted successfully with very little trouble.

ORCHARD GRASS. *Dactylis glomerata.* B: 150. Gl I: 134. This extremely common grass of hay fields will not be as important in your grasslands as you think. As the years pass away, so will it. Perhaps it needs a high level of fertility; perhaps it is short-lived, and cannot become re-established in the continuing mulch of a semi-natural Grassland. In any event, its loss is not a serious one. The foliage is often conspicuously coarse.

POVERTY GRASS. *Danthonia spicata.* B: not in. Gl I: 159. A farmer will look at your Grassland, shake his head in disgust, and say that the "grass has all run out—needs fertilizer, lots of it—nothing but poverty grass here." Every man to his liking. Danthonia spicata grows as tight little tufts of curled leaves, a few inches high. The long very slender stalks rise early in spring, topped by the delicate flowers and fruits. There is plenty of space for other plants to grow in a Danthonia grassland.

TIMOTHY. *Phleum pratense.* B: 154. Gl I: 170. Another common grass of hay-fields that you will be wondering about. Like orchard grass, it will tend to "run out," remaining an unimportant component of your Grassland. There is no reason for you either to encourage or discourage it.

CRABGRASS. *Digitaria sanguinalis.* B: (not in). Gl I: 203. This little character from Europe, now widespread in North America, together with certain close relatives, has no role whatever in Naturalistic Landscaping. It is one of those little open-land pioneers which can put up a big bold bluff when there is no one around to challenge it, but vanishes at the first sign of real aggression from other plants. I doubt whether you will ever see it in your wild unmown Grassland.

On the other hand, you may be one of those unfortunates who, because of neighborhood demands and other social infringements on one's individual freedom, have to maintain a "lawn," even tho you might sympathize with my earlier analysis of The Lawn as an anthropologic relict from pastoral days. If so, crabgrass may loom large in your life. Your local nurseryman will do his best to sell one of many crabgrass killers, containing chemicals with outlandish jaw-breaking names and deceptively simple trade-mark names. Uncertain, you will go to your agricultural agent, and he will tell you the same story! (Why not? They have both learned from the same sources, the chemical pesticide manufacturers.) Now, I believe it is reasonably true that if properly applied, just in the right concentrations and just at the right times, you probably would kill the crabgrass, and not the other grasses—if there are any others. Furthermore, I have no knowledge that these chemicals—at the date of this writing—are critical poisons lethal to a wide variety of other forms of life. Rather naively, and feeling very simple (in the most disparaging sense of the word), I ask "Why kill the poor crab grass?" There are simpler things to do.

You see, Digitaria is an annual weed. It starts from seed each year. It must have open space in which to grow. It cannot grow in a good healthy thick not-clipped-too-close lawn. The cheapest and most effective way to remove crabgrass is o t h e r g r a s s e s. Crabgrass is not the "disease" of your lawn! It is only the "symptom" of a disease! That disease can be "cured" by having good fertile soil to start with, and giving the "good" grasses an adequate start in life. My advice, if you have a chronic gastric ulcer, is not to become addicted to pain-killing drugs for every day of your life, but to give up the drugs, see a reputable M.D., and get cured (gaining the illwill of the drug pedlars in the process). And so it is with your lawn.

On the other hand, I would be the last to blame you if you have been using crabgrass killers, or wish to continue to use them. You are yourself in that respect the unwilling "symptom" of a complex "social disease." The social pressure is on to keep it that way. Crabgrass c o n t r o l is big business; crabgrass e l i m i n a t i o n would soon mean no business at all. Right; government agricultural agents should have the "scientific truth." But do not be too harsh on them. The orientation of their own research is often encouraged by industry; the source of much of their information is from industry, sometimes the only source. That source can be couched and clothed with all the smooth art of the motivational psychologist and the public relations expert. The problem of crabgrass is not for you and me to solve, but for an enlightened and aroused public.

D. sanguinalis

133

SLOUGH GRASS. *Spartina pectinata*. B: not in. Gl I: 192. This is one of the dominants of the Mid-West Prairies, found also at the upper edge of coastal tidal marshes, growing 4–6 feet high. If a few are transplanted, they serve as "fountain grasses."

SWITCH GRASS. *Panicum virgatum*. B: 148. Gl I: 215. Another dominant of low areas in Mid-West American Prairies, and also found at the upper edges of tidal marshes. Tho apparently turf-forming where found naturally, if transplanted, it behaves as a single tall "fountain grass."

BIG BLUESTEM. *Andropogon gerardi*. B: not in. Gl I: 242. This is one of the most famous of the Prairie grasses, easily growing six feet high. It has a value as a "fountain grass," tho it must be used with caution. The foliage is coarse and rank, and stands more or less erect all winter. Growth starts so late in spring that one feels sure that it has died. The flowering stalks arise in late summer, at a time when they are greatly appreciated. View it looking into the very early morning sun. Bright lights will glance from each and every curving blade of foliage in a myriad of scintillating scimitars.

LITTLE BLUESTEM. *Andropogon scoparius*. B: not in. Gl I: 242. This is the second most famous of the Prairie grasses. It is abundant on eastern American sand plains, where it is known as broom sedge, or simply as bunch grass. It is not desirable as the dominant of your Grassland! It stays erect all winter and new growth starts late in spring, both features making it a fire hazard. Its chief value is in late summer, when suddenly it starts growing. The foliage turns to reddish bronze, certainly one of the most distinctive colors of all the grasses. The fruiting heads are copiously covered with long hairs that give them a pale feathery appearance. I find this grass useful in patches 10 to 20 feet in diameter. To kill out extensive amounts of it is a real problem. I suggest buying a package of asphalt shingles; cut them into square sections; and blot out the plants one by one. It will take one full year of such "blotting" to rootkill a tussock. Follow the military tactics of enclosing the enemy, and then gradually moving in. See that rhizomatous turf-forming grasses are behind you, that will invade the land and hold it, as you move forward each year. It is not likely that the enemy will jump your line, and establish seedling outposts. If each tussock contains a large amount of dead grass, you might have to cut that away before laying on the asphalt shingle, or the shingle will not lie tightly enough to prevent new growth. If all your tussocks are bulky with dead grass, it would be wise to use heavy flat stones. They "settle" the problem! You can of course, use chemical sprays, but they may be too costly for this purpose. Furthermore, one tends to get exuberant, spray thru a good many square feet; then one finds that kill is not complete, that a shoot survives here and there. Then one sprays small shoots year after year after year, which, as they become fewer, take more time to find. The enclose-and-move-in technique (as long as not counter-acted by air-borne or underground tactics on the part of the enemy) allows you to keep your attention focussed on a narrow boundary strip, and there do a perfect job of mopping up on the adversary. If you are operating on sterile sandy soils, try fertilization alone. Andropogon may bow out gracefully to oncoming turf grasses.

INDIAN GRASS. *Sorghastrum nutans*. B: not in. Gl I: 245. Another important Prairie grass, three feet high in the northeast, with distinctive and attractive inflorescences. Tho apparently a turf-forming grass in the American Mid-West, if transplanted it behaves as a single "fountain grass."

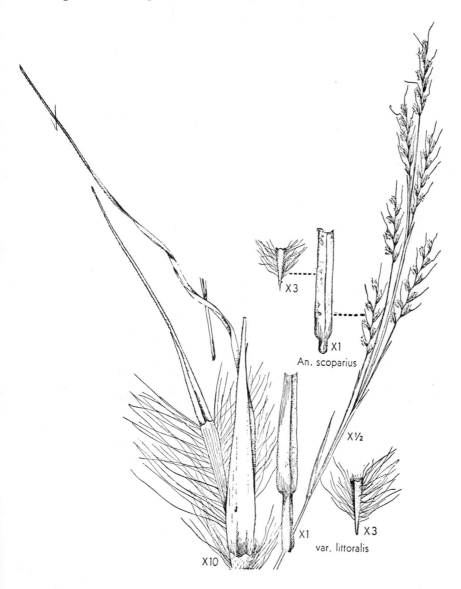

X3

X1
An. scoparius

X½

X1

X3
var. littoralis

X10

THE SPIDERWORTS

31. COMMELINACEAE. B: 197. Gl I: 377

There are two genera in this chiefly tropical family with which you might be concerned, the spiderworts (*Tradescantia*), and the day-flowers (*Commelina*), known to Asia and America, but not native to Europe. *Tradescantia virginiana* is an old-time garden favorite, also native to northeastern U.S. The author's experience has been largely with *T. ohiensis*. Others are available, both native species, and horticultural forms.

The spiderworts are plants 2–3 feet high, with grasslike foliage similar to broad-leaved panicums. The flowers are mainly blue, sometimes purple or white. Each flower lasts but a day, and is open only in the first half of the morning. When the plant grows as a clump, these flowers are sufficiently abundant to be seen at some distance.

Volunteer seedlings are abundant in bare garden soil, but have not been found in grassland. The plant can form a compact mass in the garden, but it also spreads by slender underground rhizomes that may produce a shoot at some distance from the main clump. It might even be called a pest in the garden.

In nature, these plants occur sparingly in low moist soils. On the other hand, they are also reported in dry sandy soils and on railroad embankments. They do well in full sun, or in the shade of light woods. In other words, they are relatively indifferent to light, moisture or acidity conditions.

My experience with Tradescantia in the Grassland is as yet limited. One has the choice of letting it diffuse thinly thru the grasses. In this case, the conspicuousness of its foliage, with the short morning period of flowering, may speak against it. It may be contained as a clump, in which case the brightness of the massed flowers sets off the deep green of the foliage.

THE LILIES AND RELATIVES

33. LILIACEAE. B: 200. Gl I: 403

This is a large natural plant family, of wide distribution over the earth. In all, there are about 2,000 species, in about 175 genera, including some of our choicest and most striking ornamental plants. Many of them are perennial herbs, dying down after flowering to a bulb-like organ or a crown of fibrous roots. Many of the florists' "bulbs" are in this family.

Plantain-Lilies

Hosta (Funkia). B: 206. Gl I: 412

The plantain-lilies are important mainly for their ornamental clumps of foliage, variegated green and white. The spiked flowers are blue, sometimes white or lavender, and are conspicuous when massed. There are about 40 species, native to China and Japan.

Volunteer seeding is reported by some, but not spreading by rhizomes. Each clump enlarges under favorable conditions, from which new clumps may be dug and removed.

In gardening practice, the hostas are hardy, long-lived, and do well in shade. *H. ventricosa* and *H. lancifolia* are reported to be "occasionally escaped from cultivation." More likely than not, the plants have not escaped from the garden, but the garden has escaped from the plants, and the hostas have survived in competition with invading native species.

I would suggest trying several species of *Hosta*. Plant them under the forest edge, where grass is thin or absent. Establish a clump of six or more plants, 12 to 24 inches apart. Care for them for a few years, removing woody plants and heavy forbs. Thereafter, the heavy foliage should be able to hold the site.

Day-Lilies

Hemerocallis B: 207. Gl I: 411

This magnificent genus, that holds much of promise to the Naturalistic Landscaper, is native to China and Japan. We do not know when it was introduced to Europe, but it was adequately described in a book published in 1570, and then said to be familiar in France and Holland.

These are very hardy, easily grown, easily transplantable, materials with dense grasslike foliage 1 to 2 feet high, above which are raised the funnel-shaped flowers on tall slender stalks. A new flower opens each day, whence the name.

Hybridization studies in recent years are associated with the name of A. B. Stout of the New York Botanical Garden (now deceased), whose plants are available from the Farr Nursery Co., Weiser Park, Pennsylvania. Most of the author's 25 varieties were received from this organization. In choosing *Hemerocallis*, several factors must be evaluated: the color range may be considered as being in one of three "color lines," yellows, oranges, and reds. The yellows vary from light yellow thru a dark golden. The second runs from peaches and buffs thru bright orange, to a kind of brown. The reds start with pink, and pass into dark mahogany and maroon colors. Some have dark "eyes" in the throat of the corolla; flower sizes have been both decreased and increased; a few are double. Some are highly fragrant, others have no fragrance. The flowering season has been enormously extended, with certain varieties beginning to flower in late spring, and others continuing even after frost.

Many day-lilies are sterile, and produce no seed. Others may produce fertile seed, but volunteer seedlings should not be encouraged, for the chances are at least 1 in 10,000 that the resulting plant will be inferior to its parent.

All named strains of day-lilies are clones, reproduced by division of the fleshy and bulbous roots. Most of them form dense clumps, which enlarge by rhizome offshoots close to the main clumps. In some varieties, these rhizomes may grow out six or eight inches before coming to the surface.

Behavior in the Grassland—even tho these are hardy and aggressive plants—is anything but weedy. The newer strains are not as aggressive as the common roadside orange day-lily, and even this one is not to be feared. Small slips, slit into my Grassland, have remained sterile and small for ten years! If a clump is put in, however, large enough to shade out the immediately adjacent grasses, the plant holds its own, and slowly spreads. A small plant, therefore, first needs "help" in the way of a mulch—six inches is wide enough—to kill out the adjacent grass. If this "mulch" is an asphalt shingle, it can be pulled outwards each year, to allow the clump to enlarge.

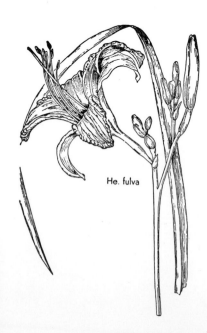

He. fulva

Hemerocallis fulva clone Europa is the common roadside orange day-lily, found now around the world. It is probably the most widespread single "individual" among plants! Tho not fragrant, it is most worthwhile—unless you are one of those snobs who despise the common, for being common. *Hemerocallis flava* is the lemon day-lily, also a clone, sometimes producing seeds. It is delightfully fragrant, and a most welcome addition to Grassland margins, or as a fountain in the open. There are also many fine hybrids from which to pick.

Lily-of-the-Valley
Convallaria. B: 211. Gl I: 430

This widely cherished spring flower, *Convallaria majalis*, is native to large areas of northern Europe and Asia. It is also said to be native to the southern Appalachians, but botanists are not sure; it may be an escape. Gardeners plant it from "pips" (the upright ends of branches from horizontal subterranean rhizomes), and thus most colonies that one sees are clones, that is, single "individuals." It is said to fruit rarely in cultivation. The author is working on the assumption that the plant is physiologically dioecious, that is, the two sexes (tho morphologically similar) are on different plants. For this reason, he grows his own seedlings, so as to get a large number of "individuals." The red fruits in fall are a chief attraction in places where there is no other color.

Altho Convallaria will grow in the full sunlight of the Grassland, it loses its effectiveness when mixed with grasses, and it is difficult to keep small patches grass-free. Plant it in the grassless forest-edges. Volunteer seedlings will probably be rare, tho the plant extends by rhizomes rapidly, almost weedily. It is easy to maintain a carpet of the plant in such sites. It is beautiful in spring with its flowers; in summer the glossy green leaves look well; and in fall the bright red fruits are a welcome addition.

False Lily-of-the-Valley
Maianthemum. B: 212. Gl I: 426

Maianthemum canadense is native to northeastern North America. (There are two or three other species, native to Eurasia and north-western North America.) This plant is similar to the above: the flowers are smaller and not fragrant, foliage is much smaller, and the fruits are mottled and not as attractive.

It is highly valuable as a ground cover, both for its carpet of white flowers, and for the compact glossy foliage that I prefer to true lily-of-the-valley. You probably will like it in the grassless forest edge. Help it. Pull up or spray out competitors. Maianthemum, with its underground rhizomes, will respond excellently. A place under pine or hemlock is especially attractive since accumulation of autumn leaves will not have a blanketing and killing effect.

Solomon's Seal

Polygonatum. B: 212. Gl I: 430

Wild-flower enthusiasts generally like the small *Polygonatum biflorum*, and the 3–4 foot tall *P. commutatum*. If you have them to start with, I would certainly keep an eye on them. In my opinion, they do not add much to the landscape, for both the greenish flowers and the fruits are pendent under the relatively unattractive foliage. Other gardeners have high regard for the plant. They belong to the forest and forest-edge.

False Solomon's Seal

Smilacina. B: 212. Gl I: 425

The native *Smilacina racemosa*, with its spreading rhizomes, can be encouraged to become predominant in semi-shaded grassless areas. Such a mass, ten or more feet across, will have a distinct attraction, not only for its spring flowers and its red midsummer berries, but for the uniformly arching leafy stems.

I do not recommend this plant for the open Grassland. Altho it will grow there, the foliage is soon bleached to a yellow tint, and its curving stem seems out of place among the erect grasses.

Bellworts

Uvularia. B: 213. Gl I: 428

The native bellworts can be an attractive factor both at the forest edge and out in the Grassland. The author's experience has been with *U. sessilifolia*. This plant spreads by rhizomes and forms a compact mass. It has the advantage of appearing very early in the season. Its foliage is up and expanded, and its pale yellow flowers are in full bloom when the grasses are still low. Later in the year the foliage is not especially attractive, and I would not want too much of it, but the grasses overtop it and make it relatively inconspicuous.

Colonies are apparently long-lived. I have known some to have lasted 20 years. Expansion into the Grassland is so slow that you cannot count upon it. To eliminate it, as you may want to in some places, is difficult. I would recommend repeated chemical mowing, just as often as new foliage appears, perhaps six or more times thru one or two years.

False Hellebore

Veratrum. B: 215. Gl I: 409

Veratrum viride is native across northern North America. It is a tall coarse-foliaged plant, slowly spreading by stout rhizomes, found in moist sites and on stream sides. The leaves have a peculiar attraction however. They are pleated, very much like a palm leaf, and I have had more than one layman tell me that it was thought to be a relative of that tropical group. They are attractive plants, and can be recommended in small groups, as background.

Asparagus

Asparagus. B: 215. Gl I: 425

Asparagus officinale is a native of Europe. Horticultural strains are cultivated for the young shoots that appear early in spring. It produces fertile seed readily, and these occasionally become established on roadsides and around the edges of tidal marshes. The fully grown 6-foot high shoots are finely divided and fern-like. (The florist's "fern" is *Asparagus plumosus*.) You might like a clump of it at the forest edge. If so, plant well-developed roots, and do not weaken the plant by breaking off the new shoots for your dinner table (if you can see them in the grass). If you have a cultivated Asparagus bed nearby, you might be concerned that the wild plants will harbor unwanted concentrations of the two kinds of beetles that are specific to this plant. If your bird populations are not high, your worry may be well founded.

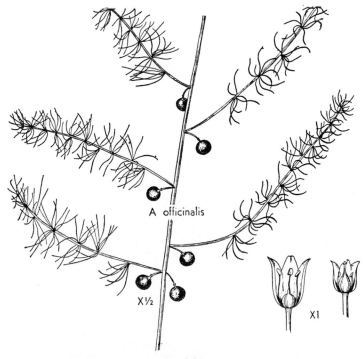

A officinalis

X½   XI

Trout-Lilies

Erythronium. B: 217. Gl I: 420

The *Erythroniums* are native mainly to North America. Other species are in Eurasia. Three are in the Northeast, of which *E. americanum* is the best known. They grow from corms, and reproduction is by lateral offshoots, either from the corm or the erect subterranean stem above it. The plants tend to form ground covers in thinly grassed or grassless areas somewhat like. *Convallaria* or *Màianthemum*. The foliage however is spotted (hence the name). Introduce a few. If they start spreading, fine. (Mine do not.) Flowers however are generally rare: 1-leaved sterile plants are the commonest.

Fritillary

Fritillaria. B: 218. Gl I: (not in)

Fritillaria meleagris, the Snakes-head, native of Eurasia, is so effectively promoted in all the bulb catalogs that you will probably be led to buy bulbs again and again. (I have. Usually they do not even come up. Only once have I seen one flower.) Apparently replacement sales are heavy enough to warrant this continued commercial promotion. Yes, I am sure it can be grown successfully, but the buyer is supposed to know what to do.

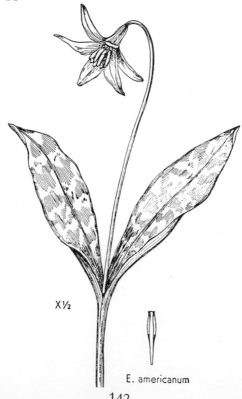

X½

E. americanum

Tulips

Tulipa. B: 219. Gl I: 419

When one mentions tulips, one thinks of those blazingly colored catalogs that come thru the mail, winning us over to fall planting of tulip bulbs. One thinks also of the tulip fields of Holland, source of those bulbs. One feels a bit of real sympathy for the Tulip Mania that once swept that country, certainly the most magnificent example of mass hysteria in the history of gardeners and gardening. Then one will plant some. In spring the plants will arise in uniform green luxuriance. Then they will burst into flamboyance, like squirts of oil pigment from an artist's tubes. They have all the uninhibited garishness of a floor show at an expense-account night club. Comes the next season; one waits with an anticipating glint in his eyes; then rubs his eyes in morning-after unhappiness. The plants are of unequal sizes, depauperate and few-leaved. A few flowers, not of full size, perhaps with one petal hanging down dejectedly. One either gives up tulips; or buys new tulips.

For Naturalistic Landscaping, I have not yet had success, tho I have tried some two dozen horticultural varieties, plus half a dozen of the "species" tulips. The former persist as a few sterile leaves, unattractive in the Grassland; the latter disappear in a few years. Yet I still have hope. The plant has some virtues: the foliage appears early, ahead of the grass growth. The flower rises on a stalk where it can be seen at a distance. I have some bulbs which persisted in a garden abandoned 20 years ago, of a brilliant red color. With heavy leaf-mulching, when the foliage is fully expanded, my hopes are returning. If there is a tulip for the Grassland, some day it will be in great demand.

Tulipa gesneriana is the name given to the cultivated tulips, a vast assemblage of hybrids, probably of Asiatic origins. In the bulb catalogs such adjectives as "giant" and "ideal" are so overused that it is difficult to sense any classification of the numerous groups. You can think of the cultivated strains as belonging to five basic groups: (1) Early Tulips, flowering in April. (The other four are May-flowering.) Most of them are single, but there are also Double Earlies. (2) Cottage Tulips are smaller, and tend to be more oval in form. Doubles in this group are named with one or all of the following adjectives: Giant, Double, Peony, May-flowering. (3) The Darwins are formal large-flowered types. The Ideal Darwins are an improved strain introduced in 1927. The Lily-flowered tulips are hybrids between Darwins and *Tulipa retroflexa*. They are also called Lily-flowered Cottage tulips. The Extra Early Darwin Hybrids are hybrids between Darwins and the very early *Tulipa fosteriana*, the Red Emperor. (4) The Breeder Tulips are large-flowered forms that tend to run to shades of bronze and mahogany. In groups 2, 3, and 4, we also have "broken" or "rectified" kinds, called Rembrandts, Bizarres, or Bijbloemen, in which the petals are striped, flaked or feathered with a dark color, due to the presence of a virus symbiont. (5) Parrot tulips have laciniated petals and fantastic coloring.

The "species tulips" are the native wild species, not horticultural strains. *T. fosteriana* of central Asia, the Red Emperor, is a gorgeous thing, flowering with the *Narcissi*, before any other tulip. I have not however, had it persist satisfactorily in grassland. *T. sylvestris* (also called *T. florentina odorata*), native of southern Europe, is said to be naturalized in Pennsylvania and Maryland, and is worth trying. The other species deserve experimentation.

Lilies. (True Lilies)

Lilium. B: 223. Gl I: 416

Lilies arouse one's enthusiasm, and so does the lily-enthusiast's enthusiasm. It is true that the sight of handsome individuals, stems literally loaded with beautiful blossoms, or the fragrance of an Easter lily, makes one succumb. But the very detail with which they describe the ease of growing lilies should make one suspicious. For example, germinating seeds remain underground the entire first year, and do not send up green leaves until the second season. Bulbs must be planted exactly at the proper depth (tho in nature they obviously have sense enough to find their own depth, after all the vicissitudes of germination.) And the surface of the soil should be kept shaded, as by low shrubs. Then one wonders whether the lily grower doth protest too much. In one standard book I read concerning the madonna lily (*L. candidum*) that "this really is one of the easiest lilies to grow." Maybe so, for a lily! In another standard, the author admits candidly that *L. candidum* "is worth taking a chance with. It may fail miserably, but if it does make up its mind to grow, it is wonderfully good." And this, from an experienced "green thumb"! Poor me! Candidly, I am still looking for lilies that satisfy the stick-em-in-and-forget-em policies of the Wild Gardener.

Lilium philadelphicum, mistakenly called the wood lily, is admirable in its manner of growth. When in the woods, it is spindly and feeble. On the other hand, two of the Norns have put about 200 of these lilies in my herbicide-induced Grassland. Here they are relatively low-growing, not rising above the level of the grass. The bright-orange 1–4 blossoms surmounting the stalk point upward so that one looks down into them. They have survived in undiminished numbers for 20 years, tho there has been no increase. I cannot start any from seed, and I cannot successfully transplant them. The botanist who develops a technique to increase their numbers in the Grassland will certainly find a place in heaven when the third Norn cuts the strand of his life.

Lilium canadense, the wild yellow lily, is seen most frequently and in best growth on shady roadsides. It will transplant readily. Seedlings will develop in your garden—if you have patience. And it does well in the Grassland. Altho I am quite sure that competition with adjacent grasses is not to its advantage, I am uncertain of the best kind of mulch with which to surround it. The plant produces a new scaly bulb each year, at a short distance from the original bulb. The size of this bulb is dependent upon the current season's growth, and thus the foliage should be allowed to mature, without mowing. This lily grows high above the general grass level, excellent in its way. The plant however, either exerts an undue fascination for deer, or wandering deer lazily prefer to take what they can without lowering their heads. A bit of "pea brush" (dead gray birch shoots) stuck in the ground will discourage the animals, and be relatively invisible at a distance. If you are growing a supply of these in the garden, keep track of your pet chipmunk, especially as he is fattening up for his winter sleep. If he discovers how good the bulbs taste, he will search until he finds every last one. I once bet with him that he wouldn't. He won.

Lilium tigrinum, the tiger lily, is native to eastern Asia. It is a clone, grown from small bulbils that form in the axils of the leaves. If you wish it in the grassland, where it can be very effective, plant six or more in a clump, close enough so that their foliage will keep out competing grasses.

Lilium superbum, the native turk's cap lily, is usually found in low wet land, but can be very abundant on roadsides. Treat it like *L. canadense*. It can be a handsome addition.

The Mid-Century Hybrid lilies, a strain recently introduced by Jan de Graaff, are widely touted for their hardiness and an almost weedy increase. They contain some *L. tigrinum* blood, which should be to their advantage. They hold promise, but so far they have been anything but weeds in my garden.

I have tried various other lilies, but with no success as would lead me now to recommend any. There are many I have not tried. I am reasonably sure that from among the world's species (about 100) or from among the horticultural hybrids, some will be found to please the Naturalistic Landscaper.

Squills

Scilla. B: 231. Gl I: 421

There are 90 or more species of squills, native to the Old World. They are small-leaved, more or less ground-covering plants developing from bulbs, of which several are grown for their spring flowers.

Scilla sibirica, the Siberian squill, the earliest and smallest, can provide sheets of an unusually intense blue. I have had it spread in the garden, probably entirely by volunteer seedlings. It is well adapted for forest edges, where grassless conditions allow for full foliage development.

Scilla hispanica (S. campanulata) is the Iberian species, which comes in white and pink. I have had more success with it where there is less grass and more shade.

Scilla nonscripta (S. nutans) is the similar English Bluebell, with blue, pink and white strains. It also does better with less grass and more shade.

Camas

Camassia. B: 232. Gl I: 421

North American plants, mostly in the West, with edible bulbs, all of which are worth trying in the Grassland. I find that the pale blue flowers of *Camassia scilloides,* native in the East, do not appear to advantage unless there is a solid mass of them.

Star-of-Bethlehem

Ornithogalum. B: 232. Gl I: 421

Ornithogalum umbellatum is the well-known Star-of-Bethlehem, from Europe. I have seen it well established in cindery waste at the edge of a city park, undeterred by excessive picking and trampling. I have found it persisting in a solid patch at a 20-year-abandoned garden, where goldenrods cover the land later in the season. Yet I have had little success in establishing it myself. It will not die, but neither will it flower. I would suggest relatively grassless sites.

Ornithogalum nutans is a west Asian species, said to be escaped in Pennsylvania, District of Columbia, and Missouri.

Glory-of-the-Snow

Chionodoxa. B: 233. Gl I: (not in)

The genus comprises half a dozen small bulbous scapose plants native to high elevations in Crete and Asia Minor. *C. luciliae*, existing in several horticultural forms, can produce striking patches of light blue in the garden. I find that it increases there, apparently by volunteer seedlings. Also try *C. luciliae* var. *gigantea* and *C. sardensis*. I have had *C. luciliae* persist for four seasons in grassland with undiminished vigor, both flowering and vegetative growth occurring before the grasses arise. It is a beauty, for early spring.

Hyacinth

Hyacinthus. B: 234. Gl I: (not in)

Hyacinthus, beloved by Apollo, from whose blood this plant arose, is known to us by *Hyacinthus orientalis*, native to the eastern Mediterranean. It has been developed by the horticulturists into mammoth-blossomed, superlatively fragrant, strikingly colored creations, ideally suited—not for Apollo—but for the formal beds of city parks, and as potted for the consolation of hospital patients and women with birthdays. I am not sure what I would do if they were fit for naturalization. They are not. I have tried it. The bulbs serve mainly for mouse food. A few may be missed, to flower only for once. My mice do not miss a second time.

Grape-Hyacinth

Muscari. B: 234. Gl I: 422

There are half a hundred species of this small plant, native to the Mediterranean region and southwestern Asia. The common horticultural form called "Heavenly Blue" is placed by Bailey in *M. armeniacum*, tho Gleason refers the cultivated plants to *M. botryoides*. In any event, the small spikes of spring flowers have the rich scent of grapes, a worthy addition to spring. In the garden, they increase too abundantly by small bulblets that produce only sterile leaves. The seed is fertile, and offspring is apparently variable: I have saved one strain that is heavier-foliaged, larger-flowered and flowering over a longer season than the others. The white "variety **album**" has barely held its own in cultivation. *Muscari* produces new foliage late in the season, a tendency that would be hindered if growing in dense grass. It is said to be often escaped in the Northeast, but I doubt if this happens in dense grassland.

Colchicum. Autumn-flowering Crocus

Colchicum. B: 235. Gl I: 412

The Old World colchicums are interesting in that the foot-high foliage appears in spring; then dries up. The flowers rise from an underground stem in autumn, with no foliage whatever. *Colchicum autumnale* is the one usually grown in gardens. Others, similar, are occasionally found, especially *C. bornmuelleri* and *C. speciosum*. I have had the small white-flowered *C. autumnale* persist for over a decade in heavy grassland, while a purple *C. speciosum* has survived four years, undiminished, tho not increasing.

Trillium

Trillium. B: 236. Gl I: 430

There are about 30 trilliums native to North America and eastern Asia. They are large-leaved woodland herbs which, with some species, can cover the forest floor with springtime color. If you have them, by all means treasure them. They transplant easily, but it would be tedious to reproduce an acre of such vegetation. They are not suitable for the grassland, since their foliage yellows in the sun and is coarse and conspicuous against the grasses. *Trillium erectum*, the wake-robin, is unusual in several respects. It has the red color of very-ripe meat; it smells like too-ripe meat; it is fertilized by the green flesh fly *Lucilia*. (Either organism if conscious—and how can we know, any more than they can know if we are?—probably considers its behavior as very clever on its own part.)

THE AGAVES

34. AGAVACEAE. B: 237. Gl I: (in fams. 33 and 35)

In this family of desert warm-region xerophytes we have, curiously, one plant that is suited for northeastern North America. This is *Yucca smalliana* (*Y. filamentosa*), Gl I: 423. It is native to the Southeast, looks amazingly like a small edition of the southwestern yuccas, and is happy enough in the Northeast to spread by lateral offshoots. There is a basal rosette of 2-foot-high, viciously spine-tipped evergreen leaves. If it flowers—and it may not do so often—one is treated to a six-foot-high cluster of cream-white flowers. If you put it in the Grassland, give it protection from grass competition until the foliage reaches full size.

THE AMARYLLISES
35. AMARYLLIDACEAE. B: 242. Gl I: 440

Onion, Garlic, Chives, Leek
Allium. B: 245. Gl I: 412 (in fam. 33)

The genus *Allium* contains the onion and its relatives. This group is by no means only of gastronomic interest, even tho the edible species—with one important exception—are of little landscape value. Other species can be serious lawn pests.

There are about 500 species of *Allium* native to the northern hemisphere. They are scapose plants, with grass-like foliage rising from the ground, or rather from a small underground bulb. The flowers are arranged in a head, in umbels, and some of them are in strikingly clear shades of yellow, pink, purple and blue.

Allium schoenoprasum, chives, is quite a remarkable plant, aside from its chives-producing ability. The deep pink blossoms can form a solid carpet in spring. Straggling flowers reappear in midsummer, and continue until frost. In the garden, volunteer seedlings will be found. I have had clumps persist in the Grassland for a decade, unaided. If you wish the best showing however, keep the clump cleaned of grass (once done, grass does not readily reinvade); and blot out contacting grass, as with asphalt shingles or leaves.

Allium moly, the bright yellow-flowered wild onion of southeastern Europe, I have found to grow well in the garden. Bulbs increase rapidly, allowing for frequent division. It is suited for thin-grassed forest edges.

Allium caeruleum (A. azureum) from central Asia has flowers of a clear and attractive blue. It is not as husky as moly, but is worth trying.

Allium tricoccum—have you known the pleasure of taking a wild leek at the edge of the woods? Do not forego the experience. One such leek, on a picnic hamburger, will raise that sandwich to divine status—if you worship leeks. The leaves of this native species dry and disappear by late spring, to be followed in late summer by inconspicuous flowers and fruits on a naked scape.

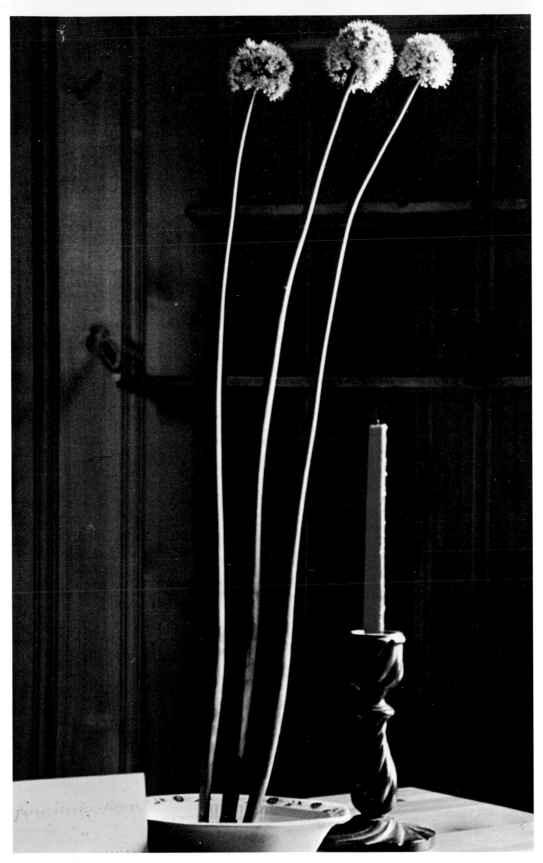

"Three slender virgins, hair-do en bouffant, by LO-CAL, the local low-calorie artiste." A local garden club exhibit. This form of *Allium cepa* requires full sunlight, and no competition from grasses.

Snowflake

Leucojum. B: 250. Gl I: 444

Leocojum aestivum, of central Europe, I am not sure is worth all the attention it gets in the spring-bulb catalogs. Such undue plugging always makes me suspicious—that sales are good on replacement orders. But any early spring bulb is to be cherished, and these demurely nodding little flowers are no exception. I have unexplainedly lost them after two or three years, yet on a hilltop a few have persisted for a decade. Gleason indicates that *Leucojum* is established in Maine, New York, Delaware, and probably elsewhere. The plant from a single bulb is likely to be lost in the grassland. I would suggest planting six or a dozen at a time, fairly close together.

Snowdrops

Galanthus. B: 250. Gl I: (not in)

I always feel warmly towards *Galanthus,* for not only is it a husky and hardy diminutive, but it is pushing up even before the last snow melts. A day or two of sun, and it is in blossom. There is none earlier.

Galanthus nivalis is the species most often grown. It is native to central and southern Europe, and on to the mountains of the Caucasus.

In the garden it does well, soon forming a carpet of white. The bulbs can be divided every two or three years so that one's supply rapidly increases. See that early spring drainage is unusually good. The bulbs can rot even in what looks like the normal mud of spring thaws, if that spring thaw is unduly long. The foliage yellows and disappears in a few weeks. The bulb is dormant until the following year.

In the Grassland, this little thing has been amazingly persistent. Tho it does not increase, plantings made a decade ago are still flowering, little spots of white and green coming up thru the flattened mulch of the preceding year's grass. Use garden-grown bulbs for planting. Once in the fibrous roots of the grass, they "cannot" be found again.

Galanthus elwesii, from Asia Minor, is a very similar species, tho slightly larger. Bulb increase in the garden is not as prolific as with *G.nivalis,* and my experience with it is less. It deserves the same respect as its smaller relative.

Daffodils, Narcissus, Jonquils

Narcissus. B: 258. Gl I: 440

To be asked what time of the year a man prefers above all others is like asking him what kind of climate, meat, or woman he prefers. Most people are not extremists, and they do not like monotony in their environment or their diet. If I could register with many votes however, I might give a majority to Narcissus Time, for reasons based largely, but not entirely, on one botanical genus. Species of Narcissus are native mainly to Europe, but some of them extend to the farthest Orient. It is accepted as native in Great Britain and other parts of western Europe, but I have strong suspicions that much that is accepted as the British botanical equivalent of the American D.A.R. is not really the result of gardening by Dame Nature. I look to some long-forgotten Roman dame who cherished these never-dying bulbs in a garden that contained much less to cherish than we have today. Who knows? Perhaps she obtained them from a forgotten hearth-site, to which a Neanderthal hunter had brought them, as a peace offering to his woman in lieu of the game he failed to catch, because of the other Neanderthal-ess he did catch. I have seen them by the thousands in western North Carolina, where they have multiplied thru breaking of the clumps by ploughing. They now grow and flower before the spring ploughing. It was amusing to wonder what might happen if the "native" people were to pass away, but not the "native" Narcissus. One could envisage some argumentative ethno-botanist of a future civilization presenting a radical theory that this plant, long thought indigenous, had really been introduced by primitive aborigenes of a country called "US" by its ego-centered inhabitants. Such is my opinion of persistence—of plants.

Just as soon as the heat of the sun becomes apparent in spring, the bold green leaves of the Narcissus emerge from the flattened brown mulch of last year's grasses. They burst into blossom—the first spectacle of a reawakening world. The sun is warm, the biting insects are not yet out; breaking buds of the trees are showing an impressionistic mist of green. All is smiling. The colors are a riotous and lavish expenditure of whites, yellows, and oranges. (Yes, there are "pink" Narcissi—but even a narcissistic Narcissus-lover should blush to call it pink.) The large-trumpeted varieties have

Early spring in an herbicide-managed old-field. Large oak and pine, juniper (*Juniperus communis*) and laurel (*Kalmia latifolia*), and a sweep of daffodils rising from the brown mulch of last year's grass. This area would be solid forest (as in the background) were it not for herbicides.

little odor, but as the flower gets smaller, the seductive fragrance seems to increase. Nor does night-time mean the end of the show, for these flowers can be snapped off at ease and brought indoors. They have sturdy stems and excellent lasting qualities. Eventually Narcissus time fades away, but as it does a sea of fresh spring grass billows up around them, submerging the maturing and yellowing foliage which have fed the bulbs for another year.

Where to plant Narcissi? If you pay attention to the eye-catching photos in the gardening literature, you will place them with a background of white birches, or clustered at the base of a beech. They look nice in such places (I have planted them there), but you will also find statements that Narcissi, after some years, fail to bloom, and die out. Of course—for such sites! I have planted Narcissi in dense maple woods and hemlock forest, close to the trunks of lawn trees, and out into full unmown grassland. In the forest and lawn-edge, the flowers get smaller and smaller, the foliage gets smaller. They may not die, they just fade away, most ingloriously. They thrive however in the full sunlight of the open Grassland. In fact, the more grass, the more they seem to thrive, contrary to most bulbs. Plant them in drifts, in solid masses of odd shapes, in crescents, or in long trails thru the Grassland, that guide you in Narcissus Time but have totally vanished a few weeks later.

The Kinds of Narcissus

Part of the joy of Narcissus time is in the great variety of plants that are available for introduction. Most of these are named clones of hybrid origin. Others are reasonably distinct botanical species. But man and nature are inextricably intermingled. It is neither possible nor very sensible to assume that we can know what early man selected, and when early man became "unnatural." Keep some varieties growing in your garden. I dig them up every three years, in which time they double or triple in number. I put the excess out to Grassland, and keep the propagating supply in the garden. I would not advise digging up grassland clumps. They are so snarled with grass roots that it is a patient man, who puts no value on his labor, that would tackle such a job.

The Royal Horticultural Society of England uses a classification of Narcissi having 11 major groups. These will be used below, coordinating the groups with the 11 species recognized by Bailey.

1. TRUMPET NARCISSI. These are the long-trumpet flowers, all included in *N. pseudo-narcissus*. The Yellow Trumpets are group 1a. King Alfred is the old standby here, but there are newer forms that are more reliable as to flowering, tho I would still not overlook the King.

White Trumpets are in 1b. Mt. Hood, a recent introduction, is one of the best. Some are white only in the sense that ivory is white.

1c are the Bicolor Trumpets, in which the trumpet is distinctly paler than the petals. Fragrance is negligible in all the trumpet Narcissi.

The Cup Narcissi embrace the next three groups: 2, 3, and 4. The trumpet has shortened to the stage where it is called a "cup." All three groups are included in the Latin binomial *N. incomparabilis*.

2. Group 2 are the INCOMPARABILIS NARCISSI. 2a have a yellow perianth; 2b have a white perianth. Fragrance starts to be found in this division.

3. The BARRI NARCISSI (*N. incomparabilis* var. *barrii*, or *N. barrii*) are intermediate between *incomparabilis* and *N. poeticus* of group 9. There are Yellow Perianth forms (3a), and White Perianth forms (3b).

4. Group 4, the LEEDSI NARCISSI (*N. incomparabilis* var. *leedsii*, or *N. leedsii*) are intermediate between *N. pseudonarcissus* (1) and *N. poeticus* (9). There are Large-cup forms, Giant Leedsi (4a), and Small-cup forms (4b).

5. The TRIANDRUS HYBRIDS are hybrids of *N. triandrus*, an Iberian species. Thalia, a white star-flowered form belongs here, and is well worth trying. It is a relatively low plant, with flowers of pure whiteness, unusual shape, and excellent fragrance, as distinct from other *Narcissi* as are the Trumpets themselves.

6. The CYCLAMINEUS HYBRIDS are hybrids of *H. cyclamineus*, a Portuguese species. They are rarely seen in the bulb catalogs, and I am unfamiliar with them.

7. The JONQUIL HYBRIDS are hybrids of *N. jonquilla*, the true jonquil, native to the western Mediterranean region and a great favorite in old gardens. It is deserving of being grown again.

8. TAZETTA and TAZETTA HYBRIDS, with other bunch-flowered varieties. In this group we have small-flowered forms, several on a stem, with possibly the finest fragrance in the entire genus. *N. tazetta* includes the Paper-Whites and the Chinese Sacred Lily that are grown indoors in winter. They are not hardy in the north outdoors. *N. poetaz* are hybrids between Tazetta and *N. poeticus* var. *ornatus* (Group 9), one of the choicest groups of all *Narcissi*. Petals vary from white to yellow, and crowns from yellow to orange. Try the pale Innocence, the deep-colored Scarlet Gem; and don't overlook St. Agnes, unexpectedly prolific.

9. POETICUS, the POET'S NARCISSUS, will make you happy even if you like neither poetry nor poets. This group, together with the preceding group 8, have neither "trumpets," nor "cups." That floral organ is here reduced to a small "crown," brightly colored, and sometimes 2-colored. The so-called "var. *ornatus*" has long existed in horticultural circles and is not of the finest texture or color. To the contrary, the Narcissus I like the best of all the lot is Actaea. (Not named from aktaia, the elder tree, but after Actaeon the Greek hunter, who peeped upon Diana at her bath—and made the fatal mistake, of being caught.) Actaea is a sturdy plant, with large flowers, petals that are translucent white, and a brilliant crown. I poked single bulbs into a dense Grassland; 15 seasons later each clump yields half a hundred blossoms.

10. The DOUBLES. I personally do not prefer the Royal Horticultural Society's idea of segregating all double forms into one group—like segregating all double-chinned people, be they Oriental, Hindu, Negro or Caucasian. Doubles occur in various groups. There are double Trumpets—which thus lose their one desirable feature, the trumpet. There are double Poetazes, aptly named Cheerfulness, solid little clusters of fragrant petals, that enrich our lives as much as their single forebears. And then, a double Campernelle appeared spontaneously in my garden, and was carefully saved. There is a double Poeticus, the Gardenia Narcissus, called *albo-pleno-odoratus*, the last of the Narcissi to bloom, if you can convince it to do so. The flowers blight in the bud unless you water it just at flowering time, even tho the soil is moist. If you wish, grow a ring of the plants at the margin of a saucer-shaped depression about two feet in diameter. Then pour in the buckets of water. For a Naturalistic Landscaper, such a demand is not neurotic, it is simply psychotic, even tho the patient has a seductive wistful beauty.

11. Called VARIOUS, is the horticulturist's basket for "what is left." And some choice things are left. Using Bailey's Manual as a guide, we find *N. bulbocodium*, the hoop petticoat daffodil, a little odd-shaped job, with a flower like a hoop-skirted doll, turned upside down. Some I have put in Grassland have survived for a decade, but with one or no flowers. It may require control of grass.

N. odorus is the Campernelle (preferably not called Campernelle Jonquil), a small and highly fragrant species from old gardens, native to Europe. *N. juncifolius* is a similar Iberian species, rarely grown in gardens.

N. biflorus of France is similar to Poeticus, also rarely grown.

One may be fascinated with *N. asturiensis* (not in Bailey), flowering when daffodils should not, with the first snowdrops as the snow recedes. It is a tiny thing, a few inches high. It has the form and color of a King Alfred, miniaturized to one-tenth its size with the perfect chiseling of a Hindu carving in ivory. It persists, barely increasing in my garden.

155

THE IRISES AND RELATIVES
37. IRIDACEAE. B: 262. Gl I: 445

Crocuses

Crocus. B: 264. Gl I: 445

Crocus is a Eurasian genus of about 75 species, a handful of which are cultivated. *C. sativus* provides the laboriously collected dried stigmas that in the kitchen we know as saffron. The crocuses, flowering after the snowdrops but before the daffodils, are for the gardener the choicest of the early spring bulbs. There is a lot of talk in the bulb catalogs about "naturalizing" them, in all their bright whites, purples and yellows. By "naturalizing" them, these people mean planting hundreds of them in grassy areas that are not mown until later in the season. They also recommend digging them up and replanting them every three years or so. (A new corm forms each year on top of the old, and thus the plant tends to rise too near the surface.) I never have any survive, to replant. If the mice do not get the bulbs, the rabbits get the foliage. Either dietetic interest is completely effective in de-naturalizing them.

I am beginning to have hopes for *Crocus susianus*, a species native from the Caucasus to the Crimea. It has appeared spontaneously in Grassland near the Garden, but whether from seed, or accidentally transported bulbs, cannot yet be said. This is a small yellow species of varying shades, with brown stripes outside, and with bright orange-red style branches. As with other early bulbs, its full growth takes place before the grasses have emerged from last year's mulch. It is a jewel of the season.

Several species are involved in the common horticultural materials. The common blues and whites are *C. vernus*. The common large yellow is *C. maesiacus*. The earlier blooming "Snow Crocus" is a combination of several species. There is no doubt that these plants would be magnificent additions to a wild landscape, but first we must train our small mammals to look—not eat.

Iris. Fleur-de-lys. Flag.

Iris. B: 266. Gl I: 445

This is a genus of about 200 species, around the northern hemisphere, but most abundant in Asia. Roots are either rhizomes or bulbs. The foliage is sword-shaped, and rises vertically from the ground. The flowers are an extraordinary variation on the basic pattern, with three parts of the perianth that fall down (the falls), and three parts that stand up (the standards), occurring in all colors. Modern hybridization has much enlarged the blossoms and increased the color range. These plants do not have the blatant severity of tulips. Rather, they have the ornate opulence of the court of the Louis'. It is no accident that this flower had become the symbol of the French. It is nature's counterpart of their decorative arts, even to its delicate temperate fragrance. The species hybridize readily in nature, and then spread vegetatively. Consequently some of the native-flora taxonomists have had hey-days describing new "species". The horticultural hybridizers have added thousands of named forms. The plants are easily moved; they naturalize readily. Altogether it is a most valuable group for the Naturalistic Landscaper.

Among the bulbous irises, the earliest blooming is *I. reticulata*, the Netted Iris from the Caucasus, a small form worth trial. The Dutch irises come next, a horticultural group derived from *I. xiphium*. Then the Spanish irises, variants from the original *I. xiphium* from the western Mediterranean. Both Dutch and Spanish start foliage growth in the fall and are harmed by snowless winters. I have not been successful with either. Later blooming are the English irises, *I. xiphioides*, native not to England but to the Pyrenees.

The non-bulbous irises comprise numerous species and hybrid groups which, for landscaping purposes, may be considered in sequence of blooming. In addition to those mentioned below, I am sure that many natural species, native to parts of Europe and Asia, are still unknown for our present purposes. These irises grow from heavy rhizomes, at the surface, and not entirely covered by soil.

They extend horizontally one to a few inches a year, and thus a colony tends to radiate outwards. Do not expect a plant to "stay put."

Iris pumila is a small early-flowering species from central Europe and Asia Minor. It is deep purple in color, and excellently scented.

Iris pseudacorus is the common yellow European iris, naturalized along many northeastern streamsides by volunteer seedlings. It is a particularly robust plant, with flower stalks five feet high. The flowers are small (as horticulturists think) but a clear yellow. I have planted it on general upland, and find it just as happy as on sloppy streambanks. Apparently nature distributed the seeds by water, and the plant had no way of moving out of the mud—until muddling man meddled.

The German irises, or bearded irises, are an enormous complex, and probably the most popular of all the irises. They are generally referred to as *"Iris germanica"*. In Bailey, *I. variegata, I. germanica, I. kochii, I. pallida,* and *I. flavescens* comprise a cosy group which does not believe in undemocratic segregation. They have crossed, and recrossed, and now form a common melting pot, from which individual clones are named. Like most melting pots, the great bulk of the plants are worthless mediocrities.

A yellow-flowered form with brown variegations was apparently the common garden iris in northwestern Connecticut, in the gardens of the now-vanished subsistence farms, from where I obtained it. It appears to correspond to the description of *Iris variegata* from the Balkans. Altho the flowers are small by present-day standards, and the flower stems are no higher than the foliage, it is admirable for naturalizing purposes. When in blossom, it forms clear patches of deep yellow, on flower stems that remain erect, and that are visible at considerable distances.

Recently developed clones among the German irises are truly remarkable. The blossoms occur in an infinite variety of subtle shades, of all the basic colors. They are gigantic in size and of an enticing fragrance. A single stalk, brought indoors, is to be admired in the same manner as one would admire an extraordinary hair-do, making its first appearance atop a countess at the court of Versailles. Lay it in the wild grass however, and it topples, understandably. These things have more beauty than backbone. I would like to find one that qualifies in all dimensions.

A colony of Japanese iris (*Iris laevigata*) perpetuating itself in an herbicide-managed grassland. This iris is apparently a relict that has survived from the garden of a house site so old it was already omitted from an 1853 map. The plant survived agricultural operations to 1938. When herbicide treatment started in 1946, the land was in brush. The colony is now slowly enlarging. It would appear that this plant was brought to America via the near East and Europe, for Commodore Perry did not open Japan to western trade until 1859.

Another view of the same herbicide-managed grassland as that facing page 41a, also with 20-year old junipers (*Juniperus communis*) selected for still further variety of size and shape.

The Siberian iris (*Iris sibirica*) starts blooming before the last of the beards. It is originally a European species, despite its name. They are very sturdy-stemmed plants, occurring in whites, blues and purples, with flat flowers that must be looked down upon for full color effect. I find them suitable for naturalizing.

The Japanese irises are the last of the season, and in some respects the most fascinating of them all. These irises seem to breathe out the spirit of Japan even as the fleur-de-lys does for the spirit of old France. The perianth segments can be of enormous size, and hang down in languorous charm, reminding one of a silk handkerchief, placed with rigorous conformity to stylized casualness.

These irises are one group for which, apparently, soil acidity (pH) is important. They do not survive in the alkaline soils of limestone regions; they thrive in acid soils. I base this statement not so much on the repeated claims of those who are forever measuring the soil acidity of plants in their "natural" haunts (tho possibly "accidental," like the streamborne *I.pseudoacorus*, mentioned above). I am impressed by the fact that nurseries in the Middle West limestone areas do not carry the plant.

Japanese iris is almost always described as a plant of moist sites. Like all other such ecological pronunciamentos, one must distinguish between a plant's toleration of such a site, and its preference for it and toleration of other sites. Long ago, I put a clump high on a sunny hillside (to see how quickly it would die out—I confess). It is still thriving, and flowering every year.

The Japanese irises comprise two botanical species. In *Iris laevigata*, the standards are fully as large as the falls, and the flower appears to be 6-petaled. In *Iris kaempferi* (*I. laevigata* var. *kaempferi*) the standards are small and erect, and the flower appears to be 3-petaled. The horticultural clones available today are probably of mixed parentage. Flower colors may be considered to run from pure white thru two color lines. One is thru shades of lavender and rose to reddish-violets. The other is thru light blue to dark purple-blues. The colors are seldom solid: coloring is effected by lines, veins, borders, stripes, and marbling. The effect is heightened by frilling and ruffling of the petals.

There is every reason to believe that Japanese iris can be long-lived and suitable for Naturalistic Landscaping. Several years ago I came upon a striking 6-petaled blue clump in an abandoned agricultural field. It had apparently found my herbicide-induced Grassland a suitable local environment, tho its origin long remained a mystery. New England archeology is hardly a science yet, but I now have convincing field evidence to indicate that this is persisting from a pre-1853 garden, at a house site that even in 1853 was no longer mapped. The plant had apparently survived subsequent agricultural operations, ploughing, mowing, grazing, existing even if only as a few small leaves, chopped and chomped by hoe and cow, but never killed. Farming stopped in 1938; brush rushed in; herbicide spraying started in 1946. The plant is there to stay—barring some uninvited human visitors with taking ways.

159

THE ORCHIDS

42. ORCHIDACEAE. B: 294. Gl I: 455

The Gods* had assembled on Mt. Olympus to recreate the plants, for Uranus had botched the job when he had brought them forth out of Ghea, or Mother Earth. Mortals were complaining—and even the Gods agreeing—that plant life was still in Chaos. It had been a long and tedious day. They had finished the Dicots by noon. They had been working on the Monocots all afternoon. Only the orchids remained. They were both weary and exhilarated, for they had not stopped for lunch tho Bacchus had seen to it that the wine-cups were never empty.

"Let us make the orchids the pinnacle of all creation in the plant world," announced Zeus; and there were murmurings of strong approval as each decided what gift he might bestow. But some of the Gods had sunk in slumber, thanks to the cup-bearers of Bacchus, and thus the orchids remain to this day devoid of some of the common attributes of other plants. For example, there are no shrubs or trees among them; they are all herbaceous. There are none in the desert. Even the goddess of economic plants was slumbering. (She opened one eye later, just long enough to breathe life into a vanilla bean.)

---

*The following myth concerning the creation of the orchids is based on a literal translation made by the author, of an ancient manuscript found quite by coincidence in the library of a monastery in southern Italy during World War II. The manuscript was in Latin, signed "Fener Al Grec", and appears to have been a 14th century copy of a classical original dating from the first century A.D. The only changes in this adaptation are of such an obvious nature, all related to modern knowledge, that it is not necessary to document them separately.

Aphrodite spoke up first. (Her wishes come first among the gods, even as among men.) "I give them superlative beauty," she decreed. And thus we have the florist's Cattleyas, those extraordinary blossoms that are considered the pinnacle of corsage beauty, that one sees perched on their prominent platforms wherever women of fashion and size try to acquire a reflection of their beauty. The smaller flowers have an ardent following, and orchid fanciers are probably more numerous, and spend more time and energy on their hobby, than any other such group.

"I give them wisdom," said Athene. "Wisdom in love," she added, for Athene always had her fingers crossed when Aphrodite was around, "and wisdom to cope with their surroundings." Just then a spritely little voice came out of the Northwest skies, "Let their wise love be turned upon insects." The Gods were not only shocked at such levity, but disturbed. Whose voice was this? And what nonsense! (They never knew. He materialized centuries later, in mediaeval England, where they called him Puck.) For these reasons, orchids take the most elaborate precautions against self-fertilization (which modern biologists consider very wise). And Puck's little afterthought has resulted in the most extraordinary entomophily that cold scientists have described. The mechanical devices in the flower for enticing insects to enter them, for sticking little masses of pollen in the proper places, for "paying" the insect in the form of nectar ("-phily" ever requires payment, in some form), then directing the insect to leave by such a route as will dust the pollen of the last flower onto the stigma of the present flower—the multitude of these devices in the different species would make a drafting board engineer envious. (I am told that the insect does not see it that way, at all. He gets what he wants, and if he pimps incidentally, that is an irrevelant side-issue. Such is the secret of symbiosis, sometimes called togetherness in the contemporary conventional wisdom.)

Zeus was a jealous God and wanted to rule over the vastest of all possible worlds, so he decreed that orchids should be greater in number of kinds than any other plant. Thus we have the largest of all plant families, probably 500 genera and 20,000 species. So many were created that man is still busy describing them.

Various other Gods had sundry ideas, but they had become too sleepy with wine to care much. Only love, wisdom and power have the ability to ward off the effects of Bacchus—within limits. One prude, disliking Aphrodite, said that their seeds should be the smallest in existence. Alas, all she accomplished was to make it extremely difficult for horticulturists to raise them from seed. Another said, "Let them be different from all other plants." That foolish comment meant that some have lost their chlorophyll, and have become colorless saprophytes. Another murmured, "Let them be in accord with life in their soil." Airborne Aeolus was worried at that, and hastily spoke up, "Let them rise into the air." So we find that all thru the tropics (where these were created), orchids are epiphytic, living high up in the branches of the forest trees—the nearest they could get to being airborne—while they obtain much of their nourishment by mycorrhizal fungi and attached "soil" surrounding the rootlets. After the Gods were gone, orchids moved out of the tropics, and to the ground as a protection from the inclement winters. The mycorrhizal fungi stayed, to add to our problems of transplanting them.

The Gods' gifts were such as to fascinate many many kinds of men, and I suspect more people are orchid-minded than are taken with any other single family of plants. There are over a dozen journals in the world, solely devoted to some aspect of orchid knowledge—orchidology it is called. The wildflower-garden books devote considerable space to finding, transplanting, and growing the native orchids.

It will come as a distinct anticlimax—after this Olympian preamble—to tell you that orchids will probably play a very very minor role in your Naturalistic Landscaping. Yet I have not thought it unwise to acquaint you with the role the Gods have played in the Orchidaceae. You are probably already a potential orchid-lover. Love them if you must, but carefully budget your time for such activities.

Of the northeastern orchids, the lady-slippers (*Cypripedium*) get the most attention. Most people say the word reverently—yet were there ever a lady with a foot to fit this shoe, she would be called a clodhopper, even in old-time wooden-shoed Holland. No doubt about it, they are magnificent plants. *Cypripedium acaule* is one of the commonest, easiest to transplant. If you have a site where it grows, be thankful. It can become almost weedy. On the other hand, I once had a completely natural colony of them, which completely died out—naturally. *C. parviflorum pubescens*, the large yellow lady-slipper, is claimed to be one of the very easiest to grow, but not necessarily with the mice and rabbits and slugs of a natural landscape. The wildflower books have much advice concerning other species, but I would advise serious consideration before you remove orchids from their native haunts, with the intent of "preserving" them.

The helleborine, *Epipactis latifolia*, is a native of Europe that has become widely established in the Northeast. There is not much you can do about it. I have had fine plants appear, with totally insignificant greenish-purplish flowers; marked the site; it has not appeared again at least for several years.

I have two orchids that are widely but sparsely scattered in sunny Grasslands. As with the helleborine, there is not much one can do about it, but these flower year after year with remarkable regularity. *Habenaria lacera* flowers in midsummer. Its white blossoms, clustered in a spike, are always a pleasure to look at closely. At the end of summer, *Spiranthes cernua*, the ladies' tresses, sends up its spike of white flowers, clearly arranged in a double spiral around the stalk. I have never seen Spiranthes grow more abundantly and luxuriantly than on a sterile gravelly roadside, where, if left alone, they would be crowded out in competition with other plants in a few years. It is a tough situation for the wildflower lovers, who think they can "preserve" plants by "protecting" them. There must be other orchids that one can naturalize, but I do not know of them.

A giant dead chestnut (*Castanea dentata*) in the forest, such as can be featured at an unexpected turn of a trail.

Beauty in death. An interesting near view of the same chestnut shown in the preceding photograph. Such views may have to be "carved out" of the forest by selective cutting and herbicide treatment.

DICOTYLEDONEAE

Family 56, the Polygonaceae (B: 347, Gl II: 64) contains the knotweeds of the genus *Polygonum*. Family 57, the Chenopodiaceae (B: 352, Gl II: 86) contains the goosefoots of the genus *Chenopodium*. And family 58, Amaranthaceae (B: 354, Gl II: 101), has the pigweeds of the genus *Amaranthus*. These genera include a large number of garden weeds that may be a great problem in bare-dirt gardening. In Naturalistic Landscaping you need not worry about these plants. They have no place where the land is already covered with plants. They are "cultivated"—even tho unintentionally—by ordinary garden practices.

THE PINKS

65. CARYOPHYLLACEAE. B: 368. Gl II: 118

The pinks involve a 2,000-species family of plants that is world-wide in distribution tho most abundant in the northern hemisphere. It includes a fair number of garden plants, notably *Arenaria* the sandworts, *Dianthus* the true pinks including the Sweet William, *Silene* the campions, *Gypsophila* or babys-breath, and *Saponaria* the soapworts. The florist's carnation is a *Dianthus*. They are all small herbaceous plants, recognizable by their opposite leaves and swollen nodes (where the leaves are attached.)

Lychnis coronaria is the Ragged Robin, a rose-purple ragged-fringed flower of old-fashioned gardens. Most of the foliage is basal, and therefore it is not successful in perpetuating itself where there is a heavy mulch of dead grass each year. It has continued for some seven years under the low branches of an apple tree where the grass is relatively thin. The flower heads are high above the other herbaceous vegetation and give the impression of the filmiest of gauze covers of the land.

Dianthus barbatus, the Sweet William, is probably a short-lived perennial, rather than a biennial. Tho it would be attractive if it could be naturalized, it dies out too quickly, and has no reliable way of reproducing itself in the grassland.

Dianthus armeria, the Deptford Pink, is a bit of a plant with such a bright pink flower that even tho small, it gets itself seen. Furthermore, it can flower all summer long. It is an annual or biennial, and has no success in a closed grassland. You might, however, like to grow it in your garden. Seedlings will pop up in the most unexpected places.

Saponaria officinalis is the pink-flowered Bouncing Bet, sometimes too common along roadsides and railway embankments, where it forms solid colonies thru spreading rhizomes. A small compact little cluster would not be undesirable in a wild grassland, but I have never succeeded. Whatever its success on sterile soils that won't grow anything else, it simply won't raise a leaf when other plants decide they want the same place in the sun.

THE CROWFOOTS

70. RANUNCULACEAE. B: 387. Gl II: 155

A large family of the north temperate and arctic regions, containing mostly herbs but sometimes small shrubs and woody climbers. A large number of attractive wild flowers and garden favorites are included. The following are worthy of special mention.

The Buttercup, *Ranunculus acris*, is actually a native of Europe. It has however, become so thoroly established in our American fields and on our roadsides that we look upon it with all the sentiment of a native wildflower. The plant depends mainly on low-growing (but not prostrate) foliage for its success. The flowers rise high on slender stalks. Thus by form, it is admirably adapted to unmown Grasslands. I have had it survive in these Grasslands for 20 years, with no evidence of diminution. The color it adds is one of the chief elements in the late spring display. It has however not invaded Grasslands where it was not originally present. Possibly it is worth while setting in mature plants.

There are many other species of *Ranunculus*—possibly 300—but to my knowledge unknown for naturalizing purposes.

Thalictrum, the Meadow-Rues, are tall perennial herbs, with finely divided and quite attractive low foliage. Flower stalks may rise to heights of 8 feet, with clouds of whitish finely divided flowers. What color there is, yellowish or purplish, is due to the stamens. The native species are generally thought of as forest edge plants. I was surprised therefore when I found a colony of a dozen or so plants developing in full light and dense grass, with their high-rising flower clusters conspicuous in season at a considerable distance. There is no evidence of spread or increase. I doubt if small plants could survive if planted in grass, but presumably if the plant is large enough (by natural coincidence or human interference) it has the "upper hand" in competition with adjacent grass.

Hepaticas, *Hepatica americana* and *H. acutiloba*, are eagerly looked for early in spring, when the white and bluish flowers form solid little patches of color. The broad liver-shaped leaves (whence the name, and its mediaeval medicinal use) survive thru the winter. A new set of leaves arise after the flowers have vanished. This life form is quite unsuited for Grassland success. It will thrive where grasses are absent, as in open woods and forest edges.

Anemones, or Windflowers, in the genus *Anemone*, contain a variety of plants, some of which are low, and suited only for relatively shaded areas. Some are cultivated plants, like the pasqueflowers. Others are native to the original Prairies, with fairly showy flowers. I have not worked with them sufficiently, but I strongly suspect that species will be found valuable to put in the Grassland.

Anemonella thalictroides, the Rue-Anemone, the only species of its genus, is a small wildflower that I have had persist for many years in a shady site. It is worth trying at the forest edge.

The Larkspurs, *Delphinium*, are a group of north temperate species, over 50 of which are found in North America, both annuals and perennials. None of the native perennials have been given adequate trial in northeastern grasslands. No one has wanted to. The western native species are among the critical poisonous plants on the cattle ranges; and the highly developed horticultural strains—which add so much to the colorfulness of the nurseryman's catalogs, and the gardens of larkspur fanciers—are totally unsuited for naturalizing. The cultivated larkspurs are short-lived, hardly winter-hardy, and often top-heavy and weak-stemmed. Two of the original cultivated forms are called *D. belladonna* and *D. bellamosum* (discussed by Bailey under *D. cheilanthum*), and by comparison are ruggedly hardy tho by no means as showy as the modern derivatives. They may prove suitable for naturalizing.

The Monkshood, *Aconitum napellus*, comes from Europe. There are three native species with less conspicuous flower stalks. All are poisonous because of the alkaloid aconitine, source of aconite. I have had *Aconitum napellus* persist for a decade in Grassland, but it becomes small, with few or no flowers. It needs the help of an "accidentally" placed rock, or an asphalt shingle, so as to restrict the grasses in immediate contact with it.

The Columbines, the genus *Aquilegia*, is an interesting group of spring-flowering plants to work with. The flowers are highly unusual, the petals prolonged backward into an elongate hollow spur. Colors are basically red, but also blue, purple, pink, yellow and white. Volunteer seedlings are common in the bare soil of gardens, and I have had volunteers appear in the thinned grass under trees. *Aquilegia canadensis* is the native eastern species. I have not found it suited to open Grassland unless the adjacent turf is matted out. The Eurasian *A. vulgaris*, in various colors, is established in several parts of northeastern U.S. and, being very hardy, is worth having. The long-spurred hybrids are largely derivatives of the Rocky Mt. *A. caerulea* and *A. chrysantha*. They are beautiful things, hardy (from the gardener's viewpoint), which in this case means that after two or three years I find they are likely not to survive the winter.

The Winter Aconite, *Eranthis hyemalis*, is a small tuberous perennial that sends up ordinary buttercup-looking flowers early in spring. It is heavily promoted in the bulb catalogs, too heavily I suspect for the good of the gardeners, but heavily enough so you will probably want to try it. It may not be favored by acid soils. In any event, its growth form does not appear to be adapted for semi-natural Grasslands.

Love-in-a-Mist, *Nigella damascena* from southern Europe, is an annual plant that I have found can become weedy in my garden with volunteer seedlings. The light blue flowers are imbedded in the very finely divided involucre, hence the name. It has not been seen to invade the Grassland, but its hardiness is such that seedlings might volunteer if you kept a small spot scratched bare, such as a skunk would do in digging for grubs.

Trollius europaeus, the Globe-Flower, hails from the mountains of Europe. Yellow, waxy, double-appearing flowers rise to a height of a foot or so from a mound of cut-leaved foliage. It will thrive in wet places, but do not hesitate to put it on the upland. If in Grassland, it may need the "accidental" placing of some asphalt-shingle "rocks" or leaves to cut down competition from adjacent grasses.

The Baneberries belong to the genus *Actaea*, a north temperate group with two species in the Northeast, both of which are worth encouraging. They are woodland species, not suited for the Grassland, but eminently adapted for the forest. They produce seeds readily. The seeds are fertile, and seedlings easy to grow. Older plants can be divided. Once established, the plants are very long-lived. *Actaea rubra*, the red baneberry, is the first of the two to flower, with short spikes of finely cut whitish flowers. Red berries appear in midsummer. For the rest of the season, the divided foliage is attractive. *Actaea alba*, the Doll's-eye Baneberry, flowers later. The autumn berries are porcelain-white with a jet black dot, whence the name. When the berries fall off, the red fleshy stalks on which the berries were attached continue to be an attractive feature.

Peonies

Paeonia. B: 405. Gl II: (not in)

Paeonia is a genus of about 30 species, mostly Asian, but with some in Europe, and with one small flowering herb in the western United States. None are considered naturalized in northeastern U.S. The so-called shrubby peonies are forms of *P. suffruticosa*, long cultivated in China.

The common cultivated herbaceous peonies are all derivatives of *P. lactiflora*, native to China and Siberia, which long played a prominent role in the gardens of China. The peony season, coming after the German iris, and before the Europa day-lilies and the Japanese iris, is one of the main calendar events in the gardening world. And well it should be! These enormous blossoms occur in an infinite variety of pastel shades of pink, and only rarely become either pure white or what might be called deep red. They are excellently fragrant—in most cases.

As a peony grower grows peonies, the procedure is impressively profound. Soil must be prepared to a depth of 18 inches before planting. Mix bonemeal with it; put wood-ashes at the top; add ground limestone if necessary. Put in your plants. Keep them from flowering for the first year, to increase the health of the roots. To control botrytis blight, the foliage should be cut below the soil surface in the fall, and burned. Plants infested with nematodes, as evidenced by gnarled swellings on the roots, should be dug up and burned. (But how to tell without digging them up first, the books do not say.) And to maintain suitable soil conditions, there should be annual applications of fertilizer. I saw no promise of pleasure in pampering peonies.

Then I realized that peonies in a garden abandoned since 1938 were flowering excellently (and still were, in 1965), even what was left of them, after vandals had stolen the main clumps. I dug up much of what remained one spring (happily not knowing that peonies should be moved in fall), and clomped them into a quackgrass Grassland, and therefore of fairly high fertility. They have blossomed excellently each year, without a single minute of gardening care. I am now adding other named strains in other areas.

In choosing peonies for purchase, consider both singles and doubles. The singles are large attractive blossoms, with heavy clusters of yellow stamens at the center. The color range of both singles and doubles is from white thru many shades of pink to deep dull reds. Some are early-blooming, some late-blooming, so that with proper choice your peony season can be lengthened. Above all, do not neglect to check as to their fragrance. I may be prejudiced, but to me a peony without fragrance is like a beautiful well-fleshed woman without perfume, and smelling too much of the earth—the peony, that is.

THE POPPIES
80. PAPAVERACEAE. B: 423. Gl II: 195

The true poppies belong in the genus *Papaver*. This group contains about 50 species, mostly Old World, but a few native to western North America. *P. somniferum* is widely cultivated for ornament, and occasionally escaped. The seeds are used in baking, and the milky juice is the commercial source of opium. Poppies are among the best known of garden flowers. The season is short, sometimes only a week, but they make up for that defect by attention-getting color. Many of the garden poppies are annual species, and beyond our present interest.

The perennial Oriental Poppy however is worthy of attention. The cultivated forms derive from *P. orientale*, often hybridized with the closely related *P. bracteatum*. Both species are native from the Mediterranean region east to Iran. The flowers can be conspicuous to the point of screaming blatancy. They can be as big as dinner plates, 10 inches across, with a distinctive crinkly texture, as if of extremely thin parchment. The basic color is called "red," actually an orange-red. Newer colors vary from white thru pink, to distinct rose-red shades. After flowering, the foliage dies to the ground. There may be minor regrowth in fall. Garden-wise, these are extremely rugged and hardy plants, increasing in size and permitting division at frequent intervals. They could be valuable additions to semi-natural Grassland because of their striking, tho fleeting, flowering period, followed by disappearance of the foliage. Success has not yet been attained however, and it is possible that they may need an "isolation-band" around them, to free them from the competition of adjacent grasses.

Sanguinaria canadensis, the native Bloodroot, a harbinger of early spring, is said to be one of the easiest wild flowers to grow. That means "in a garden" undoubtedly. Whether or not it will spread, once introduced, is another problem. It is possible that it is favored by alkaline soils. The large and attractive foliage begins to look weather-beaten by mid-summer. It is best suited for the forest edge.

Macleaya (Bocconia) cordata is the Plume Poppy from China and Japan. It is a rankly growing herbaceous plant five to eight feet in height, grown mainly for its wall of pale foliage rather than for the masses of small buff flowers. It can become rampant in a garden. To develop a mass of it at the edge of the Grassland would require careful encouragement. Data on its persistence are still not available.

The Celandine, *Chelidonium majus*, is a Eurasian species, sole member of its genus, found in old gardens and escaped in waste areas. It is a short-lived perennial, with finely divided foliage, and a long season for the small but bright yellow flowers. Volunteer seedlings can be common in bare soil, but it is not the sort of plant that would seem to have any role in the Grassland.

THE MUSTARDS
83. CRUCIFERAE. B: 431. Gl II: 202

We have here a large family—350 genera, 2,500 species—that is most easily recognized by its flowers. Four petals appear to form a cross (hence the name cruci-ferae, cross-bearing), with six stamens, two short and four long. Many have a pungent odor and taste, leading to their use as food: garden cress, radish, and horseradish. In one genus alone, *Brassica*, with different plant parts grossly over-developed for eating, we have not only the common mustard, but also kale, Brusselsprouts, cabbage, cauliflower, broccoli, kohlrabi, rape, rutabaga, turnip and several lesser known vegetables. Others can be pernicious but beautiful weeds, like the wild mustard of alfalfa fields.

Common garden plants include the woad, candytuft, the moon-wort (grown for its greatly enlarged satin-papery fruits), alyssum, arabis, aubrieta, matthiola (stocks), and others. In all this array, the crucifers have relatively little to offer to Naturalistic Gardening in the light of present knowledge.

The Toothwort, *Dentaria diphylla*, is a low rhizome-spreading colonial herb with attractive cut foliage and short spring spikes of small white flowers. It is occasionally found in nature in large patches 30 or more feet across, in open woods. Once established in grassless areas, the colony readily persists. To get it to expand, however, will require removal of plants already on the site. *Dentaria laciniata* is a closely related species with more finely divided foliage.

Dames-rocket, *Hesperis matronalis*, an old garden plant from Eurasia, is well worth investigating. It is a vigorous plant, 1–4 feet high, with large spikes of evening-fragrant flowers in late spring and early summer. Seeding is prolific, and garden volunteers are common. I am not sure it would do well out in the middle of the Grassland, nor would I want it there. But where there is a bit of shade, and a slight thinning of the grass, this species has naturalized itself. Once established, the vigor of its foliage is such as to gain the upper hand over the grass.

THE ORPINES

89. CRASSULACEAE. B: 454. Gl II: 255

A cosmopolitan family, mainly in the subtropics, with some 30 genera and 1,500 species. Many of the plants are succulent; many are cultivated in the garden; several are common greenhouse and home plants. The succulent herbaceous life form is frequently associated with sunny open vegetation of warm areas, and we do not find the family of great importance in northeastern North American Naturalistic Landscaping.

Sedum telephium (including *S. purpureum*), the Live-Forever, is a plant of old-fashioned gardens, with thick fleshy leaves that children like to blow up to resemble what they call a frog's stomach. The dense mass of flowers is rose-purple. This plant is native to a vast area from western Europe to Japan, and exists in many variations. The roots are thick and fleshy, to some extent resembling a mass of slender carrots, developing horizontally at a depth of two or three inches. I have one old-field with several thousand of these plants, the center of concentration being at an ancient house site. It is my opinion that these were broken up by ploughing, and distributed by agricultural practices. There have been no agricultural operations there for 40 years; nor any increase in the plant since that time! Neither, unfortunately, do they flower. I have seen flowers less than half a dozen times in all those years. Furthermore, they are extremely difficult to kill out with any chemical short of a soil sterilant. Even an asphalt-shingle blot-out takes time and attention, for long slender shoots can exist for an entire season under the black heat of the asphalt. With this live-forever quality, the family is worth considering for other possible introductions, which may not only live forever, but also flower.

THE SAXIFRAGES

90. SAXIFRAGACEAE. B: 469. Gl II: 260

A cosmopolitan and variable family, intermediate botanically between the Crassulaceae and the Rosaceae. It contains both herbs and such well-known shrubs as the hydrangea, and the currants and gooseberries.

The Foam-flower, *Tiarella cordifolia*, is worth consideration because of its aggressive mat-forming characteristics in shady grassless areas. In spring, the mat is a misty cloud of spikes of small white flowers. The plant reproduces by runners, which have little rooting buds at the tip and form new plants the following year. With a bit of encouragement, and removal of competitors, a dense and relatively stable mat of foliage will develop.

The Bishop's Cap, *Mitella diphylla*, is a close relative of the foam-flower, having two small leaves on the flower stalk just below the inflorescence. It can be treated the same as *Tiarella*. I would suggest keeping the plants separate, for the foliage may be difficult to distinguish when the flowers are not out.

T. cordifolia

X3

X½

THE ROSES AND RELATIVES

95. ROSACEAE. B 493. Gl II: 281

A large cosmopolitan family of some 3,000 species separated into several distinct tribes, and contributing many plants to horticulture, tho relatively few in the category of weeds. There are a large number of trees and shrubs, including blackberries and raspberries in the genus *Rubus*, peaches apricots cherries almonds and plums in the genus *Prunus*, and pears and apples in *Pyrus*. The ornamental woody plants include spiraea, roses, mountain ash, hawthorn. Some feminists in this family discovered a completely fiendish and unfair technique for assuring a matriarchy. Upon the first development of a normal and respectably fertilized embryo, the wall of the ovary—completely feminine in its tissue—produces a little false-embryo. Like the cowbird nestling, it soon becomes dominant. The original two-parental embryo withers and dies. Unlike the cowbird nestling, the false-embryo takes on all the appearance and characteristics of a decent and normal seed. It completely fooled plant taxonomists until a few decades ago. This false seed, and the plant growing from it, is identical to its mother, as much so as a root-division from the Europa clone of the day-lily. Fortunately or unfortunately, once in a while it seems as tho father's contribution is accepted by mother. Even more—tho it must offend maternal pride—the offspring is a distinct improvement, so much so that this new offspring goes on a very successful matriarchal population explosion of its own. You can't beat the matriarchy! The result is that a local colony becomes clustered around the original individual. Similar colonies may arise independently elsewhere. Occasionally one will migrate a long distance, to be discharged by a passing bird, and set up a colonial outpost. Plant taxonomists, using only the "tools" and concepts of bisexual normalcy, and not suspecting the subterfuge, could not resist the compulsions of human patriarchy by tying their own names to literally hundreds of new "species." Thus we have over a thousand native species of hawthorns (*Crataegus*) in North America. Liberty Hyde Bailey had so sired, described, over 400 species of blackberry in northeastern North America before he died as a nonogenarian; and he was still going strong, *Rubus*-wise. The situation is actually more complicated than this, in the nature and the reasons for the promiscuous variability of the populations, but fortunately other genera in the family seem to support the precise precepts expected of those who left the Ark.

Wild Strawberry, *Fragaria vesca* and *F. virginiana*, is a variable complex, partially native and partially introduced. It is highly desirable in the Grassland where it spreads by runners and forms a sort of lower layer to the vegetation. The white flowers can be a conspicuous feature in spring, and the small berries, a delectable item later.

Cinquefoil, *Potentilla simplex* and *P. canadensis*, are two closely related and variable species that can be among the most valuable components of Grassland. I have found the plants more successful and aggressive than *Fragaria*, with which they compete on essentially the same terms. Once established, they spread thru the grassland by runners, the tips of which settle into the turf and root to form new plants. The foliage thus continues to form a sort of lower stratum to the Grassland. In late spring, the entire carpet breaks out into thousands of tiny sparkling yellow flowers.

X½

var. americana

X½

F. vesca

THE LEGUMES. PEAS, BEANS, AND LUPINES

96. LEGUMINOSAE. B: 547. Gl II: 379

The Leguminosae (split by Gleason into the Mimosaceae, Cae-salpiniaceae and Fabaceae) is one of the major plant families, with possibly 500 genera and several thousand species. It contains many food plants, notably the peas and beans, and many ornamentals, herbs shrubs and trees. Many of the species have root-tubercles bearing nitrogen-fixing bacteria. The fruit is typically a one-celled pod (the edible string bean) containing a row of seeds (edible peas), occurring in an endless profusion of shapes and sizes.

Lathyrus latifolius, the Perennial Pea, is a well-known garden species from Europe, unfortunately not fragrant. On the other hand its deep pink flowers are highly attractive, and appear thru a long season. It requires continued mulching for several years, until the root system is husky enough to send out above-ground parts that dominate over Grassland. There after, it appears to be persistent.

The common Vetch, *Vicia cracca*, is native to the Northeast, as well as to Eurasia. It is a tendril-climbing herb which in season bears clusters of bright purple flowers. The mass of foliage is fairly dense in flowering time, but thins out later in the season. Where established in the Grassland, it persists excellently, tho the quantity is variable from year to year. If you do not have it, I would suggest introducing it, aiding the plants for a few seasons until the roots become well established.

The Bush-Clovers, or *Lespedeza*, are grown both for ornament and for forage. In the southeastern United States, there are some of very high wildlife value. None can be recommended as yet for northeast Grasslands, but the genus is worth consideration.

The true Lupines belong to the genus *Lupinus*, containing many agricultural and ornamental species. Many of the native species have bold conspicuous flower stalks, and are worth testing for naturalization. The famed garden Russell hybrids are variants of *Lupinus polyphyllus*, native to the west coast of North America. Seeds are fertile, and volunteer garden seedlings are frequent. Flowers on these plants tend to revert to bluish-purple, rather than the rainbow colors of the original hybrids. When planted in the Grassland, a reasonable percentage seem to persist for more than five years. Full-grown plants should be used for transplanting, or small plants should be "helped." The plant should be husky enough to send its foliage above the main mass of grass. I now find volunteer seedlings in Grassland, so the species can be considered promising for naturalization. Since it can be unsightly later in the season, one may wish to restrict it to Grassland edges.

The common garden Wild Indigo is *Baptisia australis*, native to the southeastern U.S. but naturalized in various places northwards. The flowers are deep blue. Other species of *Baptisia* are white or yellow. I find *Baptisia australis* excellently adapted for naturalization. Use garden-grown material, and plant a solid clump of it, at least 12 inches in diameter. The plant will form a conspicuous mound of foliage, rising above the general level of Grassland and thus seen at a distance. It is tall enough and dense enough to kill adjacent grasses, and even slowly to enlarge. The mound will be conspicuously green all summer, and a bright spot of blue in its season. Remember however that the foliage turns black with autumn frosts, and may then be an eyesore.

Thermopsis is a genus of hardy 1–3-foot-high plants somewhat like *Baptisia* in appearance, but yellow flowered, and with the foliage not turning black in autumn. Species are native to Siberia, to northwestern North America, and to the southern Appalachians. They are all worthy of investigation for naturalization. *T. caroliniana* is proving hardy and persistent.

The true Clovers belong to the genus *Trifolium*. You will probably know the white clover, *Trifolium repens*, from your lawn (unless you are one who uses 2,4-D for lawn-weed spraying, and kills all the clovers in the bargain). Since it is a low creeping plant, I have found it of no importance in Grassland. *Trifolium pratense*, Red Clover, is a European species, extensively planted and naturalized in North America. Farmers claim that it dies out after the second year, and this is probably true of lands planted to clover. On the other hand, I have found that after 19 years of no-mowing, no-grazing and no-burning, the red clover is an integral tho minor part of these Grasslands. Its flowering coincides with the peak of the daisy-buttercup-hawkweed season and adds one more shade to that riotous display.

The Sweet-Clovers belong to the genus *Melilotus*. *M. alba*, the White Sweet-Clover and *M. officinalis*, the Yellow Sweet-Clover, can both be found commonly along roadsides, often growing to weedy heights of 5 and 6 feet. Both are considered biennials, but one species has persisted in dense grassland, at an old house site, for a decade and a half, not spreading to other parts of the Grassland, and of no special attractiveness where it does occur, except to hordes of bees.

THE GERANIUMS
97. GERANIACEAE. B: 503. Gl II: 457

The cultivated "Geranium" belongs to the genus *Pelargonium* of this family. For naturalization purposes, the family has only one plant of interest, the Cranes-bill or Wild Geranium, *G. maculatum*, a wildflower that one almost always associates with shady roadsides and open woods. It is a perennial herb, with heavy rhizomes at the surface of the soil, and small attractive pink-purple flowers. There are some cultivated strains said to be "blue," and which are slightly bluer than the wild forms. Some years ago, I put some excess garden material into the Grassland, and to my surprise it is persisting and thriving. The foliage reaches up above the level of dense grass; the surficial rhizomes seem to receive winter protection from the mulch of dead grass (while those in the garden are often killed); and if the plants are placed 12 inches or so apart, a distinct color aspect prevails at that place, a color that is quite rare in Grassland. A few volunteer seedlings have been found in grass, so this plant may have a brilliant future.

THE MILKWORTS
108. POLYGALACEAE. B: 615. Gl II: 470

Fringed polygala, *Polygala paucifolia*, is a small woodland plant, a perennial creeping from a slender rhizome. Altho it partakes of many of the characters of low ground covers, its foliage is often too thin and sparse to be effective in that manner. It is worth introducing and encouraging for it may "take" and spread. Its small deep pink flowers can be a striking feature in the woodlands, and are so unusually formed that they repay close examination.

Polygala sanguinea is a plant of totally different appearance. It is a delicate small annual, a single stem 4–6 inches tall, surmounted by a tight head of pinkish scale-like flowers. Here is an exception to prove the rule that annuals have no place in a semi-natural Grassland. Despite the seeming illogic of the situation, this frail plant is found every year, in small quantities, in one part of a relatively thin Grassland. It flowers in the latter half of summer, when its contribution, tho minor, is appreciated by the keen observer.

THE SUMACHS AND RELATIVES
110. ANACARDIACEAE. B: 625. Gl II: 495

This is a temperate and tropical family, known to most people thru *Mangifera indica*, the Mango, *Anacardium occidentale*, the Cashew Nut, and *Pistacia vera*, the Pistachio Nut. In northeastern North America, we know it by *Cotinus* the Smoke Tree, and *Rhus*, the sumachs.

Rhus radicans (B.: not in; Gl II: 495), frequently called *Rhus toxicodendron*, is the Poison Ivy, unquestionably the most feared, most maligned, most tax-money-consuming plant of the Northeast (with the possible exception of ragweed). Yes, it is poisonous, to some people. On the other hand, it is certainly the innocent victim of much gossip and scandal, particularly on the part of those who make money by destroying it. The very mention of "poison ivy" is enough to start everyone in town on a program of eradication, at any price. And with it all, how many people really do recognize it? And could easily avoid it if they did recognize it? Alas, there is no one to sing its praises. It all goes to show what fear and insecurity are rooted in most of us.

Rhus radicans may be found, and even found commonly, in some of the areas you are landscaping. It so happens it is very rare in the lands I have most worked with, and I cherish each bit I have. It can be widely variable in form (so that taxonomists have joyfully created many named segregates). It may sprawl thinly thru the grass; it may form a thin ground cover in the forest; it may billow up and over stone walls; it may climb up tree trunks and festoon the trees. It is an excellent semi-shrubby ground cover in some places, stable and resistant to invasion by trees. The foliage turns a brilliant red in autumn and has decided value in that respect. The fruits dry and persist on the plants thru the winter, forming a most valuable food supply for wildlife, at a season when little else can be available. In areas frequented by the public, I have long recommended that it serve multiple purposes. With suitable signs, it can be used in educational and demonstration areas. These areas can be where human use has been excessive, and soil erosion is incipient or active, as on steep slopes or other spots from which the public should be barred. (My ideas have never been put into practice, to my knowledge.) Altogether, I very much like the plant. After all, one does not have to sun-bathe in a bed of it, in a bikini or less.

There is no question that many people are allergic to the oil in this plant, even to the oil that gets into the smoke of its burning wood. Drugstores carry many so-called remedies. If you know you have contacted the plant, wash yourself with much soap, as quickly as possible. The effects are worse in summer, with foliage on the plant, and sap in the stems. The federal government and state governments have ample literature on the plant. It is not difficult to eradicate it—and it should be eradicated—from areas where human use makes it distinctly undesirable. D–T sprays are useful. Tree-growing vines can be severed near the base. Water-borne sprays are reasonably effective. I would probably prefer oil-borne sprays, applied when the buds are opening in spring. Thereafter, I would keep after it as often as leaves appear, especially when it is running thru grass.

The impressive poison ivy elimination programs along our roadsides have always seemed to me one of the more interesting sociological phenonema of our age. I have talked to many highway officials on the subject. I have asked them what must seem like an insanely ridiculous question, "Why do you get rid of it?" They look at me, assuming I am not serious. I repeat the question. They look at me—differently. They answer with complete finality, "It is poison ivy," as tho no further explanation is necessary. Still I ask. "The public demands it." "Who taught the public to demand its destruction?" I ask. "Well, we can't risk the public getting poison ivy," they answer impatiently". "But does the public *ever* walk back in the brush on the side of the road, and on the tops of the stone walls?" That floors them for a moment, but then they say they cannot take any chances. Sooner or later one remembers that some other highway official had heard of some laborer who went to the the hospital with ivy poisoning, so he comes out with "We have to, or we would lose too many work-days in sick-leaves. It pays, to get rid of the stuff." Now in all these years, I have found only one highway official who seemed honest about the subject. It seems that he himself had been plagued with such sick-leaves by his work force—until he noticed that most of them started on Monday mornings. Thereafter, he does not hire men for road brush work who are unduly allergic; he gives every new man training in identification of the plant; and he claims that his men expect to be fined if they do come down with it, rather than get sick-leave. Point is, he has never had another case of ivy-poisoning, even tho the plant is common in his town. There are additional hazards for utility line workers along roadsides, altho even here, except for the areas close to the poles which can easily be kept free of poison ivy, I suspect that any poisoning is due to carelessness and failure to recognize. I strongly suspect that 95% of the roadside poison ivy, which has so many fine desirable characteristics, is the innocent victim of a human triangle, involving efficient purveyors of pesticides, acting thru willing and gullible political officials, preying upon citizens whose fears for an unknown plant are stronger than their concern for their tax dollars.

THE MALLOWS

122. MALVACEAE. B: 655. Gl II: 524

The mallows form a well-marked and distinct botanical family of herbs, shrubs and trees, occurring around the world in temperate and tropical regions. The flowers are easily recognized by having the filaments of the stamens united in a tube around the style. The anthers spread out at the top of the column in a fountain-like mass. The much-loved *Hibiscus* flowers of the tropics belong in this family, as does the fleshy mucilaginous capsule of the vegetable okra. In some, the seeds are hairy. Cotton (*Gossypium*) is in this category.

The Musk Mallow, *Malva moschata*, is a European perennial herb, commonly escaped from American gardens, and sometimes common on roadsides and open waste areas. Its abundance of flowers, white to pale purple, can be quite showy. The musk mallow does not appear to be tolerant of the competition in dense Grassland. Mature individuals can easily be transplanted however, and they are worth testing, with the immediately adjacent soil covered or mulched with leaves.

The Hollyhock, *Althaea rosea*, is one of the best-known plants of old-fashioned gardens. It is a tall-growing herb, readily flowering from seed the first year. In many cases, it is short-lived, and thus considered by some as a biennial. In gardens, it can grow to heights of 5 and 6 feet (and thus may require staking, or it will topple). Where established in the sterile soil of roadsides, it is shorter—and healthier in the sense of being able to stand by itself. The short-livedness of hollyhock and inability to seed into grass make it unsuitable for grassland naturalization. It is effective for short-term trial however.

THE ST. JOHNSWORTS

120. HYPERICACEAE. B: 675. Gl II: 536

This relatively small group of plants contains one species which should be known by every Wild Gardener at first glance, and probably destroyed at second glance. There is no other herbaceous plant mentioned in this book which in my opinion can be such an undesirable pest. The Common St. Johnswort, *Hypericum perforatum*, hails from Europe, and is now established over much of North America. It has become one of the most serious range pests in the West, poisonous to stock and occupying some lands to the exclusion of all other plants. It is combatted by chemical, biological and mechanical means. It spreads by new seedlings, and by slender stolons on the surface. One clump of it may look attractive in your Grassland, when in yellow blossom. But then the flower clusters get to look ratty and motheaten and stay that way for a long time. I had been watching it with caution, for it had been spreading. Then one year I realized, almost too late, that it was becoming a dominant, filtering all thru the Grassland as young small plants, and growing up to form dense solid masses of foliage to the exclusion of all other plants. In its way, it is quite a remarkable vegetation development, unreported in the botanical literature. The plant is very susceptible to D–T water-spraying, but the control work was far more costly of time than if the plant had been attacked in its early stages of invasion. Old-fashioned pulling, being sure to get the roots, has many advantages over spraying.

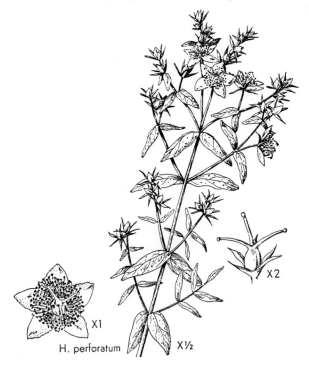

X1   X2

H. perforatum   X½

THE VIOLETS
133. VIOLACEAE. B: 682. Gl II: 552

As a family, this group of plants contains herbs, shrubs and even trees. We are likely to know it however thru only one genus, the herbaceous *Viola*. Within *Viola*, there is one old friend whom we may not have recognized as such, *V. tricolor* var. *hortensis*, otherwise known as the Pansy. A pansy is nothing more than an oversized violet, without the spur, probably of hybrid origin from ancient gardens of Europe. The pansy rarely survives a winter in northeast U.S., and is not useful for naturalization.

A wild European species, probable ancestor of the cultivated pansy, is widely escaped in North America, where it is known as Johnny-Jump-Up, *Viola tricolor*, from its habit of jumping up as volunteer seedlings in garden and lawn. Tho Gleason refers to it as an annual, I have numerous plants which survive the winters. The flowers are miniature replicas of a pansy. I only wish it would jump up in the Grassland, but it does not.

The wild violets offer many interesting opportunities to the Naturalistic Landscaper, but their way of living must be understood. Early in spring the bright and attractive flowers appear. These are mainly for show. If they have some function in the total life history—other than self-enjoyment—scientists have not discovered it. Unquestionably in the evolutionary history of the species, they served for sexual reproduction; but with the function lost, the activity remained, to give pleasure—at least to us. Later in the season, colorless closed apetalous flowers appear, close to the ground or actually within it. These are self-fertilized, and produce seed. Violets tend to spread rapidly, either from seed, or by rhizomes. Some become weedy in the garden. It is the summer foliage, which must develop unhindered, that assures the health and life of the plant. Closely related species readily hybridize, and these in turn produce viable seed. Some hybrids are quite aggressive in their reproduction. The end result of this way of living on the part of the violets is that altho the major species are fairly distinct (Gleason recognizes 51 for northeastern U.S.), what you yourself may be growing may not by any means be a typical example of any one of the 51.

Viola rotundifolia, the Round-leaved Yellow Violet, is a woodland species, flowering far ahead of any of the others. Later, the glossy leaves enlarge, lie close to the ground, and many people do not even recognize them as violets.

Viola pedata, the Bird-foot Violet is another distinctive species, with dark purple flowers, coming late in the season. You might find it does well in sunny grassless woods.

Unmowed grassland by its nature is not conducive to the growth of violets. Their low-growing foliage is covered over by the grass, and the plants soon vanish. I have found that mowing three times a year greatly encourages *Viola conspersa*, a species with such low foliage that the mowing machine passes over it, while clipping off the grass that would otherwise shade it. The position of some trails is visible in spring, before any mowing, by the abundance of this species.

Viola sororia is a fairly husky species with foliage of sufficient height to maintain itself in competition with the grasses. This species I find occasionally in the Grassland. Small individuals readily respond to any adjacent mulching out, that will give them a competitive edge.

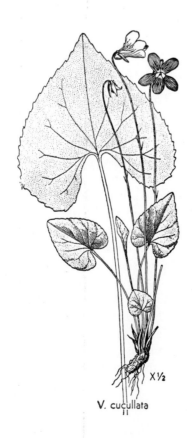

X ½

V. cucullata

185

THE LOOSESTRIFES
143. LYTHRACEAE. B: 718. Gl II: 575

The loosestrifes comprise a relatively small family of herbs shrubs and trees, most abundant in the tropics. People living in the southeastern U.S. know it from the widely planted shrub *Lagerstroemia indica*, the Crepe Myrtle. In the Northeast, it comes to our attention only thru one plant:

The Purple Loosestrife, *Lythrum salicaria*, is widely planted and exists in various horticultural varieties. Its native home is a wide area in Eurasia, but it has escaped in many parts of the Northeast. It has become so abundant in certain low areas such as river margins, swamp edges, and wet meadows that it has displaced a considerable amount of native vegetation. This plant community presents a striking carpet of rose-purple in its season. It is a rugged 3-foot perennial, with such stout stems as to remain erect far into the following season. This situation may be interesting if in small patches, but if one has several acreas of the stuff, one's attitude can change. Altho it does well in upland gardens, if placed in an upland Grassland it does not thrive satisfactorily unless given some protection from competing grasses.

THE EVENING PRIMROSES
150. ONAGRACEAE. B: 733. Gl II: 580

A small but distinctive New World family. For our interest, attention centers upon the true evening-primroses *Oenothera*. This genus is notable in botanical history for having been used by DeVries in his classical mutation studies, studies extended by American workers. *Oenothera* is self-fertilizing. Mutations frequently occur. These mutations result in a vast number of geographically isolated races that only rarely are interfertile. The ordinary "species concept" barely applies. The common and weedy *Oenothera biennis* is strictly a biennial and of no significance in mown Grassland.

Oenothera missouriensis is a low herb with showy yellow flowers 5 inches across, said to occur as a native only in dry limestone areas of the grassland states of North America. Its roots are thick and fleshy. It is worth investigation in our northeastern Grasslands. If the plant can be nurtured to the extent that its root system allows it to send its foliage above the competing grass, it may well prove persistent.

THE GINSENGS

152. ARALIACEAE. B: 742. Gl II: 603

A relatively small family, containing some well known members. *Panax quinquefolium* is the wild ginseng, collected (to the point of extinction) and cultivated (with difficulty) for export to the Orient, where it is valued for healing purposes, dependent upon the shape of the root. Tho most Americans disdain such age-old superstitions, their continued interest in this plant is interesting. "It could have medicinal value," they rationalize—as could any other plant. *Aralia spinosa* is the southeastern Hercules' Club, grown northwards for the oddity of its thick clublike branches. *Hedera helix* includes the English ivies, which I might find naturalizing, except for rabbits. *Aralia racemosa* is the American spikenard, a 5-foot herbaceous plant with fleshy roots, and berries liked by the birds. It grows vigorously in the garden, but I have not had it succeed when left in Grassland. *Aralia nudicaulis* is the common wild sarsaparilla, so-called because of the flavor of the underground parts. It occasionally may creep out into the Grassland by surficial rhizomes. In my opinion it has no landscaping value. It can be killed by repeated foliage-burning with an oil-base herbicide spray, or by mowing with a garden sickle.

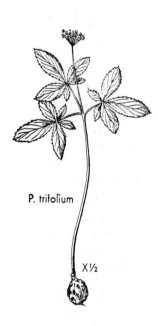

P. trifolium

X½

THE PARSLEYS AND RELATIVES

153. UMBELLIFERAE. B: 747. Gl II: 606

The parsley family is a large and very distinctive botanical group of about 300 genera and maybe 3,000 species, mostly herbs. The flowers occur in a distinct type of inflorescence called an umbel (with many branches arising from the same point), and each fruit is a small double unit separable into two parts each called a "seed." Actually, each is a single seed tightly surrounded by the ovary wall, thus making it a "fruit."

The family contains many plants commonly known. We eat the foliage of parsley and lovage, and the leaf stalks (petioles) of celery. We eat the fleshy roots of the biennial carrot and parsnip. And we season our foods with the aromatic oils in the fruits of dill, caraway, cumin, fennel and anise. Finally, we can kill ourselves with hemlock as did Socrates, under inducement.

Unfortunately for landscaping purposes, most of the umbellifers are annuals or biennials, and thus unsuited for naturalization in dense grassland.

The only attractive grassland species that has come to my attention is the Golden Alexander, *Zizia aurea*. The bright yellow inflorescences occur early in spring and are an attractive addition to the landscape. The foliage develops early in the season, ahead of the grasses. Young plants would benefit by protection from adjacent grasses.

The Goutweed is *Aegopodium podagraria*, a plant of old-fashioned gardens that often escaped and ran rampant under the shrubbery. Its aggressiveness is related to long and husky rhizomes. The flowers are more or less white, and one wonders why it was cultivated. Put in the Grassland, it promptly refuses to flower, but its rhizomes do spread out thru the grass, sending up single low leaves. I consider it a pest in the true sense of the word. Repeated burning of the foliage with an oil-base herbicide spray, or hand pulling, seems to be the only way to eradicate it. It is worth eradicating.

Levisticum officinale, the lovage, deserves more attention. It is a large celery-like plant, long persistent in abandoned gardens. The seeds, young foliage and foliage-stalks have a strong but excellent flavor for salads soups and other dishes. It is definitely worth planting in the Grassland, but if your plants are small, give them some mulching protection from adjacent competition.

An herbicide-managed forest-edge. Paper birch (*Betula papyrifera*) and flowering laurel (*Kalmia latifolia*), with a foreground of hay-scented fern (*Dennstaedtia punctilobula*).

160. PRIMULACEAE. B: 776. Gl III: 34

One of the Loosestrifes of the genus *Lysimachia* is *L. punctata*, an old garden plant rarely mentioned these days. It is a pubescent herb, to 3 feet tall, increasing slowly by short stocky rhizomes, that has often escaped to roadsides. The author found it in central New York state, brought it back, and finds it a hardy persistent plant with a very long flowering season that reaches its peak in early summer, when the entire plant appears ablaze with yellow flowers. It would appear to be able to maintain itself once it is established in Grassland.

Steironema ciliatum, another Loosestrife, is a native species, spreading by underground rhizomes, and colonial in nature. I have various patches of it, 10 to 40 feet in diameter, not dense enough to kill out other plants, but concentrated enough to form attractive yellow masses when it is in flower in early summer. It is not spreading aggressively; it is difficult to kill out with herbicides (indeed, it, and especially a close relative *Lysimachia quadrifolia*, increase on oversprayed rightofways when other plants are killed); and altho the foliage is not too attractive when not in flower, in small areas it is not objectionable. All in all, *Steironema ciliatum* is a desirable plant, within limits.

X1¼

S. ciliatum   X½

THE GENTIANS

168. GENTIANACEAE. B: 804. Gl III: 54

The word gentian to many people brings to mind the highly valued fringed gentian, *Gentiana crinita*. Unfortunately, *G. crinita* is a biennial, and perpetuates itself only if there is an ample supply of new seedlings each year. To have seedlings one must have relatively bare soil. In nature, the requirements for fringed gentian are met in swamps and lowlying areas. They are also met on roadsides (unsprayed of course), and on such unlikely places as the bare fill of some railway embankments. The propagation of fringed gentian is now thoroly understood, and to the gardener it is stated as being "easy" (for a gardener). One can also encourage it by properly scratching around in small spots in open grassland, but that for me comes quite close to "gardening." Much as we may like fringed gentian, it is not a plant of unmowed grasslands.

The Bottle Gentian, *G. andrewsii*, is another matter. This plant is unusual in that its blue flowers, a welcome sight in fall when few other plants are blooming, never open—whence the name. Bees force their way into the tops of the flowers; then maybe forgetting, or choosing an easier exit, bite their way out at the base of the flower. The escape hatches are often seen. This is a long-lived perennial. I have had one cultivated plant persist since transplanting about 30 years ago. Volunteer seedlings are not infrequent (if you do not mow your lawn too often). Tho said to be a plant of low moist areas, it seems perfectly happy in ordinary uplands. Young plants do not survive in grassland. Either protect them from grass competition for several years until their root systems are large, or cultivate them in the garden until they are well-developed.

THE DOGBANES

169. APOCYNACEAE. B: 808. Gl III: 69

This family is mainly tropical. It includes the unforgettably fragrant frangipani (*Plumeria*), as well as the too-commonly planted oleander.

In the north, the group comes to our attention thru *Vinca minor*, the Periwinkle, with lilac-blue flowers, occasionally white flowers. Vinca minor gives us possibly our most valuable evergreen ground cover, certainly for shady places. If you plant it, and wish it to spread, do not stretch the runners to their full length, and poke in the ends, hoping to cover the most ground. Frost heaves out such attempts. Rather, let the plant develop a compact mass of vegetation, and allow this compact mass to extend out more slowly. Slow but sure, in this game.

Apocynum androsaemifolium, the spreading dogbane, is a totally different sort of creature. The plant will spread thru open sunny grasslands by deep underground rhizomes. It will send up gawky stalks, surmounted by flat foliage somewhat like a bracken fern. Tho when it flowers (which is rarely, in the Grassland) the small flowers are fragrant, I consider the plant an undesirable weed. There seems to be no way of killing it except by repeated pulling, or foliage-burning with an oil spray. Keep spraying even when the leaves are miniature and but a few inches high. Once completely rootkilled, you need no longer worry.

THE MILKWEEDS

170. ASCLEPIADACEAE. B: 814. Gl III: 72

This family, tho very closely related to the preceding Apocynaceae, is a highly distinctive botanical assemblage with very few plants of either horticultural or medicinal value. In the flowers that one sees, the perianth is small drooping and inconspicuous. The colorful parts are an elaborately developed crown, arising between the petals and the stamens, and itself composed of a stalk-like limb, with spoon-shaped hoods within which are small horns. The male and female parts within the crown are themselves highly and interestingly modified.

The Butterfly Weed, *Asclepias tuberosa*, with bright orange (sometimes yellow) flowers, is a most extraordinary plant that holds one of the most unique and valuable roles in Naturalistic Landscaping. I cannot overemphasize the importance of becoming acquainted with its bright and unusual color just at that time of late summer when we feel sad that all the flush of the season is over. One refuses to think that autumn is not far ahead, and desperately needs some pyschologic assurance that the season is still in full swing. This plant supplies a two-fold biologic interest. It has a unique ability for attracting butterflies of the kind known as fritillaries, bright brown spotted ones that otherwise are not often seen. They cluster on the plants in large numbers, and on one's approach the group literally explodes, until one is surrounded with the fluttering forms.

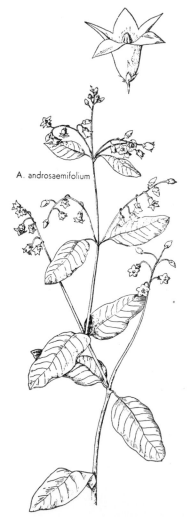

A. androsaemifolium

In nature, butterfly weed holds a strange position. It is not uncommon along rough roadsides, railway embankments, and abandoned fields. It looks "common" only because the flowers are such conspicuous beacons in the landscape. In number of individuals, I suspect it is "rare." If one digs these up carefully enough to get the entire root system (I rarely succeed, which is probably well, for then the plant remains to grow again), a surprise is in store. The roots are thick, fleshy, contorted, as tho a chimpanzee were making pretzels. This root shape is extraordinarily significant—if one knows normal seedling development. To my knowledge, it has never been described or interpreted in the ecological literature. It is my opinion that this species in nature very very rarely starts from seed. Once started however, it is extremely persistent. The plants we see in nature, considering their sites and distorted roots, have survived constructional and agricultural operations by man, ploughed over, bulldozed out, carried in fill, to flower again. To estimate their age is difficult. I would not be surprised if some of them date from colonial days.

In the garden you may grow Butterfly Weed either from seed or from sections of the root. Seedlings develop rapidly, with a remarkably deep carrot-like taproot. Plant them out in the Grassland after one year, or you will probably sever the taproot in transplanting. In using root sections, take pieces several inches long, and plant them vertically. I am not sure, but apparently some of the horizontal roots "in nature" are due to soil movements by man. Once in the Grassland, give them protection from competing grasses for a few years. Then sit back, and know that your great grandchildren will enjoy them—barring housing developments.

Asclepias syriaca is the Common Milkweed. It is native to this country, despite its epithet. I understand that when Linnaeus described this species, herbarium labels got mixed, and he thought this came from Syria. By the nomenclatural rules of priority, the original name must stand, even if inappropriate. A sensible rule, for a name is only a name. I am sure that there have been many members of the Ku Klux Klan by the name of Black, who never thought of petitioning the courts for a change.

A. syriaca has greenish purple flowers that are highly fragrant. A colony of these plants can scent the air as few other plants can do. They also attract myriads of butterflies. Unlike *A. tuberosa*, the common milkweed spreads by underground rhizomes, forming colonies. In my observations, these colonies are not long-lived. They tend to thin out after 5 to 10 years.

The plant is extremely resistant to herbicides. It is one of those to persist on roadsides that have been sprayed and sprayed with herbicides, contrary to all dictates of common sense, science and dollar economy. With other wildflowers destroyed, the milkweed carries on, its big leathery leaves drooping, and with no flowers of its own—a fitting symbol for the herbicide hucksters that have perpetrated this folly on the American people.

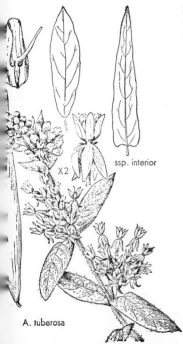

ssp. interior

X2

A. tuberosa

193

THE MORNING-GLORIES

171. CONVOLVULACEAE. B: 818. Gl III: 85

Many of us know this family from *Ipomoea batatas*, the Sweet Potato, from which we eat the tuberous starchy root; and *I. purpurea* the common Morning-Glory, an annual vine. The farmer more often knows the family from the common Bindweed, *Convolvulus sepium*, one of his most pernicious pests, spreading by fleshy underground parts that seem to defy all attempts to kill them. In the garden, this same *C. sepium* is called Rutland Beauty, until it starts spreading. Then you use the farmer's name—or worse. I am not sure it is a pest in unmowed grassland: I have given it no chance to become one. It will spread, and snarl up the grasses, seldon flowering. I know no means of control short of repeated foliage-burns with oil-based herbicides, or simple pulling.

THE PHLOXES

172. POLEMONIACEAE. B: 823. Gl III: 94

In this relatively small family, the genus *Phlox* is important to Naturalistic Landscapers, with several species holding very different roles.

Phlox subulata, the Moss Pink, can form a very dense tight almost moss-like ground cover even on sterile soils, which in spring become one of the most perfect blankets of pure color that a plant can produce. Pink was the original color, but we now have forms in white, red, and something which looks blue when it is next to pink. With a bit of weeding, this plant can be induced to form pure stands which thereafter are quite stable. It grows outward six inches a year, but not densely enough to kill out the plants it grows over. I have found that by laying strips of asphalt shingles around the clump, the phlox grows out over the shingle. The next year I pull the shingle out a bit; the phlox settles down and roots, and grows out over the new position. Sometimes I have laid down canvas or heavy cloth in a narrow strip around the clump. The phlox grows out over it, and roots down thru it. Left to itself in the Grassland, it seems to persist, meandering sparsely thru the grass.

Phlox divaricata, a Wild Phlox, is a 24-inch-high native with light blue flowers. It spreads by creeping shoots. It is not quite suitable for dense grassland, but can easily be kept in pure clumps at the forest edge. There are various other native phloxes, some of which may be suited for introduction in grassland.

Phlox paniculata is the well-known Garden Phlox. It is highly valuable because of its late flowering season, coming in at the end of the summer, before the first goldenrods. New horticultural hybrids have much improved the color range and flower size, without apparent loss of vigor, or fragrance. The Symons-Jeune hybrids from England are preferred by many. Colors range from white thru lilac to purple, and white thru buff, salmon, pink, to scarlet. Many are eyed, with darker centers. Seed is fertile; I find volunteer seedlings fairly often, even in the Grassland. The flowers of these are small, less fragrant, and of a strong magenta color which phloxophilists think is ugly. Such a plant can be encouraged to form a large dense solid clump, extremely hardy, and long-lived (I have one that is 30 years old). It would be immensely admired if it were rare and wild. The flowering periods of these volunteer seedlings can vary greatly. By selection, you may rejoice to find some that are unusually early, and others that are unusually late.

THE BORAGES

174. BORAGINACEAE. B: 830. Gl III: 109

Here is a family which can frequently, but not always, be recognized by small flowers arranged in a compact spike that appears to be curled at the end, like an unfolding fern frond. I know of no members of the family of outstanding value for Naturalistic Landscaping, tho a few have possibilities. *Mertensia virginica*, the native Bluebells, may do well and spread in a grassless forest edge. The foliage dies to the ground in late summer, so that one must mark the spot, in preliminary trials. *Myosotis scorpoides* is the true Forget-me-not of Europe, which is likely to spread very enthusiastically along any streamside to which you introduce it. *Echium vulgare* is the Viper's Bugloss, a biennial European weed that makes quite a showing on some waste lands. It is too prickly-hispid for one to handle, and I have not known it able to invade unmown grassland.

THE MINTS

176. LABIATAE. B: 847, Gl III: 139

Here is a remarkable group of plants, world-wide in distribution, with over 3,500 species. The flowers are not large and showy, but if they were ten times as large they would be some of the finest in the garden, for complex coloring and variety in form. Labiates are unique because of oil glands in the stems and foliage which give highly distinctive odors and tastes much used in flavoring and medicine. It is in this family that we find pennyroyal, lavender, marjoram, hoarhound, peppermint, spearmint, catnip, basil, rosemary, sage, savory and thyme. Regretfully, most of the desirable aromatic herbs are only annuals in northeastern U.S., or survive only under garden cultivation. There are significant exceptions however.

Nepeta hederacea, Gill-over-the-Ground, a Eurasian mat-forming spreading herb with bright blue spring flowers. It is easily naturalized in somewhat shady places. In a garden, it spreads too rapidly to be desired. It has one desirable feature however which is generally overlooked: the leaves stay healthy and bright green long after other things are dead with frost. For this reason, I have allowed it to fill up the strips between widely spaced flagstones. When it spreads out over the stones, I "clip it back" by the simple expedient of lifting the stone, and dropping it back in place on the plant.

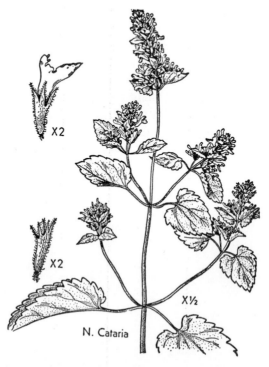

X2

X2

X½

N. Cataria

Prunella vulgaris, the Heal-All, is a cosmopolitan weed of lawns and other waste places. In the mowed grassland trails I find that it adds a minor tho significant element of color. It does not survive in the unmown grass.

The False Dragonhead, *Physostegia (Dracocephalum) virginiana*, is a desirable native species, growing 2–3 feet high, and bearing spikes of bright pink flowers late in summer. It spreads by sturdy underground rhizomes. If the plant is kept concentrated in a compact mass, it will be a solid mound of color in its season. Left to itself, it will wander off, flowering occasionally especially in low moist areas.

The Monardas or Horse-Mints have much to be said in their favor. There are two basic native species, the red *M. didyma*, Oswego Tea, or Bee Balm, and the lavender *M. fistulosa*, Wild Bergamot. There are now several horticultural strains in various shades of pink that are worth trying. The Monardas are highly attractive to hummingbirds.

M. fistulosa much enlivens our roadsides in late summer. Sometimes it is abundant to the point of being weedy in agricultural lands. It can be encouraged to form a solid clump, which in turn keeps out other plants. The clump expands by a compact mat of slender rhizomes just under the surface. This expansion can be encouraged by applying a mulch around the clump, which kills out the adjacent grasses, and allows the Monarda rhizomes to grow into it. A few clumps of these plants, strategically placed, will add bold color to your grassland.

M. didyma, with particularly striking scarlet flowers, seems to do better in moist soil, and in shade. The rhizomes are aggressive, and the plant is likely to wander off farther than what you would like.

I introduced both Monardas to my own property, where neither had occurred before. Several years later, I had set out some volunteer garden seedlings. Two proved to be *Monarda media*—on this evidence, of hybrid origin—intermediate between the two in color and in season of blossoming. It has not proved as aggressive as either parent species, but desirable for our purposes.

Satureja vulgaris, the Wild Basil, is an inconspicuous native mint, with small pink flowers and a long flowering season. It occurs sporadically all thru my unmowed Grasslands. This *Satureja* affords an interesting minor note for one with searching eyes, but it does not seem to be worth any gardening effort.

Origanum vulgare of Europe, the Wild Marjoram, is a small little mint with clusters of purplish flowers. I have seen it along some roadsides sufficiently abundant and colorful to warrant attention. I have not however been able to convince it to grow equally well on my own land.

Thymus serpyllum from Europe, Wild Thyme, is a low mat-forming almost-woody plant that can form a carpet of pink-purple in summer, highly attractive to bees. Unlike other mat-forming plants, the branches do not root readily, and continue to be dependent on the main taproot. This factor is important in transplanting: one does not cut out a chunk of sod as tho it were quackgrass. The hardy, winter cold in snowless seasons can all but eliminate it. It is an interesting plant, but not adapted for thriving in unmown grass.

The native *Pycnanthemum flexuosum*, Mountain Mint, tends to be two feet tall, with solid clusters of cream-colored flowers rising above the general level of the Grassland. Once established, it is indefinitely persistent, with the clump slowly enlarging. If it spread by seedlings, I would probably consider it a pest, but a few plants are desirable. If grown in bare soil, it is found to spread by a mat of numerous small rhizomes.

The Menthas are the true Mints. *Mentha spicata* is the Spearmint of Europe, cultivated, and widely escaped. It spreads actively by rhizomes at the soil surface, especially in slightly shady and moist places.

The Peppermint is *Mentha piperita*, believed to have originated by hybridization in Europe. The author has a cultivated strain in his garden, possibly of normal aggressiveness. It has formed such a dense mat of vegetation that for 16 years nothing has been able to invade it except *Rumex acetosella* the Sorrel. Furthermore, the rhizomes are such a pest that he had to enclose the bed literally with an iron curtain six inches high, half of it below the soil surface. He once tossed a basket of cleanings onto a fertile-soiled quackgrass area. They rooted. The quack grass, because of tall lush growth, falls over in late summer. They the Peppermint spreads up and over it.

THE FIGWORTS

179. SCROPHULARIACEAE. B: 881. Gl III: 206

If you know the flowers of the florist's snapdragon (*Antir-rhinum*) you will probably be able to recognize many other "scrophs." Most of them show family resemblances, noticeable even to the untrained non-botanical eye. Very few, unfortunately, have shown any suitability for the Wild Gardener.

The Veronicas, genus *Veronica*, include a large number of small-flowered ground-covering plants, that may occasionally meander thru your Grassland, but none to be concerned about. The European *Veronica longifolia* however, just one more Speedwell, is quite different in appearance, growing erect to heights of 2 feet, with narrow spikes of blue flowers. I have seen it abundant in a horse pasture, where the animals did not graze it. In unmowed grassland however, it deteriorates. Presumably, it needs to be given a handicap against competing adjacent vegetation, such as by a few flat stones around it, or a leaf mulch.

Verbascum thapsus is the common mullein, a true biennial. Most people know the thickly velvety cluster of basal leaves. The following year there is a tall 6–7 foot stalk with small yellow flowers on it. It is a pest in some places, but if you see a few small ones in your Grassland, do not worry. There will probably not be more. Consider yourself lucky if you have *Verbascum phlomoides*, a rare European escape with handsome large flowers.

The cultivated Foxgloves, *Digitalis purpurea*, would make quite a showing in Grassland, but they are either biennial or very short-lived. They are known to have escaped, and are worth investigation.

An old-fashioned garden and roadside species is the late-summer-flowering Butter-and-Eggs, *Linaria vulgaris*, an unusual combination of yellow and orange. In the garden, it can become quite a pest, spreading by underground rhizomes, and difficult to eradicate. If in your Grassland, it has probably spread widely already, but does not flower. Fortunately, the small vegetative shoots are not undesirable, for it would be very difficult to eradicate this plant. I have had it flower only at one place, an ancient house site, where possibly the soil acidity is still affected by buried concrete.

THE MADDERS

187. RUBIACEAE. B: 925. Gl III: 274

Coffee, quinine, and the ornamental gardenia belong to this family, which in the Northeast gives us only two groups of importance.

The Bedstraws in the genus *Galium* are slender-stemmed herbs that tend to pile up in filmy masses. Flowers are either yellow (*Galium verum*, an escaped European species), or white. Of the white species, the escaped European, *G. mollugo*, and the native *G. boreale* are common. They will persist in unmowed grassland, but they will make their best display if concentrated in small dense masses.

The Partridge-Berry, *Mitchella repens*, is a native woodland evergreen ground cover with bright red berries. It much deserves a bit of encouragement in the forest.

Bluets, *Houstonia caerulea*, is a little tuft of a small-foliaged plant that is covered with pale blue flowers in spring, and on into early summer. If you have a shady stretch of lawn (and do not compel yourself to mow it every few days), this may be a most attractive addition. And yet I know some people who pursue it with a vindictiveness, and with all manner of chemical sprays, that borders on the pathologic—just because it is not common ordinary lawn grass. In my thrice-yearly mowed grassland trails, *Houstonia* is encouraged, and becomes conspicuously frequent. Surprisingly, it is not mulched out in the unmowed Grassland. Tho scattered and sparse here, its spring flowers are an integral part of the total picture.

THE GOURDS

191. CUCURBITACEAE. B: 950. Gl III: 311

Here is a family of annual and perennial tendril-bearing vines. From Old World antiquity comes the Watermelon (*Citrullus*), the Cucumber and the Canteloupe (both in *Cucumis*), and the Gourd (*Lagenaria*). Pumpkins and Squashes (*Cucurbita*) are from America.

Herbaceous vines do not play much of a role in Naturalistic Landscaping, but some day try *Echinocystis lobata*, wild cucumber. Once it becomes established, it will probably reseed itself each year. This annual will grow up over shrubs, and in season will cover them with a filmy blanket of small white flowers. Later, the weak-spined 2-inch-long fruits will open and drop the large seeds—unless the blue jays have already pulled them out. If you have a bare spot in your grassland (by moving a flat stone you had previously placed there) poke in a few Echinocystis seeds, and a piece of peabrush, such as gray birch branches. The vine will clamber up the brush and then, after the flush of grass growth is over, roll over the Grassland as if it were a carpet.

THE BELLFLOWERS

192. CAMPANULACEAE. B: 958. Gl III: 314

A relatively small family best known for the garden bellflowers of the genus *Campanula*. The family also contains the east Asiatic Balloon-Flower (so named from the inflated flower buds), *Platycodon grandiflorum*. The color is basically blue, but horticultural strains are now known in shades varying to white. Volunteer seedlings are common in the garden. The plant is fleshy-rooted, and long-lived. Altho small plants are literally swallowed up in unmowed grassland, larger plants give some promise of surviving without attention, if you can keep them from the attention of small hungry mammals, who seems perversely (our viewpoint) to seek out the slightly fleshy foliage.

THE LOBELIAS

193. LOBELIACEAE. B: 969. Gl III: 318

Another relatively small cosmopolitan family, with only one native genus, *Lobelia*. The lobelias are relatively small plants with slender spikes of flowers. *L. cardinalis*, the Cardinal-Flower, is considered a rare native plant, tho I have found it abundant along forested stream sides. The flowers are one of the most glowing reds in the entire plant world. It transplants easily, but is apparently not long-lived. The critical foliage is mainly basal, and thus it is not suited for grasslands. Volunteer seedlings have been found in the garden where a stretch of clear ground is available. New plants will arise from the nodes of a flowering stalk if pinned to the soil.

Lobelia siphilitica, so named because of a supposed medicinal value, upon which I do not recommend your reliance, is a striking blue-flowered species well worth investigation.

Lobelia spicata seems to have attained a permanent status in my Grasslands, sparsely distributed, but remaining the same year after year. The slender pale blue spikes add a minor but much appreciated note to the yearly progression of flowers.

THE COMPOSITES
194. COMPOSITAE. B: 973. Gl III: 323

Finally we come to the *Compositae*, that culminate the sequence of dicots in much the way that the orchids culminate the monocots. The family has probably more than 15,000 species. Since the orchids are mainly tropical, the composites generally rank as the largest family of temperate regions. So varied are they in the Northeast, almost one-half of the third volume of Gleason's manual is devoted to this family alone.

The gardener knows this family by zinnia, cosmos, dahlia, marigold, ageratum, chrysanthemum, and many others. Among its wild flowers are daisies, blackeyed susans, goldenrods, sunflowers and asters. The original prairies and plains of interior North America often blazed with flowers of this family.

It is unique in other ways also. The flowers are generally extremely small, and aggregated into dense heads. Each head tends to simulate a flower, with radiating "petals." It is only the layman who picks "petals" off a daisy! The next time you do so, look closely. You will find that each "petal" is a complete flower, with all five petals united into a large flat white strap. Next time you put a daisy in her hair, let her know it is an entire bouquet.

The Chicory, *Cichorium intybus*, B: 982, Gl III: 539, is a Eurasian species, sometimes cultivated for its roots, used as a substitute for coffee. It is widely escaped in North America. Most people know it from its abundance along roadsides. Actually it thrives under occasional mowing, flowering in between cuttings and turning the landscape blue with its abundant flowers. Certain highway-men have been talked into believing it is a weed that should be sprayed out, but that is only because citizens who have the knowledge do not talk as loudly as the herbicide salesmen. *C. intybus*, (first cousin to *C. endivia*, the endive) is a long tap-rooted perennial. It is difficult to transplant. I have had no seedlings appear in the garden. It is worth the attempt to try to naturalize it in grassland, for its blue flowers are of an unusual color.

Salsify, *Tragopogon pratensis*, B: 983, Gl III: 544, is generally known as an escaped European roadside weed, that sends up large yellow heads to a height of 3–4 feet. Unless you get out in early morning, you may never see its attractive flowers, for they are closed by noon. The fruits however, are conspicuous, and may make you wonder what preceded them. I have had the plant appear in part of my unmown Grassland so I assume it is at least a short-lived perennial. The foliage is grasslike and sparse, and thus it is a desirable addition to the vegetation.

The Dandelion, *Taraxacum officinale*, B: 984, G. III: 532, is unquestionably one of the more successful plants of the world. It is native to Europe, but it is now widely naturalized, from near-Arctic areas to tropical mountains. It used to be cultivated, and still is, for the greens make a bitter salad. Immigrants to America knew and valued it. Even in the 1920's I recall seeing Italian women in New York city lots, digging up baskets of it in spring, using a penknife so as to get part of the root. The bases of the leaves taste particularly fine. In the 30's and early 40's the grassy strips on the sides of our highways were sometimes a solid sheet of gold, unquestionably a magnificent sight. That has all now vanished, banished, thanks to the efficiency of our herbicide hucksters on the highway officials who spend our taxes. In lawns, it probably has to be considered an undesirable weed, for despite the beauty of its flowers, its gawky foliage is unattractive for the rest of the year. No American housewife will stoop to cut it for the salad bowl when the spouse can "easily" spray it. As for its position in an unmowed Grassland: it is there, but very rare. The importance of the basal leaves in the growth of the plant is such that fewer of them start, and fewer survive. If you love the lowly dandelion, I would suggest you encourage the few plants you may have by laying some mulches around them. They respond handsomely.

The Hawkweeds, *Hieracium*, B: 984, Gl III: 522, represent another group of extreme beauty, easily grown and very hardy. They made the mistake of becoming "bad" weeds under certain agricultural conditions, and that attitude has spread to situations remote from cropland uses, such as certain roadsides, where highway officials pursue the plants with neurotic and unintelligent vindictiveness. The hawkweeds are characterized by a flat basal rosette of leaves, with bright orange or yellow flowers topping long stalks. They respond favorably to mowing, which cuts off the grass that would otherwise blanket them out. They used to predominate in the mowed strips along some highways. I recall one instance where the frequent mowing close to the pavement and less frequent mowing farther up the slopes resulted in the segregation of two species so that two brightly colored bands paralleled the highway. In the mowed trails thru my own Grassland, *H. aurantiacum*, the orange Devil's Paintbrush, is encouraged, and blossoms after the June first mowing in such greater abundance that it often demarcates the trail. Both this species and a Yellow Hawkweed, *H. pratense*, are considerably discouraged by the annual mulch of an unmown Grassland. Enough remains however to add some glorious color to that explosive display of the daisy-buttercup season. They are never pests.

Chrysanthemums

Chrysanthemum. B: 985. Gl III: 385

This genus of Old World northern species contains the huge florist's chrysanthemums of the football season. There are other forms of interest to landscaping.

C. coccineum, originally from southwest Asia, is commonly known as Pyrethrum, or painted daisy. It is a popular garden perennial, with flowers in a wide range of tones from white to red, and finely cut foliage. It is either short-lived or not entirely hardy in cold snowless winters, but worth further investigation.

C. nipponicum from Japan, the Nippon Daisy, is an extremely hardy late-blooming daisy-like plant that is a subshrub. It does not kill back entirely to the ground each year. I have seen it blossom magnificently in some parts of the Northeast. In my own locale however, the deep frosts get it first.

C. leucanthemum is the true Ox-eye Daisy of Europe and Asia, widely naturalized in the Northeast in a form that the botanists choose to segregate as var. *pinnatifidum*. There is no finer component of our semi-naturalized grasslands. I have had it persist for 20 years in unmown fields. Each plant is slender, with only a few flowers, but the total effect in season is to dot the fields with their gay blooms. After flowering, the foliage is not sufficiently abundant to be visible. If you wish to encourage any single plant by blotting out the immediately adjacent vegetation, you will find that the plant develops into a huge mound bearing 50 to 100 blossoms.

C. maximum, originally from the Pyrenees, has been developed in large-flowered forms known as the Shasta Daisy. All that I have tried have been short-lived perennials and unsuited for naturalistic landscaping.

C. morifolium, the chrysanthemum of commerce, is an ancient cultigen from the Orient, probably originally of hybrid ancestry. It includes the various strains of Hardy Chrysanthemums, not all of which are really hardy. But even with this limitation, these chrysanthemums promise to be the most extraordinary single addition with which we can ornament our Grasslands. They come into blossom when frosts have killed other plants and we sadly feel that the season is at an end. But there is another spurt of glory, another lease on life. The chrysanthemums extend the color season at least two weeks, and sometimes four weeks, sometimes even after the first snows.

Modern chrysanthemums come in bewildering variety. Colors range from white thru pinks to red, to deep oranges, thru ivory to bright yellow, thru lavender to violet. There are tall forms and low forms. There are small-flowered pompons, quilled varieties, singles and doubles, and a considerable spread in their flowering range. There are Arcticum and Korean Hybrids. The book "Standardized Plant Names" classifies the hundreds of named clones in over 50 kinds of types. In all this array, you can only choose blindly for ones that may be the more suitable for naturalizing. Do not put them out in fall—which is the time one is tempted to buy them. Plant them in spring. When autumn comes, leave the branches standing or fallen, to collect stray leaves, and to act as a protective mulch in winter. For best color effects, it is well to assist the plant to grow as a solid mass. Flat stones laid at the base of the plant will encourage this tendency, or use mulches liberally.

C. Leucanthemum

Golden Marguerite, *Anthemis tinctoria*, B: 990, Gl III: 383, is a bright yellow-flowered composite from Eurasia that has much to its advantage. The foliage is handsomely cut-leaved. It has a long blossoming season, thru much of the summer. Occasional plants will be found escaped to roadsides, on some of the very poorest of soils. But—there is almost always a "but"—I suspect it is both short-lived, and intolerant of competition with other plants. Its success in grassland has to date been short-lived.

The common native Yarrow, *Achillea millefolium*, B: 991, Gl III: 384, is considered one of the commonest weeds. It is an integral component of my unmown Grasslands, varying in abundance from year to year but never overly common. The dense clusters of white flowers are not exceptional, but I consider them an attractive addition to the total plant-community. The plant spreads by rhizomes, and I assume is in a more or less natural balance with the other vegetation. Many species of yarrow are cultivated, including forms with pink and with yellow flower heads. It is quite possible that some of them will be found suitable for naturalizing. I suggest they may be grown in the garden first. If they are actively rhizomatous they have a greater chance for success in naturalization.

Tansy, *Tanacetum vulgare*, B: 992, Gl III: 386, is an Old World plant, straight from medieval medicinal and herb gardens. It is now widely escaped in North America. The cut-leaved foliage is a deep dark green, especially when in partial shade, and of a distinctive and piquant odor and taste. Like all good things, it should be taken in moderation. A bit of tansy goes a long way, for those who use it in cookery, but that little is highly desirable. The small yellow button-like flower heads will keep their color in drying if brought into the house. If given a bit of encouragement and protection in the Grassland, it will form a dense solid clump that will thereafter persist. If not so encouraged, the shoots are small, and tend to be lost in the grass.

Coneflowers

Rudbeckia. B: 995. Gl III: 346

The coneflowers are so-called because of the central part of the head, which is frequently dark, enlarged and cone-like, and surrounded by the long yellow "petals". The name is also used for the closely related genera *Echinacea*, *Dracopsis* and *Ratibida*. All four genera are native to North America, with species that are typical and representative of the original Prairies in the interior part of the continent.

The common Black-eyed Susan, generally known as *R. hirta*, is a plant that, were it rare, would be grown assiduously and its blossoms considered of outstanding beauty. The long bright orange-yellow "petals" surround a dark purplish-brown center, to form one of the handsomest composites known. Black-eyed Susan is part of a highly variable population which some taxonomists would split into 10 or even 20 different named segregates. *R. hirta* (*R. serotina* in Bailey) is generally recognized as a biennial or short-lived perennial. *R. fulgida*, including *R. speciosa*, is a perennial, often stoloniferous. How many of these variations are due to the local environment in the life of the individual and how many are genetically conditioned, and to what extent geographical variants occur, and hybridization between distinct populations, are all problems for future research.

I have found Black-eyed Susan in the garden to spread aggressively by seedlings. In the Grassland, after a decade and a half, it has remained an important and valued component. In mid-summer, just as the daisies are declining, this *Rudbeckia* breaks into bloom. The abundance varies from season to season. It is as yet difficult to estimate the relative importance of new seedlings, of stoloniferous offshoots, or of persistent older plants. If anyone is garden-testing the Black-eyed Susan for introduction into areas where it does not now occur, he should choose a strain that appears to be both stoloniferous and long-lived.

Rudbeckia speciosa Goldsturm is a non-stoloniferous horticultural strain of considerable promise. Not only is its vegetative growth luxuriant, but it is especially floriferous, with the flowers coming distinctly later than the common Black-eyed Susan. A few clumps of this plant can be amazingly conspicuous.

The Brown-eyed Susan, *R. triloba*, is a later flowering species. The blossoms are smaller, with a lighter center. In the garden, it will grow to be taller than *R. hirta*, sometimes to $2\frac{1}{2}$–3 feet. It is short-lived and therefore unsuitable for any permanent introduction. However, I have found that a few small seedlings are invariably to be found in the vicinity of the old parent plant. If a few of these are protected from grassland competition with a circle of flat stones, they will attain a considerable size and will be an appreciated addition when few other things are in flower.

R. laciniata has no common name. It is the wild single form of the well-known double-flowered Goldenglow. The native species is extremely common along shady roadsides where its light yellow flowers rise on plants 5 and 6 feet high. Volunteer garden seedlings are common. Contrary to what one might expect, this plant does exceptionally well in the full light of the Grassland. Young plants need mulching protection from competing grasses. I cannot yet say whether older plants will persist without such protection. The roots are fibrous, without a distinct taproot, and I assume could become infiltrated with grass roots to their disadvantage.

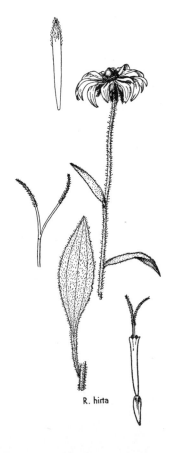

R. hirta

Ratibida pinnata, B: 996, Gl III: 350, one of the Coneflowers, is a typical prairie plant, growing 4–5 feet high, with pale yellow "petals" that droop downwards, almost as tho they were wilting. The color is distinctive enough to make it valuable. It has a heavily fibrous root system, not rhizomatous in the plants I have seen. Young plants need competition-protection in the Grassland. I do not yet have data for older plants.

Rosinweeds

Silphium. B: 996. Gl III: 367

The Rosinweeds comprise another group of native Prairie plants that added much of the color the original travelers reported. They were successful in nature on those wild grasslands, and thus we wonder if they are not suitable for naturalization. They are all coarse-foliaged plants, growing 5 to 7 feet tall, and with large yellow flower-heads.

Silphium integrifolium has leafy stems for its entire height, and a clump of it forms a solid barrier of foliage. The root system is a complex coarse mass, probably including short stocky rhizomes. The clump slowly enlarges as its age increases. Once established in grassland, its bulk and massiveness restrict the adjacent grasses, but whether it will be persistent for many years, we cannot yet say.

Silphium laciniatum is a plant with tall naked flower stems rising from a cluster of very large and deeply tho coarsely cut leaves. This is a plant with a heavy taproot, extending down to unrecorded depths. The leaves are often oriented so as to receive the morning and afternoon sun, but not the noon sun—thus the name Compass Plant. In the Prairies, it has been reported as forming clumps 5 feet in diameter, with over 100 leaves, and shading out prairie grasses in the immediate vicinity. Whether such a clump started as one seedling, or as a group of seedlings, is not known. *S. laciniatum* gives every evidence of being very long-lived. Seedlings can be started in the garden, but should be moved when one year old, before the taproots are too long. Once placed in the Grassland, I would give it some protection from adjacent grasses for a few years.

Silphium terebinthinaceum also has tall naked flower stems, but in this case rising from a clump of large coarse leaves somewhat resembling a burdock. It has a heavy woody taproot. For this reason, seedlings should be moved when young, and thereafter left in place. In its natural habitat, it forms a large clump of foliage that is apparently rarely established in nature, but once established is exceedingly long-lived, and completely able to maintain itself against the lower grasses around it.

In naturalizing the silphiums, it is a question whether one should put out single seedlings in the grass, and assume each can be encouraged to become large enough to maintain itself. Or whether one should plant a cluster, spaced 3 to 6 inches apart, in which case the aggregate mass more quickly and more easily becomes dominant over the adjacent grasses. It is quite possible that in nature individual seedlings succumb to competition from other vegetation, whereas it is the clusters of seedlings which survive and mature. Mere bulk is an important factor in survival, and thus I would favor group planting. Group planting is also more effective from a landscaping viewpoint, when dealing with these large coarse plants.

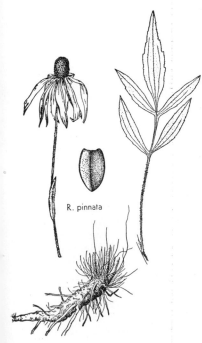

R. pinnata

Sunflowers

Helianthus. B: 997. Gl III: 332

Helianthus is a North American genus of annual and perennial fall-flowering herbs, generally large and coarse-foliaged, with large heads composed of bright yellow "petals," and with either yellow or brown-purple centers. The perennials are generally rhizomatous and actively spreading so that the plants form colonies. There are 50–100 species, depending on how one segregates the populations. Many more have been described in the botanical literature, but are probably only minor variants. Several of the major species are not sharply defined, and intergrading forms occur. Hybridization occurs in nature, and it can occur spontaneously in garden grown materials. Furthermore, semi-double and double forms are known. I have one fine semi-double form that apparently so arose, characterized by a double row of "petals" rather than the customary single row.

Helianthus annuus is the Common Sunflower, a strict annual. The seeds are a commonly used bird food, and the plant may escape. If it germinates in dense grassland, it may only grow a foot in height or less, with a very small flower. If you throw some mulch around the young plant, to restrict competing herbs, it will become much larger—and more attractive to deer. Garden-grown material, depending on moisture and fertilization, can become mammoth 12-foot plants, with blossoms a foot across.

Helianthus laetiflorus (*rigidus*) is a leafy-stemmed prairie species commonly growing 4 feet high. Heavy rhizomes spread rapidly in the garden, but the plant needs protection, at least while young, if put in the Grassland.

Helianthus giganteus is a giant only as to height, and one that is especially valuable. It produces a full-foliaged column of greenery, covered over a considerable portion of that height with relatively small flowers of a light yellow shade. From a distance it appears almost like a shrub, and should be used in that manner at the edge of the Grassland. Other sunflowers tend to have their flowers noticeably at the top of the foliage.

Helianthus occidentalis is another common rhizomatous Prairie species in which the foliage is mostly basal, and the relatively naked flower stalks rise to heights of 4–5 feet. These basal leaves are commonly six inches long, and sufficiently abundant to be conspicuous in the ground cover. The plant may spread slowly thru the Grassland, and there will probably be a limit as to how much you want of it. It may be easily controlled by herbicides, or pulling.

Helianthus decapetalus is a relatively small-leaved and small-flowered species growing 3–5 feet high. It is well to keep it concentrated in a pure clump, and let it extend only to the degree you wish. Its foliage is less conspicuous in the Grassland than the two preceding species.

Helianthus tuberosus is one of several very tall leafy-stemmed sunflowers. These grow 8–9 feet high, with stout stems covered with heavy foliage. The flowers are large, bright, conspicuous, and make a considerable showing at a long distance. This particular species is called Girasole, an Italian name of the plant, corrupted to Jerusalem, and then called Jerusalem Artichoke, in a fancied resemblance of the tuberous rootstocks. These small tubers were a valued source of food for the Indians, and can be collected in fall, or the first thing in spring when the new shoot reveals their location. There are many strains, which may differ considerably in their flowering season.

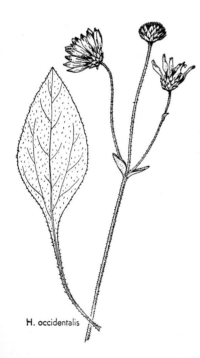

H. occidentalis

The genus *Bidens*, B: 999, Gl III: 353, is known as Beggar-ticks. They are mostly annual weeds with unnoticed flowers and barbed fruits that can be thoroly annoying in fall when they prove their migrating capacities by sticking into your clothing, and thru it, to the flesh.

There is one species quite unlike its relatives and worthy of consideration. This Sunflower-bidens, which appears to be *Bidens polylepis*, has flowers as large as a small sunflower, and just as attractive. The fruits do not adhere to clothing. It is an annual plant, which I have noticed covering some of the waste industrial areas in northern New Jersey with a solid carpet of yellow. Volunteer seedlings in the garden can be so abundant as to take over the entire area. A single seedling if kept free from garden competition will become a husky plant 5 feet high and carrying dozens of blossoms. It is mentioned here because volunteer seedlings have been found in the grass. It is true they are dwarfed individuals, less than a foot tall, and with possibly one flower, but they are a unique addition at that season. It is doubtful if seedlings would perpetuate themselves thru the years, but if an individual plant were "cultivated," it stands a chance of being a source of such seedlings the following year.

Heliopsis helianthoides, the Ox-eye, B: 1001, Gl III: 344 (including *H. scabra*), is a sunflower-like Prairie plant of North America. It is not rhizomatous, and said to be a short-lived perennial. Five feet tall, covered with flowers, it is worth investigation. *Heliopsis scabra* var. *incomparabilis* is a double-flowered horticultural form that shows promise for naturalistic landscaping. It is a husky plant, almost-bushy in appearance, with an exceptionally long flowering period, lasting most of the summer. The flowering season fades away slowly and unattractively, but in the Grassland this is not disadvantageous. Some stone-mulching or its equivalent is recommended.

Coreopsis, B: 1002, Gl III: 359, is a cosmopolitan genus, tho mainly North American, containing several cultivated species. The flowers of the different species are yellow, rarely pink or white. As garden plants they are they are especially attractive in that the "petals" are distinctly 5-toothed at their ends. (Each tooth represents the end of a separate true petal, all five of which are combined into a single strap of the single flower.)

Coreopsis lanceolata is a widely escaped and hardy species that can become exceptionally attractive on the sterile soils of some roadsides. It persists when transplanted to the Grassland, but there tends to be an excessive amount of foliage and the long flower stalks may not remain erect. Other strains may be more satisfactory.

Ragweed, B: (not in), Gl III: 372, is commonly *Ambrosia artemisiifolia.* The giant ragweed is *A. trifida.* These native species are locally abundant on open and waste lands in the Northeast. More recently they have become abundant in the northwest Pacific coast states. They are annual, starting each year from seed, often germinating continually thru the season. The ragweeds are of especial interest because many people are allergic to the pollen, one of the major sources of those allergies known as hay-fever. From 1 to 10% of the total population is said to be afflicted with this disturbance. For this reason, ragweed is of interest to the medical profession, to public health officials, and—a sordid chapter—to those groups which benefit by killing ragweed.

Altho ragweed can become an extremely abundant pest, there will be no need to fear it in your herbicide-induced Grasslands. Occasionally I find a plant, maybe one per 5 acres, small and depauperate, hardly enough to give a mouse a sniffle. The plant is very strictly a "pioneer," one that needs bare soil, with no competition from other plants. If you have any at all, you will become rather fond of them—they are among the underprivileged, with hardly a place in the sun, but...

But ragweed can become abundant, excessively abundant, especially in fallow agricultural lands after harvesting (I have seen it grow densely, over six feet tall, in southern Florida tomato lands), on abandoned city lots, and along roadsides. It can become exceedingly abundant on the barren gravelly shoulders of roads. Ragweed is the symptom of a plant-community disease; it is not the disease itself. The disease is the barren site, which can be eliminated from roadsides by hard-topping the edge, and deep-soiling the unused shoulder, preferably with the two parts separated by a curb. Herbicide-spraying these roadsides, as any botanist knows, does kill the ragweed that is sprayed (as morphine will kill the pain of a deep-seated organic disturbance). It also kills many other broadleaved herbs that are competitors of the ragweed. Perhaps a few annual grasses survive, themselves weedy. But fundamentally, the land is made even more bare, so that more ragweed comes in (from seeds in the soil, from untreated city lots, and from fallow fields), to require more spraying. Certain facets of American society have realized enormous business potential, and by means of Public Relations departments, advertising media, and other gentle and persuasive techniques, have created a thriving business. They have not hesitated in their efforts to infiltrate certain otherwise respectable government agricultural agencies, universities, non-profit health societies, and even medical groups. The situation is fascinating to a cultural anthropologist, but hardly creditable to the integrity of American scientists and scientific organizations.

Goldenrods

Solidago. B: 1005. Gl III: 413

The Solidagos usher in the autumn season with a burst of golden glory. The northeastern landscape would be entirely different were it not for its goldenrods. The genus is a large and complicated one, native mainly to North America, and reaching its greatest complexity in the eastern half of the continent. Gleason recognizes 62 species for the Northeast. Hybridization in nature frequently occurs, sometimes even between species that are not considered closely related. Since some are rhizomatous and can form dense colonies, a single aggressive hybrid, even tho unnameable, may be a conspicuous feature on the land. For the Naturalistic Landscaper, goldenrods are both beauty and bane. He cherishes some; he tries to eradicate others; and he hopes to keep others in isolated clumps. For our purposes, we can consider the different species as being: I—valued components of the mixed Grassland; II—suitable as clump or small-colony plants, or as forest-edge plants; III—weeds, to be destroyed in most places. Control of goldenrods requires recognition of the different species at all times of the season, particularly early in the spring when vegetative growth starts. Do not be discouraged if even botanists cannot identify these for you. Many plant taxonomists are very nice flower-minded and fruit-minded scientists, quite coldly unresponsive if they have no sexual organs to work upon. Get your plants identified in autumn when they are flowering brightly. Then mark the spots. Observe the vegetative growth in spring. You will find the different kinds are really very easy to identify, as easy to identify as your friends even if their faces are turned to the wall.

Group I. In this desirable group we place relatively small species, with inconspicuous or basal foliage, with relatively naked flower stalks that rise high enough to be seen, and which mat down with the winter snows. In this category, non-rhizomatous *Solidago nemoralis* is superb. It persists in undiminished numbers for many years, and its clear yellow is a welcome addition. It flowers late, and furthermore, the flowering period of individual plants seems variable, so that its season is considerably extended. *Solidago bicolor* is another highly desirable goldenrod that maintains its scattered frequency in the Grassland. This is the only common "white goldenrod," known as Silverrod, with no trace of yellow in its flowers.

Solidago tenuifolia is a low fine-foliaged plant, slowly spreading as a compact colony, and not observed to "jump" by volunteer seedlings. You may like it. It remains green long after the grasses have turned brown in autumn.

Group II. The clump and forest-edge goldenrods are those which are conspicuously leafy thruout the entire season, and which do not break down in winter, so that dead stalks mar the spring season. Some are aggressively rhizomatous, and form dense colonies that exclude all other vegetation. *Solidago juncea* comes into blossom ahead of all the others, and is certainly attractive with its bright yellow inflorescences. It slowly enlarges by a more or less prostrate stem that can hardly be called a rhizome. The foliage is coarse and rank, and undesirable in the grassland. The woody flower stalks remain standing thru another entire year. I find it suitable only for the forest-edge.

Solidago graminifolia, the Grass-leaved Goldenrod, is a rhizomatous colonial species, forming a somewhat thin colony about 2 feet high. You might like a small clump out in the open, but I prefer to restrict it to the sides.

Solidago altissima is one of the handsomest goldenrods, often growing 5 feet high, and sometimes developing as a dense colony excluding all other plants. I have had one such colony last for a decade and a half with no deterioration, and with no aggressiveness into surrounding grasses.

Solidago rugosa subsp. *aspera* is a very late-flowering colonial species about 2 feet tall that makes a very attractive clump out in the open. After a decade, the center of one clump died out.

Solidago serotina var. *gigantea* is still another common colonial species that forms a fairly open and low clump. The clumps appear to disintegrate after five years or so.

Solidago sempervirens is the fleshy-leaved tidal-marsh and sea-beach species, somewhat resembling *S. juncea*. The salt of its native environment is by no means necessary to its existence, and the plant thrives in garden soil. In the Grassland, it is much enfeebled by competition, and definitely needs protective mulches.

Solidago canadensis is a common non-rhizomatous species that can form a large and attractive clump about 4 feet high.

A colony of the Tall Goldenrod (*Solidago altissima*), spruce in background. Clones of this species can be extremely stable. This one is 20 years old.

Pasture junipers (*Juniperus communis*) and low blueberries (*Vaccinium pensylvanicum*) in the foreground of a redtop (*Agrostis alba*) grassland. Two goldenrods, *Solidago bicolor* and *S. nemoralis,* color this field later in the season. Without herbicide management, this field would now be a forest thicket 20 feet tall.

Group III. In the category of weeds I would place those species which are rank in foliage and thus detract from the continuity of grassland, without a satisfactory flowering period to compensate. Chief sinner in this matter is *Solidago rugosa*. My battle with it has been long, and not yet entirely successful. Left to itself, it fills up the land with a dense mass of foliage, excluding all else. It is brilliant for a week, then it looks moth-eaten. After several years, it tends to thin out, but even in such "normal" abundance, there is too much for my taste. I have tried all kinds of techniques of pulling and spraying. Pulling is by far the best at the start, for one generally gets a stretch of horizontal rhizome 3 to 6 inches long, or, if late in the season, half a dozen growing rhizomes that will form as many plants the next year. Oil-spray burning can be resorted to when there are fewer and smaller plants, but only if one keeps at it just as often as new plants appear, every three weeks for example.

S. juncea, *S. graminifolia*, and *S. serotina* are the three other species that I sometimes consider "weeds" and leave only at the forest edge, where their foliage and dead stalks are not too obvious.

It is very important to realize that at least 99% of my own golden-rod eradication programs has been directed to rootstocks already in the soil. I have literally pulled tens of thousands of these plants, many of them in counted experiments, and I have never found any-thing that I would assuredly call a one-year seedling! Seedlings occur, as those in bare-soil gardens testify, but those in the Grass-land apparently date back to the last agricultural operations.

S. graminifolia

X½ X4 X2 X½ X1

213

Asters

Aster. B: 1008. Gl III: 440

The genus Aster plays a role somewhat analogous to that of Solidago in its season. The plants bloom in fall after the goldenrods—the end of the season unless you have hardy chrysanthemums. They are abundant, numerous in kind, and the landscape would be vastly different without them. Whereas the goldenrods are dominantly yellow, these are blue varying to white. The change therefore from one season to the other involves a complete change in color.

The asters are predominantly a north temperate group, and most abundant in North America. Gleason recognizes 67 species for the Northeast. Identification, as with the goldenrods, is at first difficult, especially in the vegetative stages. As one gets to know them however, their personalities emerge. Soon you will be able to recognize each as easily as a farmer knows his cows. Some of the species named below are only tentatively identified.

It is likely that you will have a dozen or more species sufficiently common to merit a place in your landscape planning. As we treated the goldenrods, Group I will comprise those which diffuse thru the Grassland and form part of its overall structure. Group II includes the clump plants which should be featured as individual specimens. Group III involves the forest-edge species. I know no asters which might be considered as "weeds." *Aster acuminatus* and *Aster divaricatus* are low white-flowering species, eminently suited, and the only ones so suited, for forested areas, where they can form a fairly continuous cover on shaded ground. Most asters are aggressively rhizomatous, an important feature to consider in landscaping.

Many species of asters have been grown by the horticulturist, but Americans have done almost nothing in the way of developing garden strains. The English have taken some of our species, mainly *A. novi-belgii, novae-angliae, cordifolius, diffusus, ericoides,* and *vimineus,* also the Eurasian *A. amellus,* and turned out large numbers of highly superior Michaelmas Daisies which are now being imported into this country. It is quite possible that some good naturalizing strains may be found among them.

Group I. I have found two species to be of outstanding value in this category, the smooth-leaved *Aster cordifolius* and the pubescent *A. undulatus*. They occupy very similar roles in the Grassland, diffusing all thru it by means of the long underground rhizomes. The foliage is not conspicuous until autumn. Flower stalks rise just above the general level of the grass, and the light blue blossoms seem to cast their color over the entire stretch of land.

Aster lateriflorus is a small-flowered white species of no special attraction when it occurs in the Grassland, and not rising above the general level. I have seen no reason to encourage it, nor to consider it disadvantageous.

Aster patens in the garden is a rhizome-spreading species, blossoming at grassland height, and with flowers of an unusually clear bright blue. It is worth trying for naturalization.

Group II. There are several species that have value as individual feature plants in the Grassland. *Aster dumosus* is a small-leaved, small- and white-flowered plant. The form I know is not rhizomatous. Plants in the Grassland tend to be small and depauperate. Some encouragement in the way of stone mulches often results in conspicuously improved growth. *Aster laevis* is another medium-sized species with handsome blue flowers, not rhizomatous in the Grassland, that responds favorably to elimination of competition by adjacent grasses.

Among the larger ranker species, *Aster novae-angliae* stands supreme. Its deep purplish-blue large blossoms are the most striking of the native asters. Left to itself in Grassland it becomes small and may not flower. With the immediately adjacent vegetation blotted out, however, this fine plant grows 5 and 6 feet tall, as conspicuous as a beacon light in the distance. Both woodchucks and deer seem fond of it however, and you might have to stake in a bit of brush as a deterrent.

Aster ericoides is a late-flowering white species with small, but very numerous blossoms. Left to itself, it wanders off and is an inconspicuous component of the land. With a little aid however, it will form a dense cluster, eliminating all other plants, and slowly enlarging by stout almost woody rhizomes. It is not tall, but in season it will be a pure white spot on the landscape.

There are various smaller tussock-forming asters that are too low to be seen at any distance in the grassland, but can be used in dry open areas, or close to a trail. *Aster linariifolius* is one of the best for this purpose. The clump is less than 12 inches high, with large blue flowers. At other seasons, the foliage forms an attractive cluster of narrow-leaved stems.

Group III. *Aster umbellatus* is best relegated to the forest edge. It produces single stems 4–5 feet tall, surmounted by small white flowers. It is interesting in that it is the earliest-flowering of the asters, reaching its peak with the goldenrods. On the other hand, the stem is sufficiently woody so that the dead stalk remains erect thru the following growing season.

Aster simplex is a highly aggressive, leafy, 4–6 feet tall plant with small white or pale blue flowers, that looks nice as a clump when in blossom. Its leafiness however can become undesirable especially in slightly shady, more moist, or fertile-soiled areas. I find it is better to remove it in the open, and push it back against the forest edge.

Gaillardia aristata, the Blanket Flower, B: 1014, Gl III: 376, is a species from the Rocky Mountains and other parts of western North America, and commonly cultivated in the east. Flowers are a clear yellow and red, or orange and red. Some garden forms are called Portola Hybrids. The blossoming season is extremely long, sometimes from May to frost. Altho said to be hardy, they have not proven so for me. There are other native species in the West, and all of them deserve consideration for naturalization.

Sneezeweeds, B: 1014, Gl III: 378, belong to the genus *Helenium* The orange sneezeweed, *H. hoopesii*, is one of the most critical of poisonous plants on the western ranges, especially for sheep in Utah. It becomes abundant on overgrazed ranges, and may kill the animals after prolonged feeding upon it.

H. autumnale is a native yellow species, growing five feet tall, that may prove suitable for forest edges.

H. nudiflorum is a smaller native species. The flowers have odd-shaped "petals," contracted to a narrow base that is purple, and wide at the end with three teeth. I have seen it in dry thin sandy grasslands, indicating that it has naturalizing potentialities in some vegetation types.

Senecio, the Groundsel, B: 1018, Gl III: 397, is a cosmopolitan genus of over a thousand species that boasts annuals, perennials, shrubs and even trees. Species are often closely related, and hybridization occurs with democratic license and freedom. Various ones have entered the gardener's world. The florist's cineraria for example is *S. cruentus*.

Senecio obovatus is a common native species with glossy basal foliage, and bright orange-yellow flower clusters 12–18 inches tall. It spreads rapidly in bare land by stolons or superficial rhizomes. It is not suited for growth in grassland, but it does well at the forest edge where the grasses are thinned.

Inula helenium is the Elecampane, B: 1020, Gl III: 484, a European species grown in old gardens, and now widely escaped. It is a thoroly coarse-foliaged plant, with large 2-foot basal leaves, and leafy stalks rising 4 feet high. The flower heads are typically those of yellow composites, undistinguished in any manner. The plant is oddly interesting, but should be kept at the forest edge. When put in the grassland it is much reduced in size, and may not flower. Accidentally drop a few stones around the base however, and its growth will be amazingly improved, or liberally leaf-mulch.

Pussy-toes, *Antennaria*, B: 1022, Gl III: 478, is so named from the small woolly-white heads that might be looked upon as miniature cat-paws. The plants are low woolly-leaved ground covers, spreading by stolons. They may get into shady lawns, where they are looked upon as pests by those to whom everything but grass is a pest.

There are half a dozen species native in the Northeast, some of them from the far North. *A. neglecta* and *A. plantaginifolia* are the two best known. Both are highly variable, and such variations have been named by the taxonomists altho they are hard for any one to identify without actual herbarium material. These are interesting plants for the shady forest edge, and will often increase merely if one mows the taller ranker vegetation.

Anaphalis margaritacea, B: 1022, Gl III: 480, the well-known Pearly Everlasting, is closely related to the Antennarias, but differs from it in many important respects. It is an 18–24 inch plant that thrives in the open sunny grassland. It is densely white woolly, and the unopened flower heads are pearly white—unquestionably the whitest plant of all in the Grassland. It spreads by underground rhizomes, leading to the formation of dense circular colonies, each apparently a single clone. Some colonies are whiter than others, and occasionally a colony stands out in the distance like a cloth-covered table top. Unfortunately, such a colony disintegrates at the center after 3–5 years. A typical fairy ring is visible, and then the colony breaks up. In the meantime new clusters are forming elsewhere. It would probably be a pest if it constantly spread and never did die out. This way, it is a highly desirable changing phenomenon thru the years.

Blazing Stars

Liatris. B: 1023. Gl III: 495

For those who knew the native Prairie, some of the most brilliant plants were the handsome Blazing Stars, great long pink-purple spikes, rising high above the grassland level. They are as bright in the distance as the trail of a shooting star itself. Altho the different species occurred in the East, they were not associated with large natural grasslands—perhaps because there were no such grasslands.

It is comforting to known that these plants give every indication of being exceedingly long-lived, and that once successfully introduced they appear to be persistent without further care. They are neither rhizomatous nor heavily fibrous-rooted: instead the plants have a solid vertically oriented corm that enlarges with age, and is commonly the size of a pecan or walnut. A fountain of narrow grass-like foliage arises from this corm, and thus the plant is inconspicuous all spring and summer. One or several tall stalks arise late in summer, with the peak of blossoming falling between the goldenrod and aster seasons.

In the garden, volunteer seedlings can be so abundant as to be almost a pest. Such seedlings will reach flowering age in two or three years. The corms can be cut vertically, and the plant increased by that means. Winter heaving is critical, a situation not found in the Grassland, for the natural mulch forms a protective covering. When putting small corms out in the Grassland, give them a protective adjacent mulch for a few years, until they reach adequate size and vigor. The plants may need protection from passing deer, who seem to take a fancy for that which they do not have to bend their heads.

There are two main spike types, one with globose heads forming an interrupted spike, and one with narrow small heads forming a solid continuous spike. Of the former, *L. borealis* has been successful for landscaping. Of the latter, both *L. spicata* and *L. pycnostachya* have been rewarding. Some of my *L. pycnostachya* comes from Wisconsin, and some from southern Illinois. The Illinois form flowers one week or more later. Flowering periods of all these species vary, so that the entire season is considerably prolonged.

In the last three seasons, volunteer seedlings of all these species have been found in the Grassland! In color, season, and spectacular quality, these are potential additions of supreme importance to the Wild Gardener.

Bonesets

Eupatorium. B: 1024. Gl III: 485

Here is a vast genus of over 500 species, mainly in the American tropics. Many of the species are closely related, poorly defined, and frequently hybridizing. In the Northeast, there are at least three species, all very distinct from each other, that may be utilized in Naturalistic Landscaping.

E. rugosum (*urticaefolium*) is the White Snakeroot. It is a small 2-foot plant with clusters of very small white flowers. Tho commonly believed to be poisonous to livestock, with the poison transmissible to man in milk, I have known of no actual cases of such poisoning despite the fact that the plant is common. If put in the Grassland, the plant needs some protection from adjacent competition.

E. perfoliatum, the Thoroughwort, grows 2–3 feet tall, with dense masses of small white flowers, and with the entire plant appearing pale because of its pubescense. If you have a few such plants, they are worth saving.

E. purpureum, the Joe-Pye-Weed, is a rankly growing, heavy-foliaged plant commonly 6 feet tall, with large masses of pink flowers. The color is unusual on this size of plant, and a mass of them at the edge of the forest, particularly on a slope where one can look down upon them, is attractive.

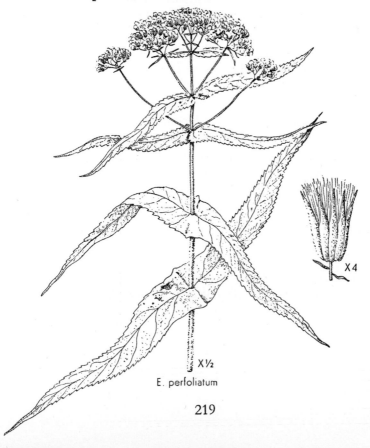

X 4

X ½

E. perfoliatum

The Star Thistles, B: 1026, Gl III: 513, belong to the genus *Centaurea*. They are not offensively spined plants, and are so-named because the flower heads of some resemble thistles, while their larger outer flowers give them a star-like radiating form. The group includes the corn-flowers and bachelor-buttons of gardens, as well as some agricultural and wasteland weeds. The genus is mostly Mediterranean in distribution, with blue-purple corollas. A few species are white or yellow. There are both annuals and perennials.

The perennial Centaureas may prove to have some value for Naturalistic Landscaping. My experience has been with European *C. maculosa*. Individual plants appear to be long-lived. Tho markedly dwarfed when growing in grassland, an adjacent stone mulch greatly improves the growth. A well-developed single plant can become a handsome mass of lavender. The foliage is finely divided and relatively inconspicuous. Do not worry about the plant becoming a pest. As is true of so many agricultural weeds, they need open land in which to become established. An unmown Grassland offers them no encouragement.

The European *Centaurea montana* is a hardy long-lived garden plant, known to volunteer in bare soil. It is worth investigation.

The Globe Thistle, B: 1028, Gl III: 512, *Echinops exaltatus* (not *E. sphaerocephalus* according to Bailey), is a tall spiny-leaved Siberian plant with a perfectly spherical bluish head of small flowers. Volunteer seedlings are common in the garden, and the plant is long-lived and fully hardy. It is greatly helped by some adjacent mulches. Since the flower heads rise on tall naked stalks, it is effective at a distance and at the forest edge, tho it is nothing that repays close observation.

The true Thistles in the genus *Cirsium*, Gl III: 506, have developed such unpleasant reputations for being obnoxious weeds, that Bailey includes none in his manual. It is true they are spiny; it is true some of them can be agricultural weeds; it is true that the Bible has prejudiced us in linking thistles to barren lands. I suspect that the main reason why the gardener is not interested in *Cirsium* is that he must forever fondle and pamper his plants. With thistles, such fondling is hard on the thumb, and may turn it from green to red. And yet we have devoted cactus fanciers, who stop just short of sleeping with their plants! Perhaps the opposition to Cirsium is just one more convention. One should look at thistles, not feel them.

Cirsium arvense, the Canada thistle, I do consider a pest in the Grassland. It spreads by deep underground rhizomes, as thick as a lead pencil. If it does flower (which it does not, in Grassland), it is a meaningless jumble of small pinkish heads. If you pull each stalk carefully, you will get a 6-or 8-inch vertical length of stem, which breaks from the deep horizontal rhizome. Keep pulling or spraying, and you will eventually starve out the plant. But wear gloves.

The Bull Thistle is another story. Several species may be involved, with *C. pumilum* one of the most attractive. From a basal rosette of leaves the flower stalk arises that bears usually a single huge head 2 or 3 inches across. It is lilac in color, fragrant, and highly attractive to bees. Altho said to be a biennial, I suspect it to be at least short-lived. I have never seen more than a dozen or so to an acre— I wish it were more aggressive in Grassland.

The Ironweeds belong to the genus *Vernonia*, B: 1030, Gl III: 500. This is a large mainly tropical genus represented in the Northeast by seven purple-flowered perennial herbs. Any two of the species will hybridize when they occur in the same region, and such hybrid swarms, often representing several basic species, can dominate locally. *V. noveboracensis* is one that is most frequently brought into gardens. The ironweeds are unusual in form and coloration. They are fairly tall and leafy, and suitable in clumps in a sunny place at the edge of the Grassland.

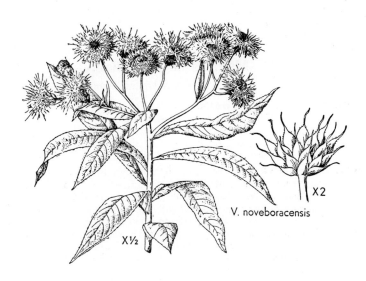

X2

V. noveboracensis

X½

There are no other books that cover the field of Naturalistic Landscaping. This particular aspect of botany may be defined—not as cultivating either wild or horticultural plants, nor as studying wild plants in their wild surroundings— but as encouraging andor planting either native or exotic species in stable semi-natural plant-communities; and then letting them take care of themselves. Many books are helpful as reference however, and some of these are mentioned below.

The English "Wild Garden"

1894. W. Robinson. The Wild Garden, or the Naturalization and Natural Grouping of Hardy Exotic Plants with a Chapter on the Garden of British Wild Flowers. 4th edition. 304 pp. Illus. London: John Murray.
———— *Mr. Robinson's concept directly paralleled our own. He is interested in "the planting of perfectly hardy exotic plants under conditions where they will thrive without further care," to form a delightful wild, tho not "unkempt," landscape. This volume is designed for the English scene, but it has much value for readers of America and Europe.*

Manuals of Cultivated American Plants

1940. Alfred Rehder. Manual of Cultivated Trees and Shrubs Hardy in North America. 2nd ed. 996 pp. Frontisp. New York: Macmillan.
———— *Restricted to woody plants, and in more detail than in the 1949 Bailey manual.*

1942. Harlan P. Kelsey, and William A. Dayton, editors. Standardized Plant Names. 2nd ed. 675 pp. Harrisburg, Penn.: McFarland. ———— *A listing of scientific and common names, including cultivated forms. A worthy attempt to standardize horticultural nomenclatorial confusion. Tho this volume did not gain either the cooperation or acceptance of a majority of botanists and horticulturists, I find the volume of considerable value. Its faults are inherent in the failure of botanists and horticulturists to cooperate—and accept a common meeting ground.*

1949. Liberty Hyde Bailey. Manual of Cultivated Plants. Rev. Ed. 1116 pp. New York: Macmillan. ———— *This is the standard botanical manual for all North American cultivated plants, and is an invaluable reference and guide.*

Manuals of Wild Plants
(for northeastern United States)

1950. Merritt Lyndon Fernald. Gray's New Manual of Botany. 8th ed. 1632 pp. New York et al.: Amer. Book Co. ———— *The standard one-volume manual for the Northeast. Fernald is more of a "splitter" than Gleason, and his keys tend to stress assumed phylogenetic relationships rather than to accept short-cuts to identification.*

1963. Henry A. Gleason. The New Britton and Brown Illustrated Flora of the Northeastern United States. Vol. I, 482 pp. Vol. II, 655 pp. Vol. III, 595 pp. New York: N.Y. Botanical Garden. ———— *Extremely valuable because of its excellent line drawings for every species, and for its practicable keys. One can often identify by the illustrations alone, analogous to what the research taxonomist does when he checks with herbarium material (tho the same man, as professor, will force his students to "key out unknowns," in order to learn the "reasons" for classification—a trying thing, to learn the reasons, which may be unreasonable reasons anyway).*

Books on Cultivating Wild Flowers

1925. Herbert Durand. Wild Flowers and Ferns: in their Homes and in our Gardens. (The 2nd ed. of Taming the Wildings). 394 pp. New York & London: Putnam's. ——— *With brief notes concerning the cultivation of many native species.*

1927. Herbert Durand. My Wild Flower Garden. 242 pp. New York & London: Putnam's. ——— *It is remarkable what can be included in a suburban area that measures only 60 by 100 feet.*

1929. E. H. M. Cox. Wild Gardening. 124 pp. London: Dulau. ——— *Mr. Cox as an Englishman recognizes what he calls the "landscape wild garden" (pp.: 59—94), altho a considerable amount of discussion is involved with woody plants.*

1935. George D. Aiken. Pioneering with Wild Flowers. 131 pp. New York: Stephen Daye Press. ——— *Senator Aiken has given us excellent horticultural notes based on his personal experiences in Vermont.*

1936. Walter Prichard Eaton. Wild Gardens of New England. Boston: W. A. Wilde.

1936. Margaret McKenney. The Wild Garden. New York: Doubleday, Doran.

1948. Frank C. Pellett. Success with Wild Flowers. 193 pp. New York: de la Mare. ——— *His gardening experience with native species supplies valuable accessory information.*

1951. Clarence and Eleanor G. Birdseye. Growing Woodland Plants. 233 pp. New York: Oxford University Press. ——— *Horticultural notes, based largely on the authors' experiences, of over 200 plants. Unusual in its emphasis on forest plants.*

1951. Samuel H. Gottscho. Wild Flowers. New York: Dodd, Mead. ——— *A guide to wildflower growing, with 103 color photographs and 122 black-and-whites by the author.*

1952. Helen S. Hull. Wild Flowers for Your Garden. 250 pp. New York: Barrows. ——— *With notes on wild flower cultivation in each state of the Union, as contributed by correspondents.*

1954. Edwin F. Steffek. Wild Flowers and How to Grow Them. 192 pp. New York: Crown. ——— *With valuable material organized and sub-divided by species and species-groups.*

1963. Kathryn S. Taylor and Stephen F. Hamblin. Handbook of Wild Flower Cultivation. 300 pp. New York: Macmillan. ——— *Precise cultural directions and descriptions are given for hundreds of wild flowers, arranged by plant families from cat-tails to composites.*

1964. Jean Hersey. Wild Flowers to Know and Grow. 235 pp. Princeton, N.J.: Van Nostrand. ——— *Wildflower gardening, with an unusual appreciation both for perpetuating the plants under seminatural conditions, and for the general subject of natural resource conservation.*

Vegetation Management and Landscaping

1963. William A. Niering and Richard H. Goodwin. Creating New Landscapes with Herbicides. A Homeowner's Guide. Connecticut Arboretum (New London) Bull. 14. 30 pp. ——— *A practical guide based on management of a tract at the Connecticut Arboretum, an application of the ideas and principles of Warren G. Kenfield.*

Index

228

Warren G. Kenfield

There are rare works produced by philosophers or literary stylists of which it is said that the book is the man. The same statement can be made only rarely of such a practical work as a book on naturalistic landscaping. The observation, however, can be applied with absolute honesty to *The Wild Gardener*. Warren G. Kenfield has brought to this work not only the self-education of a lifetime, but a carefully wrought ethical and esthetic approach to nature and its management.

Mr. Kenfield gained both his practical knowledge and love of nature early in life. He was born in Philadelphia in 1917; when he was ten his parents moved to the farm of his maternal grandparents in southeastern Ohio. Here during the years of the Depression he aided in restoring the long neglected farm to cultivation, clearing unused pasture land and cutting and grubbing the overgrown fence rows. Here also he was in constant contact with a New England Grandmother who had been one of the visitors to the last session of the Concord School of Philosophy, had seen the aged Emerson, and read Thoreau with pleasure all her life. From her, as well as in response to his own promptings, young Warren Kenfield came to feel an affinity between man and nature and to respect man's need for the spiritual restoration nature provides.

He lived with his grandmother during the last two years of her life, serving as caretaker and general gardener of her large property, supplementing his lack of formal training by extensive reading in horticulture and by taking short courses in nearby Columbus, Ohio. Upon her death in 1939, and by her wishes, he set off to inspect the gardens of Europe. He worked his passage across the Atlantic as a deck hand, toured Europe by bicycle, on foot and by rail. Two years later he left the war-disturbed countries, but carried with him his favorable impressions of English parks and continental estates which combined the use of natural forests with carefully maintained open vistas.

Mr. Kenfield returned to this country in 1942 in order to enlist in military service. 1945 found him in Japan, where he spent an extra year with the occupation forces. Even in the confusion of Japan immediately after the war, he realized that the Japanese had made an art of adapting nature to man's spiritual needs. Chiefly he came to realize that "nature" was not necessarily miles of untrodden wilderness nor even absolute allegiance to native species in their natural habitats. If the native habitat produced no early spring bloom there was no cause to believe that the gods of vegetation would blight the land as a consequence of introduced crocuses or jonquils. His vision of native landscapes, planned and managed in the manner of a garden, took shape at this time.

The chief obstacle to widespread adoption of such a mode of gardening was the labor involved. Since maintaining the wild garden was not to be an end in itself, he had to find an effective means of controlling the growth of invading shrubs and weed trees and also leaving the owner-gardeners time to enjoy their vistas. Still pondering the problem, and in reaction to his wartime experiences in both Europe and the Far East, Kenfield returned to New England to live in semi-seclusion as caretaker and landscaper for a large estate. The aftermath of the war also brought the introduction of herbicides into gardening practice, and Mr. Kenfield began to experiment with them in his own manner, recognizing in them a solution to his greatest problem.

For two decades he has worked with the natural landscape, molding, manipulating, seeking pleasing effects with a minimum of labor. Because of his lack of university education he has read extensively and has constantly sought the advice and opinion of leading horticulturists and ecologists. This book is a contemplative and practical essay upon the work of those years.

Mr. Kenfield has written two previous books, one a murder mystery and one for children, as well as an article in musicology, all under pseudonyms.

KATHRYN WHITFORD